MW00473629

2000 MOST COMMON ARABIC WORDS IN CONTEXT

Get Fluent & Increase Your Arabic
Vocabulary with 2000 Arabic Phrases

Arabic Language Lessons

www.LingoMastery.com

ISBN: 978-1-951949-44-0

Copyright © 2021 by Lingo Mastery

ALL RIGHTS RESERVED

No part of this book may be reproduced, stored in a retrieval system, or transmitted in any form or by any means, electronic, mechanical, photocopying, recording, scanning, or otherwise, without the prior written permission of the publisher.

CONTENTS

Introduction 1

The 2000 Most Common Words in Arabic 9

Conclusion...297

More Books by Lingo Mastery..298

FREE BOOK!

Free Book Reveals The 6 Step Blueprint That Took Students **From Language Learners To Fluent In 3 Months**

One last thing before we start. If you haven't already, head over to LingoMastery.com/hacks and grab a copy of our free Lingo Hacks book that will teach you the important secrets that you need to know to become fluent in a language as fast as possible. Again, you can find the free book over at LingoMastery.com/hacks.

Now, without further ado, enjoy the book!

Good luck, reader!

INTRODUCTION

If you've decided to learn Arabic, then congratulations! Arabic is a vastly rich and exciting language, and it carries both familiar and novel dimensions that can simultaneously keep you in contact with your First Language while diving into a new horizon of knowledge. It's always advised to pick your starting point carefully and thoughtfully before learning Arabic, given the multitude of learning methods. For that, Lingo Mastery is your best bet.

The Arabic Language is spoken by more than 420 million speakers, and it's the sixth most spoken language in the world. Interestingly, Standard Arabic is not spoken on a daily basis, but is still the official language of all Arab countries. And since Arabic is what unites all Arab peoples with different historical and cultural backgrounds, you will always find good assistance in your learning journey.

Lingo Mastery has designed this book to guide you through the *2000 Most Common Arabic Words in Context*. You will encounter some contexts that you may be familiar with, and others proper to the Arabic culture, or, more precisely, the *Arabic* way of saying things.

Interestingly, Standard Arabic is highly capacious with vocabulary, rhyming words, and detailed grammar, which might be frightening at a first glance. However, we think that this linguistic wealth will allow you to express yourself in a highly customized and personal fashion. We are excited to teach you how to use this flexibility to create sentences *proper to you*, ones that translate your thoughts into concrete and accurate expressions. So, use this flexibility to your advantage!

1

It is important to note that, unlike the English vowels, Arabic vowels are not letters. Words are composed of consonant sounds only, while vowels are added on top of each letter. Arabic vowels are called diacritics (or *tashkeel*), and they serve two major purposes:

- *Educational:* native speakers of Arabic are familiar with most of the Arabic words; therefore, they can understand these words without diacritics, because they have been exposed to the words time-and-time again until they were able to predict diacritics. Still, even native speakers of Arabic start their learning journey with diacritics because they're the key element in the writing and pronunciation systems.

- *Providing guidance:* vowels can change both the meaning and the grammatical category of words. They can be crucial to clarify who did what to whom, as a word can mean multiple things if pronounced differently. So, diacritics are not entirely optional. In fact, adding diacritics highlights your grammar mastery and proves how confident you are in using the language. MSA speakers, who are especially equipped with a specialized academic background in Arabic, value the use of diacritics, and find great pride in showing off their skills, which explains why they use them all the time.

Tips:

- The '*shaddah*' (Ö) is a tashkeel symbol that's similar to an upside down "3". It's the emphasis you place on sounds like /p/ in "stopped" or /s/ in "fossil", or /m/ in "common". So, instead of writing a consonant twice, all you need to do is add Shaddah above the letter, and it doubles it!

- Shaddah is not just a tashkeel symbol, but it also stands as a full letter. Make sure to always add it whenever convenient.

How can I tell if I should add Shaddah?

- Transcribe the word! If you find yourself writing double "m" or double "s" or double "t", etc., then add the Shaddah to the Arabic sound!

Recommendations for readers of 2000 Most Common Arabic Words in Context:

- *Keep practicing the language:* Find yourself good conversational pals, so that you never cease to keep your Arabic fresh. It's important to be selective while choosing your language partners, and we always recommend language teachers with an academic degree in Arabic, or the ones who practice the language on a consistent basis.

- *Don't be shy:* You may be slightly unfamiliar with the Arabic vocal system. It's a language that activates most of the jawline muscles all the way down to the throat, but mastering those sounds is not difficult. Just try to think of any sound you know that's the closest to the one you're practicing. No worries. You'll get there in no time. Meanwhile, don't let the sound system cripple you! Just use the sounds you're familiar with. Keep creating expressions, and keep voicing your opinions!

- *Start with what you know:* The Arabic language is a relatively conservative one in the sense that it does not create new terminology for modern topics such as technology, gender-related issues, and science. Instead, it resorts to direct borrowing. For example, the word "computer" is pronounced the exact way in Arabic, and the only difference is that it's written in Arabic alphabets. Start by creating expressions using borrowed words, so that you can always keep a familiar foundation for your practice. Arabic has its own way of expressing modernity, but it can never get entirely unfamiliar.

Transcription notes

ب – /b/ sound, as 'b' in "**boy**".

ت/ة – /t/ sound, as 't' in "**tea**". /t/ is alveolar but /ت/ is dental

د – /d/ sound, as 'd' in "**door**".

ك – /k/ sound, as 'k' in "**king**".

ج – /ʒ/ sound, as 's' (or phonetic "zh") in "**plea<u>s</u>ure**".

ف – /f/ sound, as 'f' in "**feet**"and "**phone**".

ذ – /ð/ sound, as 'th' in "**the**".

ث – /θ/ sound, as 'th' in "**think**".

ز – /z/ sound, as 'z' in "**zoo**".

ش – /ʃ/ sound, as 'sh' in "**wash**".

ر – /r/ sound, as 'r' in "**road**".

ه – /h/ sound, as 'h' in "**hat**".

م – /m/ sound, as 'm' in "**man**".

ن – /n/ sound, as 'n' in "**near**".

ل – /l/ sound, as 'l' in "**leave**" and "**people**".

ص – /s/ sound, as 's' in "**son**"

> ➤ English vowels are: "a" "e" "o" "I" "u" but Arabic vowels are: "ي" "و" "ا".
>
> ي – /i:/ sound, as 'e' in "**beat**".
>
> و – /u:/ sound, as 'ou' in "**soup**".
>
> ا – /æ/ sound, as 'a' in "**cat**".

Easy, isn't it?

A Few Grammar Notes

The science of the Arabic language is known as (نحو /nahw/) – basically translated as Arabic grammar and Arabic syntax. Words are divided into three categories:

1. 'Nouns' (اسم) /ism/
2. 'Verbs' (فعل) /fe'l/
3. 'Particles' (حرف) /harf/

Each category has:

اسم	nouns pronouns adjectives adverbs
فعل	Verbs
حرف	prepositions articles conjunctions particles (such as most interjections)

There are two main types of sentences: nominal and verbal. The former is for the sentence which effectively begins with a noun, and the latter is for the sentence which effectively begins with a verb.

sentence	
فعليّة Verbal	اسميّة Nominal

5

- **Nouns**

In the English language, a noun can be many things, and can take multiple forms as well. Similarly, Arabic has its own use of the Noun, making it the most flexible grammatical category in the language. A noun can refer to:

- Gender: all nouns are either
  - Masculine, or
  - feminine

- Plurality: all nouns are either
  - singular,
  - dual, or
  - plural

- Definitions: all nouns are either
  - Indefinite, or
  - definite

- **Verbs**

Arabic morphology has its own way of classifying and dealing with verbs. Grammar divides verbs into the following categories.

- ماضي(perfect): the past tense verb
- مضارع(imperfect): this includes the present, future, prohibition, and all variations
- أمر حاضر(imperative): this includes only the active, second-person conjugations of the command verb

- **Particles**

There are less than 80 particles in the entire language., it is possible to categorize them based on their meanings and their effects.

Abbreviations

adj	*Adjectives* used to qualify, quantify or modify nouns
adv	*Adverbs* functioning to qualify, quantify or modify verbs
part	*Particles are words that do not impart meaning on their own. As in prepositions, conjunctions, and articles. Thus, vocative particles (voc.part)*
attach.pron or suf.	Attached pronouns are always added to the end of the word
Excla.	*Exclamation is the act of exclaiming; sudden, vehement utterance*
Elat.	*The elative (Arabic: اِسْمُ تَفْضِيل ismu tafḍīl, literally meaning "noun of preference") is a stage of gradation in Arabic that can be used to express comparatives or superlatives.*
n	Nouns which refer to names of people, concepts, or objects.
Un.n	The unit noun is an individual thing that is part of something larger.
Masc.	*Masculine pronoun which refers and belongs to males.*
a.p.	*The active participle is that noun derived from a gerund which is used to indicate upon the one who has, is, or will enact something. It is loosely referred to as the 'doer'.*
prep	*Prepositions* functioning as temporal, spatial, or referential units which are always placed *before* words and meaningless on their own.

pron	*pronouns* referring to or standing for subjects or nouns such as possessive pronouns (poss.pron), subject pronouns (sub.pron), demonstrative pronouns (dem.pron), and relative pronouns (rel.pron).
imperf	The imperfect is a verb form which combines past tense and imperfective aspect.
perf	*Perfect is a verb form that indicates a complete ("perfected") action.*
v	*verbs* expressing actions, happenings, or states of being.

Let's go! And good luck! Or as you will be saying after learning the language, *bit-tawfīq*!

THE 2000 MOST COMMON
WORDS İN ARABİC

Building your vocabulary with some of the most common words used in the Arabic language is a great start for your journey in learning this beautiful language. Using everyday common words is the most convenient way to learn Arabic. The more you hear these words, the better it is for you to process and understand them.

1. لا [neg.part] *no/not*

لا تَتَعَاطَى المُخَدِّرَاتْ.

Do **not** take drugs.

هَلْ تَنَاوَلْتَ الفَطُورْ؟ لا

Did you have breakfast? **No.**

2. من [prep] *of*

مَجْمُوعَةٌ مِنَ الفَتَيَاتِ.

A group **of** girls.

3. فِي [prep] *in*

اللُّعْبَةُ فِي السَّيَّارَةِ.

The toy is **in** the car.

4. أَنَّ [part] *that*

عَلِمْتُ أَنَّ المَدْرَسَةَ غَداً.

I knew **that** school is tomorrow.

9

5. هَذَا [dem. pron, masc.] *this*

هَذَا هُوَ الْكِتَابُ.

This is the book.

6. عَلَى [prep] *on*

ضَع سِلَاحَك عَلَى الطَّاوِلَةِ.

Put your gun **on** the table.

7. مَا [interrog] *what*

مَا الْهَدَفُ مِنْ قِرَاءَةِ هَذَا الْكِتَابِ؟

What is the purpose of reading this book?

8. أَنَا [pron] *I*

أَنَا أُحِبّ عَصِيرَ الْبُرْتُقالِ.

I love orange juice.

9. هَلْ [interrog] *Is*

هَلْ مِنْ أحدٍ هُنَا؟

Is anyone here?

10. وَ [part] *and*

أُحْضِر لِي عَصِيراً وبسكويت.

Bring me juice **and** cookies.

11. أوه [exclam] *oh*

أوه، أَنَا حَقّاً لَسْت بَارِعاً فِي هَذَا.

Oh man, I'm really terrible at this.

12. ذَلِكَ [dem. pron] *so*

رُبَّمَا لَا تَعْتَقِدُ ذَلِكَ وَلَكِنَّك تَفْعَلَه.

You might not think **so**, but you're doing it.

13. لقد+فعل ماضي [pres. perf] *I have*

لَقَد فَحَصْتُ كلّ الْمَنَازِل. لَقَد غَادَر الْجَمِيعُ.

I have checked all the houses. Everyone's gone.

14. لَمْ [neg] *not*

لَمْ يَتِمَّ إِنْشَاءُ حِسَاب فيسبوك جَدِيد.

A new Facebook account has **not** been created.

15. مَاذَا [interrog] *what*

مَاذَا تَفْعَلُ؟

What are you doing?

16. هُنَا [adv] *here*

تَعَالَ إلى هُنَا!

Come **here**!

17. كَانَ [v] *was*

كَان جاك رجلاً مهذباً.

Jack **was** a polite man.

18. أَنْتَ [pron] *you are*

أَنْتَ شابٌّ مُهذَّب.

You are a gentleman.

19. إِلَى [prep] *to*

ذَهَبَ جَاك إِلَى السُّوقِ.

Jack went **to** the market.

20. هُوَ [pron] *is*

الْخِيَارُ الْوَحِيدُ هُوَ النَّجَاحُ.

The only option **is** success.

21. هَذِهِ [dem. Pron. Plur] *these*

مِنْ أَيْنَ أَحْضَرَت هَذِه الزُّهُور؟

Where did you get **these** roses from?

22. عَنْ [prep] *about*

أَعْلَم الْقَلِيلَ عَنْ الْقَانُونِ.

I know a little **about** the law.

23. إِنَّ [emphatic the] *the*

إِنَّ نَقْصَ الأُكْسِجِين يُؤَدِّي إِلَى الاخْتِنَاق.

The lack of oxygen causes asphyxiation.

24. نَعَمْ [interjection] *yes*

هَل تُحِبُّ عَصِيرِ الْعِنَبِ؟ نَعَم.

Do you like grape juice? Yes.

25. هناك [adv] *there are*

هُنَاك أَسْرَار عَنْ هَذِهِ الْقَلْعَة.

There are secrets about this castle.

26. كُلُّ [adv. quantifier] *all*

هَذِه **كُلّ** تَجَارِبِنَا الْعَامَ الْمَاضِي.

These are **all** our experiences last year.

27. لَيْسَ [neg] *not*

الْفَقْرُ **لَيْس** عائقاً أَمَام النَّجَاح.

Poverty is **not** a hindrance to success.

28. كنت [imperf] *I was*

كُنْتُ فِي الْمَطْعَمِ.

I was at the restaurant.

29. فَقَطْ [adv] *only*

رَأَيْتُه مَرَّةً وَاحِدَةً **فَقَط**.

I've **only** seen him once.

30. الآنَ [adv] *now*

لَيْس **الآنَ**.

Not **now**.

31. مَعَ [prep] *with*

مَا حَصَلَ هُنَا **مَعَ** جيني لَن يَحْصُل مجدداً.

What happened here **with** Jinny will never happen again.

32. شَيْء [n] *something*

كَانَ هُنَالِكَ **شَيْءٌ** ثَمِينٌ عَلَى ذَلِكَ الْقُرْص الصَّلْب.

I think there was **something** valuable on that hard disk.

33. الَّذِي [rel. pron] *which*

مِنْ الْمُرَجِّحِ أَنَّهُ الْعَلَمُ الَّذِي اخْتَفَى مِنْ الْمَكْتَبَة.

It appears to be the flag **which** disappeared from the library.

34. لَكِنْ [coordinating. Conj] *but*

يُمْكِنُنِي تَعْلِيمُك، وَلَكِن فَقَطْ لَوْ أَرَدْتَ أَنْتَ ذَلِك.

I can teach you, **but** only if you're willing.

35. يَجِبُ [v] *must be*

يَجِبُ أَنْ تَكُونَ جَاهِزاً.

You **must be** ready.

36. لَكَ [poss. pron] *yours*

هَذَا لِي وَهَذَا لَك.

This is mine and this is **yours.**

37. لَنْ [part] *will not be*

لَن أَكُون هُنَاك غداً.

I **will not be** there tomorrow.

38. كَيْف[interro] *how*

كَيْفَ حَالُك؟

How do you do?

39. من أَجْلِ [prep] *for*

خَبَزْتُ كِيكَة مِنْ أَجَلِك.

I baked a cake **for** you.

40. أَنا [pron] *I am*

أَنَا مُعَلِّمٌ.

I am a teacher.

41. حَسَناً [discourse marker] *well*

حَسَناً، سَأَزُورُهُ غَداً.

Well, I will go to see him tomorrow.

42. لي [prep+poss. pron] *at me*

اِبتَسَمَتْ لي.

She smiled **at me**.

43. إنه [إنْ -> it "ه" -> is.] *it's*

إنَّهُ خَبَرٌ رَائِع.

It's amazing news!

44. نَحْنُ [sub. pron] *we are*

نَحْنُ مَجْمُوعَةٌ مِنَ الْمُهَنْدِسِين.

We are a group of engineers.

45. سوف [part] *will*

سَوْفَ أَذْهَبُ إلى البَحْرِ.

I **will** go to the sea.

46. كانَ [imperf] *was*

كانَ الكَلْبُ نَائِماً

The dog **was** asleep.

47. عَندَما [adv] *when*

كُنتُ أَشَاهِدُ التَّلْفَازَ عِنْدَمَا أَتَيْتَ.

I was watching TV **when** you came.

48. إِذَا [part] *if*

إِذَا أَمْطَرَت غَداً، فَسَنَذْهَبُ لِلسِّينِمَا.

If it rains tomorrow, we'll go to the cinema.

49. لِمَاذَا [interrog] *why*

لِمَاذَا لَمْ تَذْهَبْ إِلَى الْمَدْرَسَةِ؟

Why didn't you go to school?

50. أَيْ [part] *i.e.*

اتّفقنا على المغادرة يوم الخميس، أي اليوم.

We agreed to leave on Thursday, **i.e.** today.

51. قد [perf/part] *has*

لَقَدْ كَانَ في الحَانَة طِيلَة الظَّهِيرَة.

He **has** been in the pub all afternoon.

52. أنه [أن -> part., "ه" -> attached pron.] *that*

يَعْلَمُ أَنَّهُ مُحِقٌّ.

He knows **that** he is right.

53. الأَمْرُ [n] *it*

الأَمْرِ لَا يَتَعَلَّقُ بِالشَّجَاعَة، بَل بِالثِّقَة.

It's not about courage, it's about trust.

54. هي [pron] *is*

أَوْلَوِيَّتي الْآنَ هِيَ تَأْمِين الْمَبْنَى.

My priority right now **is** to secure the building.

55. بَعْدَ [adv] *after*

سَأُغَادِرُ بَعْد الْمُبَارَاة.

I'll leave **after** the match.

56. كذلك [n] *as well as*

نَتَوَقَّعُ اِعْتِذَاراً مِنْه، وَمِنْك أَنْتَ كَذَلِكَ.

We expect an apology from him, and from you **as well**.

57. لِمُدَّةِ [prep] *up to*

بَقِيتُ لِمُدَّةِ سَبْعِ سَاعَاتٍ.

I stayed **up to** seven hours.

58. إنَّهُ [إنْ -> part., "ه" -> attached pron.] *he*

إنَّه مُتَهَوِّر.

He's reckless.

59. قَبْل [adv] *before*

سَأُغادِر قَبْلَ أَنْ يَأْتِي.

I'll leave **before** he comes.

60. أوْ [part] *or*

رُبَّمَا مَرَّة أَوْ مَرَّتَيْن.

Maybe one **or** two times.

61. لَوْ [part] *if*

سَتَفْعَلُ نَفْسَ الشَّيء لَوْ كُنْتَ مَكَانِي

You would have done the same **if** you were in my shoes.

62. أَيْنَ [interrog] *where*

أَيْنَ ذَهَبَ عَلِيَّ؟

Where did Ali go?

63. الَّتي [rel. pron] *which*

ألا تَعْرَف الْمَحَلَّاتِ الَّتِي تَبِيعُ هَدَايَا النِّسَاء؟

Do you not know **which** shops sell gifts for women?

64. هيا [voc. part] *come on*

هَيَّا، إِنَّهُ مَوْعِد الْمَدْرَسَة.

Come on, it's school time.

65. تلك [dem. pron] *those*

تِلْك الجينات تَسَبِّب التَّوَحُّد.

Those genes cause autism.

66. رُبَّمَا [adv] *maybe*

رُبَّمَا تَحْتَاجُ إِلَى بَعْضٍ الْوَقْتِ.

Maybe you just need some time!

67. إنها [إنْ -> part, "ﻫ" -> pron.] *it is*

إِنَّهَا السَّاعَةُ الَّتِي أَخْبَرْتُك عَنْهَا.

It's the watch I've told you about.

68. أعرف [v] *I know*

أَعْرِفُ مِنْ أَنْتَ.

I know who you are.

69. بعض [adv] *some*

أَحْتَاج بَعْض السَّلَامِ هُنَا.

I need some peace here.

70. يكون [v] *be*

يُرِيدُ أَنْ يَكونَ الأَفْضَلَ.

He wants to **be** the best.

71. أريد [v] *I want*

أُرِيد أَلْفِ عَامٍ!

I want a thousand years!

72. أعتقد [v] *I think*

أَعْتَقِدُ أَنَّهُ مُحِقٌّ.

I think he is right.

73. مِن قَبِيل [n] *such as*

يمكنك اختيار أيّ حيوان أليف، **من قبيل** القطط والكلاب والأرانب.

You can pick any domestic animals, **such as** cats, dogs, and rabbits.

74. عليك [n] *you have*

عَلَيْكَ أَنْ تَدْرُس جيداً.

You have to study well.

75. به [n] *by*

هذا هو السوق الذي مررت به بالأمس.

This is the market I walked **by** yesterday.

76. بخير [adv] *fine*

أَنَا بِخَيْر.

I am **fine**.

77. أنك [أن -> part, "ك" -> pron.] *that you*

ظَنَنْت أَنَّك لَنْ تَأْتِي فِي الْمَوْعِدِ.

I thought **that you** wouldn't come on time.

78. صحيح [adj] *true*

هَلْ صَحِيحٌ أَنَّك أَرْسَلْت شرطياً إلى المستشفى؟

Is it **true** that you sent a policeman to the hospital?

79. الوقت [n] *time*

حانَ الوَقْتُ لِلْقِيَام بِشَيْء جَدِيد.

It's **time** to do something new.

80. أحد [n] *one*

لم يأتني أحد.

No **one** came to me.

81. شخص [n] *person*

أَنْت شَخْصٌ ذُكِّي.

You are a clever **person**.

82. رجل [n] *man*

أَنْت رجلٌ رَائِع.

You are an amazing **man**!

83. أعلم [v] *I know*

أَنَا أَعْلَمُ بِذَلِكَ.

I **know** that.

84. جيد [adj] *good*

إِنَّهُ شَابٌ جَيِّد.

He is a **good** guy.

85. أمريكي [n] *American*

إنه رجل أمريكي.

He is an **American** man.

86. أكثر [elat] *more than*

أُحِبُّ الشَّاي أَكْثَر مِنْ القَهْوَة.

I like tea **more than** coffee.

87. تكون [v] *be*

يَجِبُ أَنْ تَكُونَ هُنَا عَلَى السَّاعَةِ السَّادِسَة مساءً.

You must **be** here at 6 p.m.

88. علي [n] *Ali*

جَاءَ عليٌّ.

Ali has arrived.

89. يمكن [v] *can*

يُمْكِنُك فِعْلِهَا!

You **can** do it!

90. لذا [part] *so*

شعرت بالملل، **لذا،** شاهدتُ فلما.

I was bored, **so** I watched a movie.

91. كما [n] *as*

الأمر ليس صعبا **كما** يبدو.

It's not as difficult **as** it seems.

92. اليوم [adv] *today*

سَتَأتِي عَمَّتِي الْيَوْم.

My aunt will come **today**.

93. يبدو [v] *it seems*

يبدو من المستحيل إقناعه باللعبة الجديدة.

It seems impossible to get him into the new game.

94. أليس [n] *Alice*

أليس في عَالَمِ الْعَجَائِب.

Alice in Wonderland.

95. إنها [إن -> part, "ها" -> pron.] *it's*

إنَّها أثَرية جِداً.

It's very antique.

96. يُمْكِنُكَ [v] *you can*

يُمْكِنُكَ فِعْلُ ذَلِك.

You can do it.

97. لَدَيَّ [n] *I have*

لَدَيَّ ثلاثُ أَخَوَاتٍ.

I have 3 sisters.

98. كِلا [masc.] *both*

كِلا الْفَرِيقَيْن رائعَيْن.

Both teams are great.

99. آخَرُ/أُخرى [n] *another*

أريد شراء سُتْرَة أُخرى.

I want to buy **another** jacket.

100. عَلَيْه [n] *it*

إذَا أَرَدْت الْمَال، عَلَيْك الْعَمَل لِلْحُصُول عَلَيْه.

If you want money, you need to work for **it**.

101. مُنْذُ [adv] *since*

أَعْرِفُه مُنْذ صِغَرِي.

I've known him **since** I was a child.

102. غَيْرُ [n] *is not*

إنَّها غَيْرُ مُتَّصِلَة بالانترنت.

She **is not** connected to the internet.

103. لست [imperf] *I'm not*

لستُ غبياً.

I'm **not** stupid.

104. يلعب [v] *plays*

يَلْعَب أَخِي فِي الْمَلْعَبِ.

My brother **plays** in the stadium.

105. لديك [n] *you have*

لَدَيْكَ ثَلاَثَةُ إِخْوَة

You have 3 brothers.

106. تُرِيدُ [v] *want*

مَاذَا تُرِيدُ؟

What do you **want**?

107. أَسْتَطِيعُ [v] *I can*

رُبَّمَا لَا تَسْتَطِيعِين فِعْلِهَا، لَكِنْ أَنَا أَسْتَطِيع.

Maybe you can't do it, but I **can**.

108. لَهُ [n] *has*

أَخِي لَهُ سُمْعَةٌ رَفِيعَةٌ.

My brother **has** a fine reputation.

109. مَرَّةَ [un. n] *once*

رَأَيْتُه مَرَّةً وَاحِدَةً فَقَطْ.

I've only seen him **once**.

110. بِأَنْ [part] *that*

وعدتُ صدِيقَتِي **بِأَن** أقابِلَهَا غَداً.

I promised my friend **that** I'll meet her tomorrow.

111. لَدَيْنَا [n] *we have*

لدينا ثلاثَةُ أطفالٍ.

We have three children.

112. وَاحِد [n] *one*

رَقْمُ وَاحِدْ.

Number **one**.

113. لا شَيْء [n] *nothing*

-هَلْ قُلْتَ شَيْئاً؟ - لا. لا شَيْء.

- Did you say anything? - No. **Nothing.**

114. يُمْكِنُنِي [v] *I can*

يُمْكِنُنِي فِعْلُهَا.

I can do it.

115. حَدَثٌ [n] *event*

إنَّه أَسْعَد حدثٍ فِي حَيَاتِي.

It's a blessed **event** in my life.

116. بِهَا [n] *her*

وَعَدْت ابنتي بِأَنَّنِي سَأَتَّصِل بِهَا اللّيْلَةَ.

I promised my daughter I'd call **her** tonight.

117. الناس [n] *people*

لَا تَهْتَمَّ لِكَلَام النَّاس.

Don't care about what **people** say.

118. أوه [excla] *Oh!*

أُوه ! مَاذَا حَدَثَ؟

Oh! What happened?

119. الأفضل [elat] *the best*

أَنْت الْأَفْضَل.

You are the **best**.

120. مكان [n] *place*

سأساعدك عَلَى إيجَادِ الْمَكَان.

I'll help you to find **the place**.

121. تفعل [v] *do*

مَاذَا تَفْعَلُ؟

What are you **doing**?

122. سيّدي [n] *sir*

سَيِّدِي، هَل يُمْكِنَني المغادرة؟

Sir, can I leave?

123. لم يكن [v] *was/were not*

لَمْ يَكُنْ دَوْرَك.

It **wasn't** your line.

124. الكثير [n] *a lot*

لَدَيْنَا **الْكَثِير** مِن الْحَلْوَى.

We have **a lot** of sweets.

125. بهذا [dem. pron] *this*

يُمْكِنُك كِتَابَتُهَا **بِهَذا** الشَّكْلِ.

You can write it like **this**.

126. جداً [adv] *very*

أَنَا أُحِبُّك جداً.

.I love you **very** much.

127. لي [n] *to me*

ماذا قُلْتَ لِي؟

What did you say **to me?**

128. علينا [verb phrase] *we have to*

عَلَيْنَا أَنْ نُسْرِع.

We have to hurry.

129. أخرى [adj] *other*

لِيسَتْ لديّ كلماتٌ أُخْرَى.

I have no **other** words.

130. رائع [adj] *Fantastic*

أَنْت شَخْصٌ رَائِع.

You are a **fantastic** person.

131. آسِفٌ [adj] *Sorry*

آسِفٌ، لَمْ أَقْصِدْ ذَلِكَ.

Sorry. I didn't mean it.

132. بذلك [adv] *thus*

وَبِذَلِك حَقَّقْت البرازيل نجاحاً واسعاً.

Brazil had **thus** made considerable progress.

133. ـك [possess] *your*

حَاسُوبُك مُعَطَّلٌ.

Your computer is broken.

134. كم [interro/excla] *how*

كَم أَنْت مَشْغُولَةُ الْبَال!

How pensive you are!

135. يوجد [v] *there are*

يُوجَد الْكَثِيرُ مِنْ الْحَلْوَى.

There are a lot of sweets.

136. يحدث [v] *happen*

حسناً، لَن أَدَعَ ذَلِك يَحْدُثُ.

Well, I won't let it **happen.**

137. قلت [v] *I said*

نَعَم، قلتُ ذَلِك.

Yes, **I said** that.

138. ثُمَّ [adv] *then*

نضع البيض، ثُمّ نضيف السّكّر.
We put the eggs, **then** we add sugar.

139. يوم [n] *day*

سَنَذْهَبُ يَوْماً مَا.
One **day**, we will do.

140. سيد [adj] *Mr.*

سَتَجِد السَّيِّد حَمْزَةَ فِي الْمَقْهَى.
You'll find **Mr.** Hamza in the café.

141. مرحبا [n] *hello*

مَرْحَباً، كَيْفَ حَالُكَ؟
Hello, how are you?

142. معك [مع -> adv., "ك" -> attach. pron] *with you*

خُذْنِي مَعَكَ.
Take me **with you**.

143. شكراً [n] *thanks*

شكراً جَزيلا كثيراً!
Thanks a bunch!

144. أَبِي [n] *dad*

أَحِبّ أَبِي.
I love my **dad**.

145. مَعي مع [adv., "ك" -> attach. pron] *with me*

تَعَال مَعِي.

Come **with me**.

146. أتعلم [v] *learn*

أُرِيدُ أَنْ أَتَعَلَّمَ الْعَرَبِيَّةَ.

I want to **learn** Arabic.

147. لها [pron] *her*

مَاذَا فَعَلْت لَهَا؟

What did you do to **her**?

148. بالطبع [adv] *of course*

بِالطَّبْع، يُمْكِنُك الاتِّصَالُ بِهَا.

Of course, you can call her.

149. إذن [part] *so*

إِذْن، الْمَكَان الْوَحِيد لِمُشَاهَدَة التِّلْفَاز سَيَكُونُ فِي الْأَسْفَلِ.

So, the only place to watch TV will be downstairs.

150. الليلة [adv] *tonight*

اللَّيْلَة حَفْلُ عيد مِيلَادِي.

Tonight is my birthday party.

151. العمل [n] *work*

مَتَى ستذهب لِلْعَمَلِ؟

When will you go to **work**?

152. المكان [n] *location*

هَل يُمْكِنُك مراسلتي بِالْمَكَان؟

Could you message me with **the location**?

153. إله [n] *God*

هيرميس هُوَ إلَاهُ التِّجارَةِ عِنْدَ الإغْريق.

Hermes is the Greek **god** of trade.

154. يفعل [v] *doing*

مَاذَا يَفْعَلُ؟

What is he **doing**?

155. لا [part] *do not*

لا تَكْذِبْ.

Do not lie.

156. هكذا [conj] *thus*

سَوْف يَعِيش هَكَذَا إِلَى الأَبَدِ.

Thus, he will live forever.

157. الحقيقة [n] *truth*

سنعرف الْحَقِيقَة، لا تقْلقْ.

Don't worry, we'll know the **truth**.

158. أمي [n] *mom*

أحبّ أمِّي.

I love my **mom**.

159. لِ [prep] *for*

هَل صَنَعْتِهَا لِي؟

Did you make it **for** me?

160. كادَ [v] *about*

كادَتْ أَنْ تَنْجَحَ.

She was **about** to succeed.

161. بما فيهم [adv phrase] *including*

عَلَيْهِمْ أَنْ ينجحوا، بِمَن فِيهِمْ أَنْت.

They should succeed, **including** you.

162. لذلك [part] *so*

كنتُ مريضاً، لِذَلِكَ لَمْ أَذْهَب إلى المَدْرَسَة

I was sick, **so** I didn't go to school.

163. حقاً [adv] *really*

أَنَا حقاً أُحِبُّك.

I **really** like you.

164. الجميع [n] *all*

أحِبُّكُم جميعاً.

I love you **all**.

165. يمكننا [v] *we can*

يُمْكِنُنَا فِعْلِ ذلك.

We can do it.

166. لَنا [poss. pron] for **us**

اشتَرِ **لَنَا** ألعاباً.

Buy **us** toys.

167. لأَن [part] **because**

لَم أَذهَب إلى الحفلة **لِأَنَّنِي** مَريضٌ.

I didn't go to school **because** I am sick.

168. خِلال [adv] **during**

ماذا فَعَلت **خِلال** الْحَجر الصّحّيّ؟

What did you do **during** the quarantine?

169. فقط [adv] **only**

أحتاج هذا **فقط**.

I **only** need that.

170. العالم [n] **world**

سأسافر حَوْل الْعَالم.

I'll travel around the **world**.

171. عنه [part+pron] **about**

هَل يُمْكِنُك إِخْبَارِي أَيّ شَيْء **عَنْهُ**؟

Could you tell me anything **about** it?

172. الذهاب [n] **go**

يَجِبُ عَلَيَّ الذَّهَابُ.

I have to **go**.

173. فعلت [v] *I did*

فَعَلْت مَا يَكْفِي مِنْ أَجْلِهَا.

I did enough for her.

174. هم [sub. pron] *they are*

هُم الْأَفْضَل.

They are the best.

175. قال [v] *he said*

قَالَ مَا يُرِيدُهُ.

He said what he wants.

176. المنزل [n] *home*

أُرِيد الذَّهَابَ إِلَى الْمَنْزِلِ.

I want to go **home**.

177. أفعل [v] *I do*

مَاذَا عَلَيَّ أَنْ أَفْعَلَ؟

What should **I do**?

178. فيه [part+pron] *in which*

هَذَا هو المَبدأ الذي أُومِنُ بِهِ.

This is the value **in which I believe**.

179. أعني [v] *I mean*

أَعْنِي، هَذِهِ خطوتي الْأُولَى فِي الْعَالَمِ الْحَقِيقِيّ.

I mean, this is my first step into the real world.

180. كثيرا [adj] *very*

أحبّ الْعِنَب كثيراً.

I like the grapes **very much**.

181. بين [prep] *between*

مَا الِاخْتِلَاف بَيْنَ هَذَا وَذَاكَ؟

What is the difference **between** this and that?

182. فيك [part+pron] *of you*

لَكِنَّ هَذَا الْجَانِبِ الْجَدِيد فيك سَاكِتٌ.

But this new side **of you** is quiet.

183. جيدة [adj] *good*

إنَّهَا فِي حَالَة جَيِّدَة.

She is in a **good** condition.

184. بِشَأْن [n] *about*

مَاذَا فَعَلْت بِشَأْن الحَفْلَة؟

What did you do **about** the party?

185. اللعنة [n] *curse*

اللَّعْنَةَ عَلَى الْحَظِّ السَّيِّءِ.

Curse on bad luck.

186. نحن [pron] *we are*

نحن الأَفْضَل.

We are the best.

187. ها [part] *ha*

هَا. مَا الَّذِي فَعَلْتَهُ؟

Ha! What did you do?

188. متى [interrog] *when*

مَتَى ستغادر اسطنبول؟

When will you leave Istanbul?

189. يعني [v] *it means*

شكراً لكَ تيد، هَذَا يَعْنِي لِي الْكَثِير.

Thanks Ted, **it means** a lot.

190. فكرة [n] *idea*

هَل لَدَيْك أَيّة فِكْرَةٌ؟

Do you have any **idea**?

191. الأمور [n] *things*

لَا أُرِيدُ أَنْ أَكُونَ إِحْدَى هَذِهِ الْأُمُورِ.

I don't want to be one of those **things**.

192. أظن [v] *I think*

أَظُنُّ أَنَّهُ ذَهَبَ إِلَى عَمَّتِي.

I think he went to my aunt.

193. أنني [part+poss. pron] *I*

قُلْتُ أَنَّنِي لَمْ أَفْعَل ذلك.

I said I didn't do it, okay?

194. كنّا [v] *we were*

كُنَّا فِي الْمَقْهَى.

We were in the café.

195. مجرد [adv] *just*

إِنَّهَا مُجَرَّدٌ صَدَفَةٍ.

It's just a shell.

196. المال [n] *money*

هـلْ تَمْلُك الْمَال؟

Do you have money?

197. أقول [v] *I say*

دائماً ما أقول "يمكنك تَحْقِيقٍ مَا تَصْبُو إِلَيْهِ"

I always say, "You can achieve what you're looking for."

198. ستكون [part+v] *will be*

أَثِق بِك، سَتَكُون الْأَفْضَل.

I trust you; you'll be the best.

199. تقول [v] *is saying*

لَا أَعْلَمُ مَاذَا تَقُولُ.

I don't know what she is saying.

200. أم [part] *or*

كَبِيرٌ أُم صَغِيرٍ؟

Big or small?

201. هؤُلاء [pron] *those*

أنتِ أَكْبَرُ مِنْ **هَؤُلاءِ** الأَطْفَال بِعَشْرِ سَنَوَاتٍ.

You've got about 10 years on most of **those** kids.

202. الطريق [n] *road*

نَحْتَاج لِمَعْرِفَةِ مَا كَانَ يَفْعَلُهُ فِي ذَاكَ **الطَّرِيقِ** اللَّيْلَةَ الْمَاضِيَةَ.

We need to find out what he was doing on that **road** last night.

203. بالنسبة [n] *for*

لَا أُرِيدُ أَنْ يَكُونَ الْمَوْقِف غريباً **بِالنِّسْبَةِ** إِلَيْك.

I just don't want it to be awkward **for** you.

204. أي/أيّة [prep] *any*

لَيْس هُنَاك أي نِقَّاش اللَّيْلَةَ **بِأيّة** لُغَةً ماعدا الْعَرَبِيّة.

There shall be no discussion tonight in **any** language but Arabic.

205. أمر [n] *order*

هَـلْ جَـاءَ **الأمر** مِنْ "أليكس"؟

Did the **order** come from Alex?

206. معه [مع -> prep, "ه" -> attach. pron] *with him*

هَل ستهرب مِنْ حَيَاتِهَا الْجَدِيدَة **مَعَه**؟

Will she run away from her new life **with him**?

207. منه [من -> prep, "ه" -> attach. pron] *him*

لَقَدْ كَانَ الطَّقْس سيئاً لِلْغَايَة فَطَلَبَتْ **مِنْهُ** الْمَبِيت.

The weather was so bad, so I asked **him** to stay overnight.

208. توقف [v] *stop*

أَرَدْتُكَ أَنْ **تُوقِفَ** المعتدي.

I was hoping you'd be able to **stop** the aggressor.

209. نفس [n] *the same*

لَا تَحْتَاجُ إلى اتباع النَّمط **نفسِه**.

You don't need to follow **the same** style.

210. لما [part] *when*

لمَّا أَتَيتَ، كُنْتُ أُشَاهِدُ التِّلْفَازَ.

When you came, I was watching TV.

211. انظر [v] *see*

انظر إلَيْه.

Look at him.

212. الحياة [n] *life*

أَعْلَمُ أَنَّ **الحَيَاةَ** مِنْ دُونِكَ بَائِسَةٌ.

I know that **life** without you is misery.

213. مِنْ دُونِ [n] *without*

غَادَرَتْ **مِنْ دُونِ** أَنْ تَأْكُلَ.

She left **without** eating.

214. بأس -> n] لا بأس[لا -> part, *it's fine*

-هَل أنتَ غاضِب؟

-لا **بَأْس**.

-Are you mad?

-**It's fine.**

215. بسبب [n] *because of*

ارْتَكَبْتُ جَريمَةً بِسَبَبِ رَغْبَتِي في كَسْبِ المَالِ.

I committed a crime **because of** my foolish desire to earn money.

216. جحيم [n] *hell*

الحَيَاةُ مَعَه جحيم.

Life with him is **hell**.

217. حصلت [v] *I got*

حَصَلْتُ عَلَى وَظِيفَةٍ جَيِّدَةٍ فِي مَجَالِ البِنَاءِ.

I got a good job in construction.

218. أشعر [v] *I feel*

أشْعُرُ بِالمَلَلِ.

I feel bored.

219. أرى [v] *I see*

هَلْ تَعْلَمُ فِيمَا أُفَكِّرُ عِنْدَمَا أَرَى هَذِهِ المُنْحَنَيَاتِ؟

Do you know what I think when **I see** these curves?

220. لكم ["ل" -> prep, "كم" -> plural pron.] *you*

أُوَكِّدُ لَكُمْ أَنَّ الحُكُومَةَ تَتَّخِذُ جَمِيعَ الاحْتِيَاطَاتِ الوَاجِبَةِ.

I assure **you,** the government is taking all the necessary measures.

221. عند [adv] *when*

لقد كنتِ فَخُورَةً عند شِرَائِكِ هَذَا المنزل.

You were so proud **when** you bought this place.

222. الذي [rel. pron] *which*

حَقِيقَةً لا يَهُمُّ الاتجاه **الذي** ستتبعينه.

Actually, it doesn't matter **which** way you go.

223. تبدو [v] *look*

تَبْدُو هَادِئاً عَلَى غَيْرِ العَادَةِ.

You **look** abnormally calm.

224. الذين [rel. pron, masc. plural] *who/ who are*

هَلْ النَّاسُ **الذِينَ** سَرَقُوا الكُرَةَ هُمْ نَفْسُ الأَشْخَاصِ **الذِينَ** يَتَّهِمُونَنِي؟

Are the people **who** stole the ball the same people **who are** accusing me?

225. تحت [adv] *under*

هُنَالِكَ طِفْلٌ صَغِيرٌ **تَحْتَ** مَكْتَبِكَ.

There's a young boy **under** your desk.

226. الأشياء [n] *things*

اشتريتُ الكَثِيرَ مِنَ **الأَشْيَاءِ**.

I bought many **things**.

227. ليلة [adv] *night*

ليلَةً سَعِيدَةً.

Good **night**.

228. لكي [pron] *in order to*

يَجِبُ أَنْ تَتَّبِعُوا هَذِه القَاعِدَة **لِكَيْ** تُصْبِحُوا تَلامِيذِي.

In order to become my students, you must follow this rule.

229. حيث [adv] *where*

قَالَ أَنَّهُ عَائِدٌ إِلَى **حَيْثُ** يَنْتَمِي.

He said that he was going back to **where** he belongs.

230. مشكلة [n] *problem*

مَا الْمُشْكِلَةُ؟

What's the **problem**?

231. الـ [part] *the*

سَأَذْهَبُ إِلَى الـبَحْرِ.

I'll go to **the** sea.

232. نفسك [نفس -> n, ك -> attach. pron] *yourself*

اعْتَنِي بِنَفْسِكَ.

Take care of **yourself**.

233. تَعَالَ [v] *come on*

تَعَالَ، دَعْنَا نَنْزِل إِلَى البُحَيْرَة وَنَتَمَتَّعُ بِذَلِكَ الغُرُوبِ.

Come on, let's get down to the lake and enjoy that sunset.

234. شيئاً [n] *something*

اعْزِفْ شَيْئاً أَكْثَرَ بَهْجَةً، مِنْ فَضْلِكَ.

Play **something** a little more upbeat, please.

235. أذهب [v] *go*

لا أَسْتَطِيعُ التَّحَدُّثَ أَكْثَرَ. عَلَيَّ أَنْ أَذْهَبَ.

I can't talk anymore; I have to **go**.

236. حَاجَةٍ [n] *need*

هَذَا عَظِيمٌ، وَلَكِنَّي بِحَاجَةٍ لِأَكْثَر مِنْ مُجَرَّدِ دَعْمِكَ.

That's great, but I **need** more than your support.

237. يريد [v] *want*

مَاذَا تُرِيدُ؟

What do you **want**?

238. آسفة [n] *sorry*

أَنَا آسِفَةٌ!

I'm **sorry**!

239. بالفعل [n] *already*

كَانَ قَدْ وَعَدَهَا بِالزَّوَاجِ، لَكِنَّهُ كَانَ مُتَزَوِّجاً بِالفِعْلِ.

He had promised to marry her, but he was **already** married.

240. مِنْ فَضْلِكَ [n -> من] prep, فضلك <- n] *please*

هَلْ يُمْكِنُكَ مُسَاعَدَتِي مِنْ فَضْلِكَ؟

Could you help me, **please**?

241. عَزِيزَتي [n] *My dear*

عَزِيزَتي، لَنْ يَتِمَّ شَيْءٌ قَبْل عَوْدَتِه.

My dear, nothing can be done until he returns.

242. الوَحِيدُ [n] *only*

إِنَّهَا الشَّخْصُ الوَحِيدُ الذِي كَانَ يُؤْمِنُ بِي.

She's the **only** person who ever really believed in me.

243. قَتَل [v] *killed*

إِنَّنِي فَقَطْ أُحَاوِلُ اكْتِشَافَ الشَّخْصَ الذِي قَتَلَ صَدِيقَتِي.

I'm just trying to figure out who **killed** my friend.

244. بِحَقّ [noun phrase] *against*

لَنْ يَرْتَكِبَ تِلْكَ الجَرَائِمَ بِحَقِّ أَصْدِقَائِه.

He won't commit this crime **against** his friends.

245. طوال [adv] *throughout*

كُنْتُ أَخْشَى التَّحَدُّثَ مَعَ الفَتَيَاتِ طَوَالَ حَيَاتِي.

Throughout my life, I was afraid to talk to girls.

246. الشرطة [n] *police*

سَوْفَ نَطْلُبُ المُسَاعَدَةَ مِنْ قِسْمِ الشُّرْطَةِ.

We'll ask for help from the **police** department.

247. رأيت [v] *I saw*

عندما رأيت هَذَا الفُسْتَانَ، ظَنَنْتُهُ رَخِيصاً.

When **I saw** this dress, I thought it was cheap.

248. بنا [نا <- poss. pron, بـ <- prep] *us*

إِنْ اسْتَطَعْنَا تَجَاوُزَ حَرَكَةِ المُرُور، يُمكنكم الالْتِقَاءُ بِنَا هُنَاكَ.

If we can get through the traffic, you can meet **us** there.

249. ما الذي [rel. pron] *what*

أَنَا مُسْتَعِدٌّ، مَا الذِي تَنْتَظِرِينَهُ؟

I'm ready, **what** are you waiting for?

250. أريد [v] *I want*

أُرِيدُ أَنْ أَشْتَرِيَ سَيَّارَةً جَدِيدَةً.

I **want** to buy a new car.

251. أحب [v] *love*

أُحِبُّكَ!

I **love** you!

252. فعله [فعل <- v, ه <- attach. pron] *to do*

هَلْ تُدْرِكِينَ مَا تَطْلُبِينَهُ مِنَّا فِعْلَهُ؟

Do you realize what you're asking us **to do**?

253. أرجوك [أرجو <- v, ك <- attach. pron] *please*

يَجِبُ أَنْ تَسْمَحَ لِي بِرُؤْيَةِ ابْنِي، أَرْجُوكَ.

You have to let me see my son, **please**.

254. أيضاً [n] *also*

لَقَدْ رَبِحْتُ أَيْضاً بِضْعَةَ مُبَارَيَاتِ مُلَاكَمَةٍ.

I've **also** won a few boxing matches.

255. بل [part] *but*

أَنْتَ لَا تُرِيدُ زَوْجَةً، بَلْ مُرَبِّيَةَ أَطْفَالٍ.

You don't want a wife, **but** a babysitter.

256. إنهم [إن <- part, هم <- pron] *they are*

إِنَّهُمْ إِخْوَةٌ، لِذَلِكَ نُحِبُّ أَنْ نُبْقِيَهُمْ سَوِياً.

They're brothers, so we'd like to keep them together.

257. نار [n] *fire*

لا تَلْعَبْ بِالنَّارِ، سَتَحْرِقُ يَدَكَ.

Don't play with **fire**; you will burn your hand.

258. لم أكن [v] *wasn't*

لَقَدْ أَصْبَحَ جَاداً جِداً وَلَمْ أَكُنْ مُسْتَعِدَّةً لِذَلِكَ.

He got really serious, and I **wasn't** ready for it.

259. أردت [v] *I wanted*

كَذِبْتُ لِأَنَّنِي أَرَدْتُ لِعَائِلَتِي أَنْ تمضِيَ قُدُماً.

I lied because I **wanted** my family to move on.

260. من أجل [n -> أجل prep, من <-] *for*

لَمْ تُخْبِرْنِي أَنَّكَ غَادَرْتَ مُبَكِّراً مِنْ أَجْلِ حُضُورِ الحَفْلِ.

You didn't tell me you left early **for** the party.

261. كبير [adj] *large*

ضَعْ المُكَوِّنَات في وِعَاءٍ كبِيرٍ.

Put the ingredients in a **large** pot.

262. نذهب [v] *go*

عَلَيْنَا أَنْ نَذْهَبَ إلى البَحْرِ.

We have to **go** to the sea.

263. سَمِعْتُ [v] *I heard*

سمعت بِأَنَّكَ اسْتَقَلْت.

I heard you retired.

264. رِجال [pl. n] *men*

مُقَابَلَتِي لِرِجالٍ آخرين لا يعني أنَّنِي أَخُونُهُ.

Going out with other **men** doesn't mean that I'm cheating him.

265. يعرف [v] *he knows*

أنا مُنْبَهِرٌ لِأَنَّهُ يَعْرِفُ الكَثِيرَ عَنِ المُحَرِّكَاتِ.

I'm impressed that **he knows** so much about engines.

266. فيها [في -> prep, ها -> attach. pron] *where*

أَهَذِهِ هِيَ القَاعَةُ الَّتِي تَحْدُثُ فِيهَا أَكْثَرُ الاحْتِفَالاتِ؟

Is this the room **where** most of the parties happen?

267. لابد [n] *must*

لابُدَّ أَنَّهُمَا خَرَجَا لِتَنَاوُلِ الإِفْطَارِ قَبْلَ الجَنَازَةِ.

They **must** have gone out for breakfast before the funeral.

268. فتاة [n] *girl*

إِنَّهَا أَحْلَى وَ أَجْمَلُ فَتَاةٍ فِي العَالَمِ.

She is the sweetest and prettiest **girl** in the world.

269. البَاب [n] *door*

لا يمكنكِ المُرُورُ مِنْ خِلَالِ ذَلِكَ البَابِ حَتى تَحْصُلِينَ عَلَى المِفْتَاحِ.

You can't go through that **door** until you have the key.

270. السيارة [n] *car*

ابقوا في السَّيَّارَةِ.

Stay in the **car**.

271. يريد [v] *want*

مَنْ يُرِيدُ أَنْ يَلْعَبَ "كُرَةَ القَدَم"؟
Who **wants** to play kickball?

272. دولار [n] *dollar*

سَأُعطيكِ خَمْسِينَ سنتاً على كل دُولارٍ نَكْسِبُهُ.
I will give you fifty cents of every **dollar** we make.

273. أعرف [v] *know*

أَنَا أَعْرِفُ كُلَّ شَيْءٍ عَنْ مُنَى.
I **know** everything about Mona.

274. حَيَاتِي [pron <- ي <- n, حياة] *my life*

لَقَدْ دَمَّرْتَ حَيَاتِي.
She ruined **my life**.

275. انتظر [v] *hold on*

حَسَناً، انْتَظِرْ، سَآتِي مَعَكَ.
Well, **hold on**, I'll come with you.

276. أين [interrog] *where*

أَيْنَ المَفَاتِيح؟
Where are the keys?

277. خارج [adv] *outside*

سَنَلْتَقِي خَارِجاً.
I'll meet you **outside**.

278. ثلاثة [n] *three*

لَدَيَّ ثَلاثَةُ إِخْوَةٍ.

I have **three** brothers.

279. السبب [n] *the reason*

السَّبَبُ وَرَاءَ مُغَادَرَتِي مُبَكِّراً هُوَ اتِّصَالُ أُمِّي.

The reason why I left early is because mom called.

280. قَضِيَّةٌ [n] *cause*

فَلْنَدْعَمْ هَذِهِ القَضِيَّةَ.

Let's support this **cause**.

281. يقول [v] *says*

ا افْعَلْ مَا يَقُولُ، اتَّفَقْنَا؟

Do what he **says**, okay?

282. دون [n] *without*

لا أَعْتَقِدُ أَنَّنِي كُنْتُ سَأَفْعَلُ ذَلِكَ دُونَ مُسَاعَدَتِكَ.

I don't think I could have done it **without** you.

283. كانوا [v] *they were*

كَانُوا يَلْعَبُونَ كُرَةَ الطَّائِرَة.

They were playing volleyball.

284. حقًّا [adv] *indeed*

هنالِك حَقَّاً حَاجَةٌ مُلِحَّةٌ لِتَحْسِينِ كَفَاءَةِ عَمَلِيَّاتِنَا.

Indeed, there is an urgent need to improve the efficiency of our operations.

285. قُمْتُ [v] *I did*

عِنْدَمَا غَادَرْتَ، قُمْتُ بِبَعْضِ التَّحَرِّيَاتِ.

When you left, **I did** some research.

286. هنالك [n] *there*

سَتَكُونُ **هُنَالِكَ** طَائِرَةٌ بِانْتِظَارِكَ لِأَخْذِكَ لِلْوَطَنِ.

There will be a plane waiting to take you home.

287. جميلة [adj] *beautiful*

أَنْتِ فَتَاةٌ جَمِيلَةٌ.

You are a **beautiful** girl.

288. دائماً [adv] *always*

أَنَا **دَائِماً** أَسْتَيْقِظُ عَلَى السَّاعَةِ الثَّالِثَةِ.

I **always** get up at 3:00.

289. مما [part] *than*

كَمَا قُلْتُ لَكَ، التَّشْفِيرُ أَكْثَرُ تَعْقِيداً مِمَّا تَوَقَّعْنَا.

As I told you, the encryption is much more complex **than** we had anticipated.

290. ثانية [n] *second*

أَفْتَقِدُهَا كُلَّ **ثَانِيَةٍ** خِلالَ اليَوْمِ.

I miss her every **second** of the day.

291. نوع [n] *type*

أَيُّ **نَوْعٍ** من الحلوى تُحِبُّ؟.

What **type** of sweets do you want.

50

292. دعنا [v] *let us*

أَتَوَسَّلُ إِلَيْكَ، **دَعْنَا** نَحُلُّ ذَلِكَ وِدِّياً.

I beg you, **let us** resolve this peacefully.

293. جديد [n] *new*

سَأَشْتَرِي سَيَّارَةً جَدِيدَةً.

I'll buy a **new** car.

294. للتو [n] *just*

لَقَدْ مَنَحْتَنِي **لِلتَّوِّ** المِثَالَ الأَرْوَعَ لِلغَيْرَةِ الجَامِحَةِ.

You've **just** given me the perfect example of unbridled jealousy.

295. سعيد [n] *Saed*

سَعِيد شَخْصٌ نَاجِحٌ.

Saed is a successful person.

296. الحصول على [prep] *get* [n -الحصول -> , على ->]

بِوِسْعِهِ **الحُصُولُ عَلَى** أَشْيَاءَ لا يُمْكِنُ لِلآخَرِين إِحْضَارُهَا لَكِ.

He can **get** you things that other people can't get you.

297. دقيقة [n] *minute*

لا أَسْتَطِيعُ الجُلُوسَ عَلَى الأَرِيكَةِ **دَقِيقَةً** أَكْثَرَ.

I can't sit on this sofa one more **minute**.

298. بالضبط [n] *exactly*

بِالضَّبْطِ. أَعْرِفُ كُلَّ حركاتها.

Exactly. I know all her moves.

299. غرفة [n] *room*

دَعِينَا فَقَطْ نَتَظَاهَرُ أَنَّكِ فِي **غُرْفَةِ** مَعِيشَتِي.

Let's just pretend that you are in my living **room**.

300. المدينة [n] *city*

إِنَّهُمْ لا يَفْهَمُونَ مَا أُحَاوِلُ فِعْلَهُ لِصَالِحِ هَذِهِ **المَدِينَةِ**.

They don't understand what I'm trying to do for this **city**.

301. الأرض [n] *earth*

لديك أكثر مخلوق مُذْهِلٍ عَلَى **الأَرْضِ** يَعْمَلُ بِمَزْرَعَتِكَ.

You have the most amazing being on **Earth** doing chores on your farm.

302. لحظة [n] *moment*

قَدْ تَكُونُ هَذِهِ أَفْضَلَ **لَحْظَةٍ** فِي حَيَاتِي كُلِّهَا.

This may be the best **moment** of my entire life.

303. طريقة [n] *way*

عَلَيْنَا إِيجَادُ **طَرِيقَةٍ** أُخْرَى.

We have to find another **way**.

304. بسرعة [adv] *quickly*

يَجِبُ أَنْ نَبْدَأَ تَحْقِيقَاتِنَا **بِسُرْعَةٍ** قَبْلَ أَنْ تَخْتَفِيَ الأَدِلَّةُ.

We must begin our investigation **quickly** before the evidence disappears.

305. أنتم [sub. pron] *you are*

أَنْتُمُ الأَفْضَلُ!

You are the best!

306. إجازة [n] *holiday*

كَانَتْ فِي إِجَازَةٍ فِي مَانِيلا مَعَ وَالِدَتِهَا.

She was on **holiday** in Manila spending time with her mother.

307. جون [n] *John*

أَيْنَ جُونْ؟

Where is **John**?

308. عظيم [adj] *great*

إِنَّهُ لَشَرَفٌ عَظِيمٌ لِي أَنْ أُخَاطِبَ هَذِهِ الهَيْئَةَ.

It is a **great** honor privilege to address this body.

309. التحدث [n] *talk to*

هَلْ تَعْتَقِدُ أَنَّنِي يُمْكِنُنِي التَّحَدُّثُ مَعَهَا؟

Do you think I could **talk to** him?

310. جاك [n] *Jack*

جَاكْ رَجُلٌ عَظِيمٌ!

Jack is a great man!

311. مات [v] *died*

هَلْ تَعْلَمِينَ كَيْفَ مَاتَ عَمِّي؟

Do you know how my uncle **died**?

312. تعمل [v] *works*

إِنَّهَا تَعْمَلُ فِي شَرِكَةٍ لِلإِعْمَارِ.

She **works** in a construction company.

313. نفسي [نفس -> ن, ي -> pron] *myself*

بَعْدَ أَنْ قُتِلَ، فَقَدْتُ نَفْسِي لِفَتْرَة.

After he got shot, I lost **myself** for a while.

314. خاص [adj] *special*

هَلْ تَعْلَمِينَ أَنَّهَا تُصَوِّرُ بَرْنَامَجاً وَثَائِقِياً خَاصّاً؟

Do you know that she's shooting a **special** documentary?

315. ألم [n] *pain*

فَجْأَةً، لم يَسْتَطِعْ التَّنَفُّسَ بِسَبَبِ أَلَمٍ فِي الصَّدْرِ.

He can't even breathe because of sudden **pain** in his heart.

316. دعني [v] *let me*

دَعْنِي أَمُر.

Let **me** pass.

317. عام/سنة [n] *year*

أَتَوَقَّعُ أَنْ تَتَحَسَّنَ الأُمُورُ مَعَ حُلُولِ السَّنَةِ القَادِمَةِ.

I expect things to get better by next **year**.

318. لديها [لدي -> ن, ها -> pron] *she has*

لَدَيْهَا أَرْبَعُ أَخَوَاتٍ.

She has 4 sisters.

319. ساعة [n] *hour*

زوجكِ يَتَّصِلُ بِهَذِهِ الفَتَاةِ كُلَّ سَاعَةٍ.

Your husband calls this girl every **hour**.

320. تتحدث [v] *talking*

عَمَّ تَتَحَدَّثُ؟

What are you **talking** about?

321. خير [adj] *good*

لا خَيْرَ يَأْتِي أَبَداً مِنْ نَبْشِ المَاضِي.

No **good** ever comes from dredging up the past.

323. لم [part] *wasn't*

لَمْ تَأْخُذْ الشُّرْطَةُ تَصْرِيحَهُ بِجِدِّيَّةٍ.

His statement **wasn't** taken seriously by the police.

323. إليك [إلى -> prep, ك -> poss. pron] *here are*

إلَيْكَ بَعْضُ النَّصَائِحِ.

Here are some tips.

324. سأكون [v] *I'll be*

سَأَكُونُ الأَفْضَلَ.

I'll be the best.

325. رفاق [n] *guys*

يَا رِفَاقْ، هَلا خَرَجْتُمْ مِنَ المَطْبَخِ رَجَاءً؟

Guys, can you step out of the kitchen, please?

326. بينما [adv] *while*

أُرِيدُكِ أَنْ تُمْسِكِي بِالأَلْوَاحِ بَيْنَمَا أَقْطَعُهَا.

I need you to hold these boards **while** I cut them.

327. ترى [v] *see*

هَلْ تَرَى مَاذَا يَجْرِي فِي الشَّارِعِ؟

Do you **see** what's going on in the street?

328. مَرَّةً [n] *time*

جَعَلْتِنِي أَتَّخِذُ الخَطَوَاتِ الأَرْبَعِ مَرَّةً وَاحِدَة.

You made me take four steps at a **time**.

329. فقد [part] *it has*

فَقَدْ أَصْبَحَتْ ضَاحِيَةً حَيَوِيَّةً وَمُتَنَوِّعَةً فِي هَذِهِ المَدِينَةِ.

It has become a vibrant and diverse suburb in this city.

330. أحاول [v] *try to*

يَجِبُ أَنْ **أُحَاوِلَ** نِسْيَانَ المَاضِي.

I should **try to** forget the past.

331. القيام [n] *to do*

شكراً لكِ، ولكن عليّ **القِيَامُ** بِهَذَا وَحْدِي.

Thank you, but I have **to do** this alone.

332. طريق [n] -> عن [prep, طريق عن -> *through*

قالوا بأن المُرُورَ **عَنْ طَرِيقِ** السَّفَارَةِ سَيَكُونُ أَسْرَعَ.

They told me it's faster if I go **through** the Embassy.

333. سعيدة [adj] *happy*

إنّني **سَعِيدَةٌ** لِلْغَايَةِ لِأَنَّنَا تَحَدَّثْنَا أَخِيراً.

I'm so **happy** we finally got a chance to talk.

334. الموت [n] *death*

لَمْ يَعْتَقِدْ أَنَّ المَوْتَ سَيَبْتَسِمُ لَهُ أَوَّلاً.

He didn't think **death** would smile at him first.

335. رقم [n] *number*

أَعْطَيْتُهُ أَخِيراً رَقْمَ هَاتِفِي.

I finally gave him my phone **number**.

336. معها [مع -> prep, ها -> pron] *with her*

هَذَا هُوَ المَكَانُ الذِي أَحْتَفِظُ فِيهِ بِكُلِّ ذِكْرَيَاتِي مَعَهَا.

This is where I keep all the memories I have **with her**.

337. أقصد [v] *I mean*

أَعْنِي، الأَمْرُ لَيْسَ مِنْ شَأْنِي فِعْلاً.

I mean, it's really none of my business.

338. تأتي [v] *come*

إِذَا فَعَلْتَهَا مُجَدَّداً، لا تَأْتِ بَاكِياً إِلَيّ.

If you do it again, don't **come** crying to me.

339. أتمنى [v] *I wish*

لا أَتَمَنَّى لَكُمَا سِوَى السَّعَادَةَ.

I wish you both nothing but happiness.

340. المزيد [n] *more*

لا نَسْتَطِيعُ تَحَمُّلَ المَزِيدَ مِنْ أَخْطَائِك.

We can't afford any **more** of your mistakes.

341. ذهبت [v] *I went*

ذَهَبْتُ مُبَاشَرَةً مِنْ أَجْلِ العُثُورِ عَلَيْهَا، لَكِنَّنِي كُنْتُ مُتَأَخِّراً.

I immediately **went** to find her, but I was too late.

342. صغيرة [adj] *small*

هُنَاكَ سَبَبٌ لِكُلِّ لَحْظَةٍ صَغِيرَةٍ مِنْ حَيَاتِنَا.

There is a reason for every **small** event in our life.

343. الأول [n] *the first*

هَمِّي الأَوَّلُ هُوَ سَلامَةُ عَائِلَتِي.

My **first** concern is the safety of my family.

344. صديقي [n] *my friend*

سَأَزُورُ صَدِيقِي غَداً.

I'll visit **my friend** tomorrow.

345. صباح [n] *morning*

صَبَاحُ الخَيْرِ!

Good **morning**!

346. على الأقل [n -> على - prep, الأقل -> n] *at least*

عَلَى الأَقَلِّ، عَرَفْنَا أَنَّكَ لا تَسْتَطِيعُ هَزِيمَتِي بِنَزَاهَةٍ.

At least we know you can't straight-up beat me.

347. فرصة [n] *chance*

أَعْطِنِي فُرْصَةً لتفسِيرِ مَا حَدَث.

Give me a **chance** to explain what happen!

348. علاقة [n] *relationship*

التَّواصُلُ هُوَ المِفْتَاحُ الأَسَاسِيُّ لِأَيَّةِ **عَلاقَةٍ** نَاجِحَةٍ.

Communication is the key to any successful **relationship**.

349. غريب [adj] *strange*

هُنَالِكَ شَيْءٌ **غَرِيبٌ** يَحْدُثُ هُنَا.

Guys, there's something **strange** going on here.

350. نستطيع [v] *we can*

رُبَّما **نَسْتَطِيعُ** اللَّحَاقَ بِعَرْضِ السَّاعَةِ العَاشِرَة.

Maybe **we can** still catch a 10:00 show.

351. مدرسة [n] *school*

عَلَيْكَ الذَّهَابُ إِلَى المَدْرَسَةِ الآنْ.

You must go to **school** now.

352. الرئيس [n] *the president*

يَجِبُ أَنْ تَسْتَعِدِّي لِشَرْحِ هَذَا الأَمْرِ إِلَى **الرَّئِيس**.

You need to be prepared to explain this to **the president**.

353. يكفي [n] *enough*

المَالُ الذِي أَرْسَلْتَهُ بِالكَاد **يَكْفِي** لِيُطْعِمَنَا وَيَكْسِينَا.

The money you sent is barely **enough** to keep us fed and sheltered.

354. عشرة [n] *ten*

أَعْطِنِي **عَشْرَ** دَقَائِقَ. أُرِيدُكَ أَنْ تُقَابِلَ الرَّئِيس.

Give me **ten** minutes; I want you to meet the president.

355. تقوم [v] *you do*

وَظِيفَتُكَ مُسْتَحِيلَةٌ، وَلِكَنَّكَ تَقُومُ بِهَا بِبَرَاعَةٍ.

You have an impossible job, yet **you do** it brilliantly.

356. يتم [v] *it is*

عِنْدَمَا يَتِمُّ بِنَاؤُهَا، سَتَرْكَبُهَا المَلِكَةُ إِلَى مَكَانِ تَتْوِيجِهَا.

When **it is** built, the queen will ride it to her coronation.

357. أتعلم [v] *learn*

أَرَدْتُ دَوْماً أَنْ أَتَعَلَّمَ عَزْفَ الجِيتَارِ.

I've always wanted to **learn** to play the guitar.

358. إلا [part] *however*

يَبْدُو أَنَّ هَذَا القَرَارَ لَيْسَ صَالِحاً إِلَّا عَلَى الأَرَاضِي الأُورُوبِّيَّةِ.

This decision, **however**, is valid only on European territory.

359. أطفال [pl. n] *children*

هَلْ تُحِبُّ الأَطْفَالَ؟

Do you love **children**?

360. يرام [n] -> على ما يرام [pron, ما -> prep, على -> *fine*

إِنَّهَا فَتَاةٌ قَوِيَّةٌ وَسَتَكُونُ عَلَى مَا يُرَامٍ.

She's a tough girl. She'll be **fine**.

361. أفهم [v] *I understand*

لَمْ أَفْهَمْ لِمَاذَا، لَكِنَّنِي أَرَدْتُ مُسَاعَدَتَه.

I didn't **understand** why, but I wanted to help him.

60

362. سأذهب [v] *I'll go*

سَأَذْهَبُ لِشِرَاءِ بَعْضِ المَشْرُوبَات.

I'll go get some refreshments.

363. لأنك [لأن <- part, ك <- pron] *because you're*

الجَمِيعُ يَبْدُو صَادِقاً مَعَكَ لِأَنَّكَ رَجُلٌ كَرِيم.

Everyone seems sincere to you **because you're** a gracious man.

364. حالة [n] *case*

اترِكِ المُحَرِّكَ يَعْمَل فِي حَالَةِ مَا تَتَبَّعُونَا.

Leave the engine running, in **case** they follow us.

365. كونك [n] *being*

لابُدَّ أَنْ يَكُونَ هُنَاكَ تَوَازُنٌ بَيْنَ كَوْنِكَ مُحِبّا وحازِماً فِي الوَقْتِ ذَاتِه.

There must be a balance between **being** loving and firm at the same time.

366. أفكر [v] *I think*

أُفَكِّرُ بِكَ عِنْدَمَا أَذْهَبُ لِلنَّوْمِ لَيْلاً.

I think about you when I'm going to sleep at night.

367. حالك [حال <- n, ك <- pron] *are you*

كيف حالك؟

How **are you**?

368. دقائق [pl. n] *minutes*

أُرِيدُ رُؤْيَتَكَ فِي مَكْتَبِي خِلالَ خَمْسِ دَقَائِق.

I want to see you in my office in five **minutes**.

369. الحب [n] *love*

إِنَّهُ وَاجِبِي أَنْ أُقَدِّمَ لَهَا الحُبَّ وَالدَّعْمَ.

It's my duty to give her **love** and support.

370. حين [adv] *while*

اذْهَبْ حين تسْنَحَ لَكَ الفرصة.

Go **while** you have the chance.

371. النهاية [n] *the end*

زُمَلَائِي أَوْفِيَاء إلى النِّهَايَة.

The people I work with are loyal to **the end**.

372. أخبرني [v] *tell me*

عِنْدَمَا يُصْبِحُ قَادِراً عَلَى المَشْي، أَخْبِرْنِي.

When he can walk, **tell me**.

373. الهُوِيّة الجندريّة [n] *gender*

يَجب أَنْ نُرَكِّزَ عَلَى التَّعْليم وَالهوِيّة الجندريّة والصحة.

We need to focus on education, **gender,** and health.

374. لنذهب [v -> نذهب <- prep, ل -> *let's go*

لِنَذْهَبْ، لَيْسَ لَدَيْنَا وَقْتٌ كَافٍ.

Let's go, we don't have enough time.

375. سيدة [n] *lady*

كَيْفَ تَتَجَرَّأُ عَلَى مُضَايَقَةِ سَيِّدَةٍ أَمَامِي؟

How dare you harass a **lady** in front of me?

376. أَليس [أ - > prep, ليس - > imperf] *isn't*

أَلَيْسَ الأَفْضَلِ مُنَاقَشَةُ الأَمْرِ كَأُنَاسٍ مُتَحَضِّرِينَ؟

Isn't it better to discuss it like civilized people?

377. الخاصة [adj] *private*

سَيَكُونُ مِنَ الأَفْضَلِ لَوْ ابْتَعَدْنَا عَنْ حَيَاتِه الخَاصَّة.

It would be better if we stayed out of his **private** life.

378. عني [عن - > prep, ي - > pron] *about me*

يَتَحَدَّثُ عَنِّي مَعَ تِلْكَ الفَتَاةِ طَوَالَ الوَقْت.

He talks **about me** with that girl all the time.

379. بدأت [v] *began*

عِنْدَمَا بَدَأَت الفِرْقَةُ بِالعَزْفِ، أَصَابَنِي صُدَاع.

When the band **began** to play, I had a headache.

380. نعرف [v] *we know*

لَسْتَ بِحَاجَةٍ لِلْكَذِبِ، فَنَحْنُ نَعْرِفُ الحَقِيقَة.

You don't need to lie, **we know** the truth.

381. كي [part] *to*

نَحْنُ نَشْرَبُ كَيْ نَتَذَكَّرَ، ولَكِنْ يَبْدُو أَنَّكِ تَشْرَبِينَ كَي تَنْسَي.

We drink **to** remember, but it seems you drink **to** forget.

382. معنا [مع - > prep, نا - > pron] *with us*

هَلْ تَوَدِّينَ فَتْحَ حِسَاب تَخْزِين مَعَنَا؟

Would you like to open up a savings account **with us**?

383. أسمع [v] *hear*

أَسْمَعُ أَنَّكِ مُهْتَمَّةٌ بِالسَّفَرِ عَبْرَ الفَضَاء.

I **hear** you're interested in space travel.

384. حصل على [prep] <- على -> [v, حصل] -> *got*

حَصَلَ أَبِي عَلَى تَرْقِيةٍ أُخْرَى فِي العَمَل.

Dad **got** another promotion at work.

385. البيت [n] *house*

هُنَاكَ شَىٌ مُظْلِمٌ فِي أَرْكَانِ هَذَا البَيْت.

There's something dark in the corners of this **house**.

386. ماذا [interrrog] *what*

مَاذَا تَدْرُسُ؟

What are you studying?

387. صغير [adj] *little*

لَيسَ لَدىّ وقتٌ لِأخبِركَ بِكُلّ شَيءٍ صَغِيرٍ يَحْدُث.

I don't have time to tell you every **little** thing.

388. رؤية [n] *vision*

أَنْتَ رَجُلٌ ذُو رُؤْيَةٍ عَظِيمَة.

You are a man of great **vision**.

389. طفل [n] *child*

أَيُّ طِفْلٍ يُمْكِنُه القِيَامُ بِذَلِك؟

Any **child** could do that?

390. قليلاً [adj] *little*

إنّني أتنزّه **قليلاً** قَبْلَ اجْتِمَاعِي القَادِم.

I'm just taking a **little** constitutional before my next meeting.

391. تحتاج [v] *you need*

حسناً، **تَحْتَاجُ** لتَحْسِينِ مَهَارَاتِكَ.

Well, **you need** a little work on your skills.

392. تعني [v] *means*

أَرَى أَنَّ العَائِلَة **تَعْنِي** الكَثِيرَ بِالنِّسْبَةِ لكَ.

I see that family **means** a lot to you.

393. أكبر [elat] *the largest*

سَيَكُونُ هَذَا **أَكْبَر** فُنْدُقٍ عَلَى السَّاحِل الغَرْبِي.

This will be **the largest** hotel on the West Coast.

394. أُريدك [pron] <- ك ,v <- أُريد -> [pron] *I want you*

مَهْمَا سَيَحْدُثُ مَسَاءَ الغَد، **أُرِيدُكِ** إلَى جَانِي.

No matter what happens tomorrow night, **I want you** by my side.

395. لطيف [adj] *nice*

كوْنُكَ **لَطِيفاً** لا يَكْفِي لإرْضَاءْ امْرَأَة.

Being nice isn't enough to satisfy a woman.

396. مهما [adv] *whatever*

مَهْمَا فَعَلْتَ، سَأحتّبك دَائِماً.

Whatever you do, I will always love you.

397. أود [v] *I would like*

أَوَدُّ العَوْدَةَ إِلَى المَنزِلِ لِرُؤْيَةِ زَوْجَتِي.

I would like to go home to see my wife.

398. سام [n] *Sam*

هَلْ رَأَيْتَ سَامْ؟

Did you see Sam?

399. بعض [n] *some*

أَرْغَبُ فِي شِرَاءِ بَعْضِ القُمَاشِ لِأَخِيطَ لِنَفْسِي القَلِيلَ مِنَ المَلابِس.

I'd like to buy some fabric to make myself some clothes.

400. أكثر [elat] *more than*

لَدَيْكَ قُدْرَة على التّنَبّؤ أَكْثَر مِمَّا تَوَقَّعْتُ.

You're more predictable than I thought.

401. الهاتف [n] *phone*

لَمْ تَتْرُكِي الهَاتِفَ طَوَالَ اليَوْم.

The phone hasn't left your side for the whole day.

402. تماماً [adv] *fully*

أَنَا أُؤيدُكَ تَمَاماً وَأُؤمِنُ بِسِيرَتِكَ المِهَنِيَّة.

I fully support and believe in your career.

403. فهمت [v] *I understand*

لا أَعْتَقِدُ أَنَّنِي فَهِمْتُ مَاذَا تُرِيدِين.

I don't think I understand what you want.

404. السيدة [n] *Ms.*

هل تمانع إذا تَحَدَّثْتُ مَعَ السيِّدَة أَماني لِلَحْظَة؟

Do you mind if I steal **Ms.** Amany for a moment?

405. طويل [adj] *long*

هَذَا الفستان لَيْسَ طَويلاً بما يكفي.

That drss is not not **long** enough.

406. أحدهم [pron <- هم ,n -> أحد] *one of them*

سَأتَعَرَّفُ عَلَى أَحَدِهِم غَداً.

I can say I'll get to know **one of them** tomorrow.

407. السجن [n] *jail*

حاوَلْتُ جَاهداً أَنْ أُلْقِيَ بِكَ في السِّجْنِ لِمُدَّةِ ثَلاثَةِ أَعْوَام.

For three years, I tried hard to put you in **jail**.

408. سيدتي [n] *madam*

سَيِّدَتي، هَلْ تعرفين كَيْفِيَّة إِصْلاحِها؟

Madam, do you know how to fix it?

409. أقل [adj] *less*

سَأُحَاوِل أَنْ أَكونَ أَقَلَّ وَقَاحَة.

I'll try to be **less** abrasive.

410. والدك [pron <- ك ,n -> والد] *your father*

أنا ووالدك نُريدُ إِخْبَارَك بِشَيْءٍ مَا.

Your father and I have something we want to tell you.

411. ظننت [v] *I thought*

ظننتُ أَنَّكَ كُنْتَ فِي البَيْت.

I thought you were at home.

412. أتحدث [v] *I'm talking*

كيف تجرؤ على طَرْحِ سؤالٍ سَخِيفٍ بَيْنَمَا أَتَحَدَّث؟

How dare you raise such a random question while **I'm talking**?

413. عبر [n] *through*

لَقَدْ وَضَعْتُ قفلاً عَلَى البَاب وَلَكِنَّهُم يَأْتُونَ عَبْرَ الغَابَة.

I put a padlock on the gate but they come **through** the wood.

414. أيام [pl. n] *days*

أُرِيدُك أَنْ تُخْلِيَ الغُرْفَة خِلال ثَلَاثَةِ أَيَّام.

I want you to vacate the room in 3 **days**.

415. ترجمة [n] *translation*

الشَّكْوَى مُرْفَقَة بِالمِلَف، مَعَ تَرْجَمَة إلى الفِرَنْسِيَّة.

The complaint is attached to the file, with a French **translation**.

416. أخي [n] *my brother*

أُحِبُّ أَخِي.

I love **my brother**.

417. أبداً [adv] *never*

لَنْ تُقَدِّرَ تِلْكَ الفَتَاةُ أَبَداً مَا أَفْعَلُه من أجلِهَا.

That girl will **never** appreciate how much I do for her.

418. فوق [adv] *above*

هَلْ تَعْرِفِينَ قِصَّةَ الطِّفْلَة البَيْضَاء الَّتِي تَسبَحُ **فَوْقَ** الغُيُوم؟

Do you know the story of the white child that floats **above** the clouds?

419. العودة [n] *go back*

لِمَاذَا تُرِيد **العَوْدَة** إلَى هُنَاكَ أَيُّهَا الصَّبِي؟

Why do you want to **go back** there, boy?

420. الماضي [adj] *last*

لَمْ أَرَهُمْ إِطْلاقاً مُنْذُ الأُسْبُوع **المَاضِي**.

I didn't see them at all since **last** week.

421. ينبغي [v] *should*

اعْتَقَدْتُ أَنَّه **يَنْبَغِي** عَلَيْنَا التَّحَدُّث بِمُجَرَّد وُصُولِك.

I thought we **should** talk as soon as you got in.

422. نفس [n] *same*

لا أُرِيد مِنْكِ أَنْ تَرْتَكِبِي **نَفْسَ** الخَطَأ.

I don't want you to make the **same** mistake.

423. حان [adv] *it's*

حَانَ وَقْتُ المُغَادَرَة.

It's time to leave.

424. عامة [n] *general*

لا تَزَال الخَدَمَاتُ الصِّحِّيَّة **العَامَّة** غَيْرَ مُتَاحَة.

General health services remain inaccessible.

425. نكون [v] *be*

قَدْ **نَكُون** صِغَاراً، لَكِنَّنَا لَسْنَا عِمْيَان.

We might **be** young, but we are not blind.

426. حياتك [pron] < -n, ك- > < -حياة] *your life*

الشُّكْرُ هُوَ الطَّرِيقِ لِتَحقيق الإضَافَة فِي **حَياتِك**.

Gratitude is the way to bring more into **your life**.

427. مايكل [masc. n] *Michael*

مَايْكِل، الفُرَصُ الثَّانِيَةُ لا تَأْتِي كَثيراً.

Michael, those second chances don't come too often.

428. طعام [n] *food*

لَدَيْنَا **طَعَام** فِي الوَقْتِ الحَاضِرِ وَيُمْكِنُنَا بِنَاءُ مَأْوَى.

We have **food** for the moment and we can build a shelter.

429. أصبحت [v] *I became*

اتَّصَلْتُ بِالأسْتَاذُ وَأَصْبَحْتُ تِلْميذَه.

I called the professor and I **became** his student.

430. خطأ [n] *error*

لابّدّ أنّ هُنَالِك **خطأ** فِي النَّظَام.

There must be an **error** in the system.

431. الماء [n] *water*

المَاءُ أَسَاسُ الحَيَاة.

Water is the foundation of life.

432. نصف [n] *half*

ثَلاثُ سَاعَاتٍ وَنِصْفُ هُوَ وَقْتٌ طَوِيل للعَشَاء.

Three and a **half** hours is a pretty long time for dinner.

433. سيئة [adj] *bad*

إنَّها فَتَاة سَيِّئَة.

She's a **bad** girl.

434. المفترض [n] *supposed*

كان من المُفْتَرَضِ أَنْ تَلْقَانِي هُنَا مُنْذُ خَمْسٍ دَقَائِق.

She was **supposed** to meet me here about five minutes ago.

435. معرفة [n] *know*

يجب عَلَيَّ مَعْرِفَةُ التَّفَاصِيل.

I need to **know** the details.

436. داخل [n] *inside*

لا أَهْتَمُّ حَقّاً لِمَا في دَاخِل الحَقِيبَة.

I don't really care what's **inside** the bag.

437. منزل [n] *home*

لَدَيَّ مَوْعِدٌ لِلْقَاءِ نَظْرَةٍ عَلَى مَنْزِل نَمُوذَجِيّ.

I have an appointment to take a look at a model **home**.

438. سَيِّدِي [n] *sir*

مَازِلْنَا نُحَاوِلُ اكْتِشَافَ ذَلِكَ، سَيِّدِي.

We're still trying to figure that out, **sir**.

439. البقاء [n] *stay*

بِإِمْكَانِكَ البَقَاءُ لِبِضْعَةِ أَيَّامٍ حَتَّى تَحُلَّ مَشَاكِلَكَ.

You can **stay** for a few days till you figure things out.

440. أتساءل [v] *I wonder*

أَتَسَاءَلُ مَاذَا سَيَحْدُثُ لَوِ انْكَشَفَتْ أَسْرَارُهُم.

I wonder what will happen as their secrets come out.

441. تشعر [v] *feel*

لَقَدْ مَضَتْ سَاعَتَانِ، بِمَاذَا تَشْعُرُ؟

It's been two hours. How do you **feel**?

442. فريق [n] *team*

أَنَا فَخُورٌ بِفَرِيقِي.

I am proud of my **team**.

443. دكتور [n] *doctor*

رُبَمَا يَجِبُ عَلَيْكَ زِيَارَةُ طَبِيب.

Maybe you should go to the **doctor**.

444. أخبرك [pron -> ك, -> v أخبر -> ك] *tell you*

أَصْغِ جَيِّداً وَافْعَل مَا أُخْبِرُكَ بِه.

Listen very carefully and do exactly as I **tell you**.

445. وضع [v] *put*

هَلْ تُرِيدُ مِنِّي وَضْعِ السَّلَطَةِ فِي الثَّلَّاجَة؟

Do you want me to **put** the salad in the fridge?

446. مَرْحَباً [n] *hi*

مَرْحَباً، كَيْفَ حَالُك؟

Hi, how are you?

447. بخصوص [n] *about*

لَيْسَ عَلَيْنَا أَنْ نَكُونَ دَقِيقِينَ بِخُصُوصِ التَّفَاصِيل.

We don't need to be specific **about** the details.

448. جزء [n] *part*

أَخْذُ الأَطْفَالِ إلى المَدْرَسَة هُوَ أَفْضَلُ جُزْء في يَوْمِي.

Taking the kids to school is the best **part** of my day.

449. أعمل [v] *work*

لَطَالَمَا حَلَمْتُ بِأَنْ أَعْمَلَ في هَنْدَسَةِ الطَّيَرَان.

It's always been my dream to **work** in aeronautics.

450. أخذ [v] *take*

أَنَا أَعْرِضُ عَلَيْكَ أَخْذُ هَذَا المَشْرُوع مِنْك.

I'm offering to **take** this project off your hands.

451. تحاول [v] *try*

لا تُحَاوِلْ أَنْ تَسْتَنْشِقَ الكَثِير، فَهُوَ سَامّ.

Don't **try** to inhale too much; it's poisonous.

452. كلمة [n] *word*

سوف تُخْبِرُهم كُلَّ كَلِمَةٍ أَقُولُهَا لَك.

You are going to tell them every **word** I say.

73

453. حق [n] *right*

جِئْتُ مِنْ بَلَدٍ حَيْثُ تَتَمَتَّعُ المرأة بِحَقِّ التَّصْوِيت.

I come from a country where women already have the **right** to vote.

454. الماضية [adj] *the last*

مَاذَا فَعَلْتَ فِي السَّاعَاتِ المَاضِية؟

What have you done in **the last** hours?

455. ممكن [n] *possible*

سَتَفْعَل أَيَّ شَيءٍ مُمْكِن لِتُبْقِي ابنَهَا سَالِماً.

She'll do everything **possible** to keep her son safe.

456. يأتي [v] *comes*

هل يَأْتِي وَالِدُكَ لِمُرَاقَبَتِه؟

Will your father **come** to keep an eye on him?

457. اللعين [adj] *dreaded*

لِنَخْرُجْ مِنْ هَذا المَكان اللَّعِين.

Let's get out of this **dreaded** place.

458. الآخر [n] *the other*

أَحَدُنَا مِصرِيٌّ، والآخَرُ تُونِسِيٌّ.

One of us is Egyptian, and **the other** is Tunisian.

459. يمكنه [pron -> v, ك <- يمكن] *he can*

يُمْكِنُهُ فِعْلُهَا.

He can do it.

460. تظن [v] you *think*

أَلَا **تَظُنُّ** أَنَّهُمْ سَيَعْلَمُونَ بِمَا أَفْعَلُه؟

Do **you** not **think** they're going to know what I'm doing?

461. عرفت [v] *I knew*

تَوَقَّفْ عَن الكَذِب، **عَرَفْتُ** الحَقِيقَة.

Stop lying; **I knew** the truth.

462. خذ [v] *take*

خُذْ هَذِهِ الرِّسَالَة إلى القَرْيَة بِأَسْرَعِ مَا يُمْكِن.

Take this message to the village as fast as you can.

463. النوم [n] *sleeping*

انْعَمْ بِبَعْضِ **النَّوْم** يَا صَاح. تَبْدُو مُنْهَكاً.

Get some **sleep**, dude. Seriously, you look ill.

464. تقلق [v] *worry*

لا **تَقْلَقْ**! نَحْنُ بِخَيْر.

Don't **worry**! We are fine.

465. لمدة [adv] *for*

سَأَكُونُ في المَكْتَبَة لِمُدَّة 10 دَقَائِق.

I'll be at the library **for** the next 10 minutes.

466. أسبوع [n] *week*

أَمَامَنَا **أُسْبُوع** وَاحِد لِإِثْبَاتِ أنفسِنَا.

We have one **week** to prove ourselves.

467. نظرة [n] *look*

أَلْقِ نَظْرَةً، رَجَاءً.

Take a **look**, please.

468. المرأة [n] *woman*

أَلْهَمَتْني تلك الكلمات المُذْهِلَة التي قُلْتَها لتلك المَرْأة الشَّابَّة.

The wonderful words that you said to that young **woman** illuminated me.

469. وجود [n] *the presence of*

يُمْكِنك أَنْ تَتَكَلَّم بِحُريَّة في وُجُود وَالِدِك.

You may speak freely in **the presence of** your father.

470. مشكلة [n] *problem*

هَلْ لَدَيْكَ أَيَّةُ مُشْكِلَة؟

Do you have a **problem**?

471. الخروج [n] *exit*

قَابِلْني عِنْدَ بَاب الخُرُوج.

Meet me at that **exit** door.

472. ذهب [n] *gold*

أَنَا مُتَأَكِّدٌ أَنَّ لَدَيْهَا قَلْباً من ذَهَب.

I'm sure she still has a heart of **gold**.

473. الوحيدة [n] *the only*

أنتِ الفَتَاةُ الوَحِيدَةُ التي أُحِبُّها.

You are **the only** girl I love.

474. الحرب [n] *war*

لا تَقْلَقُوا، هَذِهِ الحَرْبُ سَتَنْتَهِي قَرِيباً.

Don't worry, this **war** will soon be over.

475. أفعل [v] *doing*

أَنَا أَفْعَلُ مَا فِي وِسْعِي لِتَجَنُّبِ المَشَاكِل.

I'm **doing** my best to steer clear of trouble.

476. بلا [part] *without*

لَدَيْكُمْ سَاعَة وَاحِدَة لِتَسْلِيمِهِمْ بِلا عِقَاب.

You have one hour to turn them in **without** punishment.

477. حاولت [v] *I tried*

سَيِّدِي، لَقَدْ حَاوَلْتُ انْقَاذَهُمْ، وَلَمْ أَسْتَطِعْ.

Sir, **I tried** to save them, and I couldn't.

478. وشك [n] *about*

كَانَا مَخْطُوبَيْن وَعَلَى وَشَك الزَّوَاج.

They were engaged and **about** to marry.

479. عائلة [n] *family*

أَمْلِكُ أَعْظَم عَائِلَة عَلَى الإِطْلاق.

I have the greatest **family** ever.

480. الفتيات [n] *girls*

تَعَالِينَ يَا فَتَيَات لِنُحَضِّرَ لَكُنَّ شَيْئاً تَأْكُلْنَهُ.

Come on, **girls**. Let's get you something to eat.

481. أَخْبرتك [pron -> كَ -> v] *I told you*

أَخْبَرْتُكَ أَنِّي سَأَتَّصِلُ بِكَ بَعْدَمَا تَنْتَهِي المُحَادَثَة.

I told you I'd call you after it was over.

482. آخر [adj] *last*

لَقَدْ أَتَيْتُ لآخُذ آخِرَ مُسْتَحَقَّاتِي.

I'm here to pick up my **last** check.

483. الخارج [n] *abroad*

كُلَّمَا شَعُرْتُ بِالمَلَل، سَافَرْتُ إِلَى الخَارِج.

Whenever I'm bored, I travel **abroad.**

484. ذا [part] *of*

تُسْعِدُنِي مَعْرِفَةُ أَنَّكَ رَجُلٌ ذُو مَوَاقِفَ حَاسِمَة.

I'm glad to know you're a man **of** decisive action.

485. عدم [n] *not*

بَعْدَ دِرَاسَةٍ دَقِيقَةٍ، قَرَّرْتُ عَدَمَ المُصَادَقَةِ عَلَى حَدِيقَتِكَ.

After careful consideration, I've decided **not** to endorse your park.

486. العديد [n] *many*

عِنْدَمَا تَتَغَيَّرُ كُلُّ الأَضْوَاء، سَيَأْتِي العَدِيدُ مِنَ الزَّبَائِن.

When all the lights are changed, **many** customers will come.

487. الموضوع [n] *topic*

أَعْطَتْنَا أُسْتَاذَتُنَا مَوْضُوعاً مُضْحِكاً.

Our teacher gave us a funny **topic.**

488. المساعدة [n] *help*

لَدَيْنَا مُشْكِلَةٌ وَنَحْتَاجُ بَعْضَ المُسَاعَدَة.

We have a problem, and we need some **help**.

489. نيويورك [n] *New York*

هَلْ سَبَقَ وَذَهَبْتَ إلى نْيُويوزُك؟

Have you ever been to **New York**?

490. العشاء [n] *dinner*

هَلْ تَنَاوَلْتَ طَعَامَ العَشَاء؟

Did you have **dinner**?

491. خمسة [n] *five*

يَتَكَوَّنُ فَرِيقِي مِنْ خَمْسَةِ أَعْضَاءٍ.

My team consists of **five** members.

492. مهلاً [adv] *wait*

مَهْلاً، مَا الِذي نَفْعَلُه؟

Wait a minute, what are we doing?

493. فتى [n] *boy*

هَذَا فَتَى رَائِع.

He is an amazing **boy**.

494. نساء [n] *women*

أنتِ تَغْضَبِين عِنْدَمَا يَتَكَلَّمُ مَعَ نِسَاءٍ أُخْرَيَاتٍ.

You don't like it when he talks to other **women**.

495. جورج [masc. n] *George*

أَيْنَ ذَهَبَ جُورْج؟

Where did **George** go?

496. رئيسي [n] *prime*

اذْهَبْ وجِدْ لَنَا مَكَاناً رَئِيسِيّاً لِلْمُشَاهَدَه.

Go find us a **prime** viewing spot.

497. رسالة [n] *message*

هَلْ أَرْسَلْتَ رِسَالَة إلى أُمِّك؟

Did you send a **message** to your mom?

498. حسب [n] *according to*

سَأَقُومُ بِذَلِكَ حَسَبَ القَانُون.

I'll do it **according to** the law.

499. يهم [v] *matter*

لا يهم.

It doesn't **matter**.

500. أتذكر [v] *I remember*

أَتَذَكَّرُ أَوَّلَ يَوْمٍ فِي صَدَاقَتِنَا.

I remember our first day of friendship.

501. حينما [adv] *when*

تُغَنِّي حِينَمَا تَكُونُ سَعِيدَة، وَتَبْكِي حِينَمَا تَكُونُ مَجْنُونَة.

She sings **when** she's happy and cries **when** she's mad.

502. أشخاص [pl. n] *persons*

دَخَلَ أَرْبَعَةُ أَشْخَاص فَقَطِ المَنْزِلَ خِلالَ الحَفْلَةِ المُوسِيقِيَّة.

Four **persons** entered the home during the concert.

503. حقيقي [adj] *real*

إِنَّهُ يَبْدُو كَزُومْبِي حَقِيقِي.

I mean, he does look like a **real** zombie.

504. مباشرة [adv] *directly*

لِما لا تدع مُحَامِيكَ يُرْسِلُهَا مُبَاشَرَة؟

Why can't you get your lawyers to send these **directly**?

505. أهذا [أ -> prep، هذا -> dem. pron] *is that*

سَوْفَ أَبْدَأ بِالتَّسْجِيل، أَهَذَا جَيِّد؟

I'm going to start recording, **is that** cool?

506. القادمة [adj] *next*

مَا سَنَفْعَلُه فِي الأَشْهُر القَادِمَة سَيُغَيِّرُ التَّارِيخ.

What we'll do in the **next** few months will make history.

507. فترة [n] *period*

حَسَناً، قَرِيباً سَأَنْتَهِي مِنْ فَتْرَة تَدْرِيبِي.

Well, I'm nearly finished with my training **period**.

508. اسم [n] *name*

مَا اسْمُك؟

What's your **name**?

509. ضد [n] *against*

أَصْبَحَ رَمْزاً لِلأَمَل ضِدَّ نِظَام الظُّلْمِ وَالفَسَاد.

He became a symbol of hope **against** a system of injustice and corruption.

510. مجنون [adj] *crazy*

هل أنتَ مَجْنُون؟

Are you **crazy**?

511. أصدق [elat] *truer*

لَيْسَ هُنَاك دَلِيلٌ أَصْدَقُ مِنْ قَلْبِك.

There is no **truer** guide than your heart.

512. متأكدة [n] *sure*

هَلْ أَنْتِ مُتَأَكِّدَةٌ أَنَّكِ تَفْهَمِينَ طَرِيقَةَ عَمَلِهَا؟

Are you **sure** you understand how they work?

513. يحصل على [prep -> على, v -> يحصل] *get*

يَجِبُ عَلَى الجَمِيعِ أَنْ يَحْصُلَ عَلَى بَعْضِ الرَّاحَةِ اللَّيْلَة.

Everyone should **get** some rest tonight.

514. يوجد [v] *there are*

يُوجَدُ عَدَدٌ مِنَ العَيِّنَات هُنَا يُمْكِنُكُمْ فَحْصُهَا.

There are a number of samples that you may examine.

515. فرانك [masc. n] *Frank*

فَرَانْك فَتى جَيِّد.

Frank is a good guy.

516. دعونا [v] *let's*

دَعُونَا نَحْتَفِل بِعِيدِ مَوْلَدِهَا.

Let's celebrate her birthday.

517. سوف [n] *I'll*

سَوْفَ أَزُورُ جَدَّتِي.

I'll visit my grandma.

518. قصة [n] *story*

هَلْ يُمْكِنُكَ اخْبَارِي بِقِصَّتِك؟

Could you tell me your **story**?

519. امنحني [امنح -> v, ي -> pron] *give me*

امْنَحْنِي خَمْسَ دَقَائِقَ وَسَأَكُونُ فِي المَكْتَبِ.

Give me 5 minutes and I'll be in the office.

520. هذه [هذه -> dem. pron] *these*

المَوَارِدُ التِي تُوَفَّرُ لِهَذِهِ الأَنْشِطَة غَيْرُ كَافِية.

These activities are insufficiently resourced.

521. زوجتي [زوجة -> n, ي -> pron] *my wife*

أَوَدُّ العَوْدَةَ إِلى المَنْزِل لِرُؤْيَة زَوْجَتِي.

I would like to go home to see **my wife**.

522. لقاء [n] *meetings*

أَنَا لا أُرِيدُ أَنْ أُرَتِّبَ أَيَّ لِقَاءٍ مَعَكَ.

I don't want to arrange any **meetings** with you.

523. مثلك [n] *like you*

رُبَّمَا خَبِيرَةٌ مِثْلُكَ قَدْ تُقَدِّرُ مَا أَعْرِضُهُ عَلَيْهَا.

Perhaps a connoisseur **like you** would appreciate what I have to offer.

524. في [prep] *in*

سَتَجِدُ اللُّعْبَةَ فِي الخِزَانَة.

You'll find the toy **in** the closet.

525. أراك [أرى -> v, ك -> pron] *see you*

أَرَاكَ غَداً فِي الحَفْلَة.

See you tomorrow at the party.

526. النهاية [n] *finally*

فِي النِّهَايَة، غَابَاتُ أَشْجَارِ النَّخِيلِ تَنْتَشِر.

Finally, the sugar palm forest takes over.

527. ذاهب [a.p.] *going*

إِلَى أَيْنَ أَنْتَ ذَاهِب؟ أَنَا أَشْعُرُ بِالتَّوَتُّر.

Where are you **going**? I am feeling a bit tense.

528. لعبة [n] *games*

كَمْ لُعْبَةً أَنْهَيْتَ حَتَّى الآن؟

How many **games** have you finished so far?

529. حفلة [n] *concert*

ظَنَنْتُهَا تَذَاكِر حَفْلَة أَوْ شيئاً كَهَذَا.

I thought they were **concert** tickets or something like that.

530. بواسطة [n] *by*

كُلُّ دُيُونِكَ سَتُلْغَى بِوَاسِطَة وَلِي العَهْدِ.

All your debts will be cleared **by** the Crown.

531. حقيقة [n] *fact*

تِكْرَارُ سَرْدِ الذِّكْرَيَاتِ الكَاذِبَة يُحَوِّلُهَا إِلَى حَقِيقَة.

The act of recounting a false memory hardens it into **fact**.

532- بالتأكيد [n *absolutely* ,prep التأكيد -> بِ]-

أَحْبَبت هيئتك بالتَّأْكِيد.

You know, I **absolutely** love your outfit.

533. بعد [adv] *after*

عِنْدِي زِفَافٌ بَعْدَ خَدَمَاتِ صَبَاحِ غَد.

I've got a wedding **after** morning service tomorrow.

534. حديث [adj] *modern*

نحتاج الى شيء حديث في القرن الحَادِي والعِشْرِين!

This is the 21st century, we need something **modern**!

535. مجموعة [n] *group*

لَقَدْ طَرَحْتُ مَوْضُوعَ اجْتِمَاع مَجْمُوعَة الدَّعْمِ مِنْ قَبْل.

I've broached the subject of a support **group** meeting before.

536. طلب [n] *order*

أَحْتَاجُ إِلَى مَعْرِفَةِ مَكَان الأَلَم حَتَّى أَسْتَطِيعَ طَلَبَ الأَشِعَّةِ السِّينِية الصَّحِيحَة.

I need to know where it hurts so I can **order** the right X-rays.

537. أمام [adv] *in front of*

لَقَدْ جَعَلْتَهُ يَبْدُو ضَعِيفاً أَمَامَ امْرَأَةٍ جَمِيلَةٍ.

You made him look weak **in front of** a beautiful woman.

538. الثاني [n] *second*

حَصَلَتْ عَلَى المَرْكَزِ الثَّانِي.

She got **second** place.

539. صورة [n] *image*

هَلْ هَذِهِ أَفْضَلُ صُورَةٍ لَدَيْنَا للسَّائِقِ؟

Is that the best **image** we have of the driver?

540. طيلة [n] *over*

ازْدَادَتْ عَمَلِيَّاتُ الاحْتِجَازِ التَّعَسُّفِيِّ **طِيلَةَ** الفَتْرَةِ المَشْمُولَةِ بالتَّقْرِيرِ.

Arbitrary arrests increased **over** the reporting period.

541. يحاول [v] *tries*

يُحَاوِلُ الذَّهَابَ إلى وَطَنِهِ كُلَّمَا اسْتَطَاعَ، لَكِنَّ ذَلِكَ لَيْسَ سَهْلاً.

He **tries** to get home as often he can, but it's not easy for him.

542. عندي [عند -> adv, ي -> pron] *I have*

عِنْدِي مَوْعِدُ أَسْنَانٍ.

I have a dental appointment.

543. أصدقاء [n] *friends*

يَجِبُ عَلَيْكَ اخْتِيَارُ أَصْدِقَائِكَ بِحِكْمَةٍ أَكْثَرَ.

You should choose your **friends** more wisely.

543. مثير [adj] *interesting*

عُنْوَانٌ **مُثِيرٌ** لِقِصَصِهَا، ألا تَظُنِّينَ ذَلِك؟

Interesting title for her stories, don't you think?

544. كلها [n] *whole*

اتَّضَحَ أنَّهُ اخْتَلَقَ القِصَّةَ **كُلَّهَا** لِكَيْ يَدْخُلَ لِلبِرْنَامَج.

Turned out he fabricated the **whole** story to get into the program.

545. تحدث [v] *occur*

تَحْدُثُ هَذِهِ الأحْدَاثُ بِضْعَةَ أيَّامٍ فَقَطْ كُلَّ عَامٍ.

These events only **occur** for a few days each year.

546. تفكير [n] *thinking*

هَذَا هُوَ جَمَالُ عَلاقَتِنَا، لا **تَفْكِير**.

That's the beauty of our relationship. No **thinking**.

547. لكل [n] *per*

سَأدْفَعُ لَكَ عِشْرِينَ دُولاراً **لِكُلِّ** سَاعَةٍ.

I will pay you 20 dollars **per** hour.

548. لن [part] *won't*

لَنْ نَذْهَبَ لِلحَدِيقَةِ اليَوْم.

We **won't** go to the garden today.

549. بيننا [بين <- adv, نا <- pron] *between us*

هذَا سِرٌّ **بَيْنَنَا**.

It's a secret **between us**.

550. تَفْهم [v] *understand*

بِالطَّبْعِ لَنْ تَفْهَمَ لِأَنَّ هَذَا عَمَلُ الشُّرْطَةِ الحَقِيقِيُّ.

Of course, you wouldn't **understand** because this is real police work.

551. كَهَذا [ك -> prep, هَذا -> dem. pron] *such a*

تُوجَدُ نِعْمَةٌ تَأْتِي مِنْ زَوَاجٍ كَهَذَا.

There is a grace that comes in **such a** marriage.

552. أَتُريد [أ -> prep, تُريد -> v] *do you need*

أَتُرِيدُ قِنِّينَةَ مَاءٍ أَوْ بَعْضَ الثَّلْجِ لِرَقَبَتِكَ؟

Do you need a water bottle or some ice for your neck?

553. أحضر [v] *bring*

سَوْفَ أُحْضِرُ أَكْيَاساً صَغِيرَةً مِن الفُولِ السُّودَانِيِّ مَعِي.

I'd **bring** a couple of tiny bags of peanuts with me.

554. سوى [n] *only*

الخبر السّيء هُوَ أَنَّهُ لاتُوجَدُ سِوَى وَظِيفَةٍ شَاغِرَة وَاحِدَةٍ كَمُدَرِّب.

The bad news is, there's **only** one trainer position available.

555. موعد [n] *date*

انْظُرْ، أَنَا أَنْتَظِرُ فَقَطْ مَوْعِدَ مُحَاكَمَتِي.

Look, I'm just waiting on my trial **date**.

556. أشهر [n] *months*

مَكَثْتُ تِسْعَةَ أَشْهُرٍ بَيْنَ أَنْسِجَةِ شَجَرَةِ البَلُّوطِ.

I have spent nine **months** within the oak tree's tissues.

557. مدينة [n] *city*

انْظُرْ إِلَى هَذَا المَكَانِ، إِنَّهُ مِثْل مَدِينَةِ الزُّمُرُّدا!

Look at this place, it's like the Emerald **City**!

558. بعضنا [pron *-> n, نا <- pron*] *some of us*

مَشَاكِلِي تَحْتَ السَّيْطَرَة، عَلَى عَكْس بَعْضِنَا.

I got my stuff under control, unlike **some of us**.

559. لسنا [imperf] *we are not*

لَسْنَا الوَحِيدِينَ مَنْ نَشْعُرُ بِهَذَا الشُّعُور.

Apparently, **we're not** the only ones who feel that way.

560. واضح [adj] *obvious*

وَاضِحٌ أَنَّهُمْ لَنْ يَصِلُوا إِلَى النِّهَايَة.

It's **obvious** they're not even going to finish.

561. كبير [adj] *big*

أَعْتَقِدُ أَنَّكَ اقْتَرَفْتَ خَطَأً كَبِيراً بِإِحَالَتِهِ مِنْ هُنَا.

I think you made a **big** mistake transferring him out of here.

562. انتهى [v] *end*

أَنَا آسِفٌ لأَنَّ لِقَاءنَا الأَخِير انْتَهَى بِسُوء.

I'm sorry that our last meeting had to **end** so badly.

563. الملك [n] *king*

سَتَلْتَحِقُ بِالجَيْشِ لِتُحَارِبَ في سَبيلِ المَلِكِ والدَّوْلَة؟

Will you be joining the army fighting for the **king** and country?

564. الوضع [n] *situation*

لَسْنَا أَسْعَدَ مِنكُمْ بِشَأْنِ هَذَا الوَضْعِ.

We are no happier about this **situation** than you are.

565. ذو [nom.] *has*

إنهُ **ذُو** قَلْبٍ طَيِّبٍ.

He **has** a good heart.

566. أسمع [v] *I hear*

لا أَسْتَطِيعُ رؤْيَة أيَّ شَيْء، لَكِنَّنِي **أَسْمَعُ** ضَحِكَاتِهِم.

I can't see anything, but **I hear** them laughing.

567. قادم [a.p.] *coming*

لَدَيْهِ صَدِيقٌ **قَادِمٌ** إلَى المَدِينَة مِنْ نْيُويوْزْك.

He has a friend **coming** into town from New York.

568. شركة [n] *company*

لا أَعْمَلُ لَدَى **شَرِكَةِ** الكَهْرَبَاء.

I don't work for the electric **company**.

569. بنفسك [n] *yourself*

قُمْتَ بالتَّضْحِيَةِ **بِنَفْسِكَ** لِحِمَايَةِ أَحِبَّائِكَ.

You sacrificed **yourself** to protect your loved ones.

570. تأخذ [v] *take*

لا **تَأْخُذْ** هَذَا الأمْرَ بِجِدّيَةٍ. أَخْبَرَتُكَ بِأَنَّهَا جَيِّدَة.

Don't **take** it so hard. I told you she was good.

571. تخبرني [pron -> ي - v <- تخبر <- v, ي] *tell me*

لَمْ تُخْبِرِني السَّيِّدة فُوزِهِييس أَنَّ لَدَيْهَا فَتَاة!

Mrs. Voorhees didn't **tell me** that she had a daughter!

572. الزواج [n] *marriage*

أَنَا أَكْذِبُ بِدَافِعِ الحُبِّ، وَبِهَذِه الطَّرِيقَة يَفْلَح الزَّوَاجُ.

I lie out of love; that's how **marriage** works.

573. أتيت [v] *come*

إِنْ أَتَيْتَ إِلى هُنَا، فَسَتَجِدُ الكَثِيرَ مِنْ الأَصْدِقَاء.

If you **come** over here, there are lots of our friends.

574. مليون [n] *million*

هُنَالِك عشرة مَليونِ شَخْصٍ في مَدِينَة نْيُويوزْك.

There are 10 **million** people in New York City.

575. صاح [v] *shouted*

لَقَدْ صَاحَ عَلَيَّ.

He **shouted** at me.

576. نسيت [v] *forget*

نَسْيت أَنْ أَقُولَ لَك، عِنْدِي مَوْعِدُ أَسْنَان.

I **forgot** to tell you but I have a dental appointment.

577. قضية [n] *case*

أُرِيدُك أَنْ تُقْنِعِيني بِأَنَّ هَذِه قَضِيَّةٌ خَاسِرَةٌ.

I want you to convince me this is a losing **case**.

578. عملية [n] *process*

عَمَلِيَّةُ التَّحْنِيطِ تَحْتَاجُ لِسَاعَاتٍ، صَحِيح؟

The embalming **process** takes a couple of hours, right?

579. حبيبتي [n] *baby*

حَبِيبِتِي، تَعَالَي لِمُقَابَلَتِي، أَنَا أَحْتَاجُكِ.

Come see me, **baby**. I need you.

580. مستحيل [n] *impossible*

تَعْتَقِدِين أَنَّهُ مُسْتَحِيل، وَلَكِنَّ ذَلِكَ غَيْرُ صَحِيح.

You think it's **impossible**, but it's not.

581. فعلته [pron <- ه ,v <- فعلت] *you did*

أَنَا أَحْتَرِمُ مَا فَعَلْتَهُ حَقاً.

I really admire what **you did**.

582. الرب [n] *Lord*

ارحَمْنَا أَيُّها الرب.

Lord have mercy.

583. ذاك [dem. pron] *that*

حَسَناً، ذَاكَ الأُسْتَاذُ عَلَّمَنِي دَرْساً جَيِّداً.

Well, **that** professor did teach me one good lesson.

584. عدة [n] *several*

طَلَبْتُ مِنْهُ عِدَّةَ مَرَّاتٍ أَنْ يَدْخُلَ المِصْعَدَ.

I asked him **several** times to step into the elevator.

585. آمل [v] *hope*

أَنَا آمُلُ فَقَطْ أَنْ يُسَامِحَنِي عِنْدَمَا أَجِدُهُ.

I just **hope** he forgives me when I find him.

586. كل [n] *each*

تَتِمُّ اسْتِضَافَةُ **كُلِّ** سِبَاقٍ سَنَوِيّاً مِنْ قِبَلِ مُنَظَّمَة مُخْتَلِفَة.

Every year, **each** race is hosted by a different organization.

587. يدرك [v] *aware of*

الكَلْبُ **يُدرِكُ** مَا حَوْلَ رَأْسِهِ بِثَلَاثِ بُوصَاتٍ.

This dog is **aware of** three inches around his head.

588. تذكر [v] *remember*

هَلْ **تَذْكُرُ** عِنْدَمَا أَخْبَرْتُكَ بِأَنَّنِي قَابَلْتُ جَانِباً مُخْتَلِفاً مِنْكَ؟

Do you **remember** when I told you I once met another version of you?

589. مواعدة [n] *dating*

هَلْ سَمِعْتُكِ تَقُولِين "مُوَاعَدَة"؟

Did I just hear you say "**dating**"?

590. أمك [n] *your mother*

مالذِي سَتَظُنُّهُ بِكَ **أُمُّكَ** بِمُضَايَقَتِكَ لِإمْرَأَة؟

What would **your mother** think of you harassing a woman?

591. اعتقدت [v] *I thought*

اعْتَقَدْتُ بِأَنَّنِي لَنْ أَرَاكِ إِلَّا بَعْدَ الإِجَازَة.

I thought I wouldn't see you until after the holidays.

592. سيحدث [v] *will happen*

ماذا **سَيَحْدُثُ** حِينَمَا يَلْتَقِطُ رَائِحَتَنَا؟

What do you think **will happen** when he picks up our scent?

593. يحتاج [v] *needs*

زَوْجُكِ **يَحْتَاجُ** للْكَثِيرِ مِن العِنَايَة.

Your husband **needs** a lot of care.

594. أثناء [adv] *during*

أَثْنَاءَ العَاصِفَة، عَلِقَ أَبِي تَحْتَ إِحْدى الأَعْمِدَة.

During the storm, my father was trapped beneath a column.

595. طلبت [v] *I asked*

طَلَبْتُ مِنَ الفَتَيَاتِ أَنْ يَأْتِينَ بَعْدَ سَاعَةٍ.

I asked the girls if they'd come an hour later.

596. قيد [adv] *under*

إِنَّهُ **قَيْد** الاعْتِقَالِ لِتَقْدِيم مَعْلُومَاتٍ للعَدُوِّ.

He's **under** arrest for supplying information to the enemy.

597. وصلت [v] *I reached*

لا أَتَذَكَّرُ اللَّحْظَة التي **وَصَلْتُ** فيها إلى هُنَا.

I don't remember the moment when **I reached** this place.

598. الحظ [n] *fortune*

كَيْفَ تَجْرُؤُ عَلَى إِهْدَار هَذَا **الحَظّ** الجيّد؟

How dare you waste that good **fortune**?

599. تعتقدين [v] you *think*

تَعْتَقِدينَ أنَّهُ مُسْتَحيلٌ وَلَكِنَّ ذَلِكَ غَيْرُ صَحيحٍ.

You **think** it's impossible, but it's not.

600. صعب [adj] *tough*

من الصَّعْبِ الحُصُول عَلَى أيَّة مَعْلُومَاتٍ مِنْهُ.

We're having a **tough** time getting any other information out of him.

601. قل [v] *say*

قُلْ بأنَّ هَذَا الشَّيء يَسْتَمِرُّ دَائِما.

Say that this sort of thing is going on all the time.

602. نعلم [v] *we know*

نَعْلَم يَقيناً بأنَّ هَذَا القَلْبِ يُعْتَبَر خِياراً جيّداً.

We know without a doubt that this heart is a viable option.

603. ابن [n] *son*

لَقَدْ أدَّيْتَ وَاجِبَكَ وَكَأنَّكَ ابْنُ أخْتي الحَقيقي.

You've acted like the true **son** of my sister.

604. تصبح [v] *become*

قَدْ تَتَعَلَّمُ كَيْفَ تُصْبِحُ شَخْصاً أكْثَر تَوَاضُعاً.

You may learn to **become** a far more humble person.

605. سؤال [n] *question*

هَذَا سُؤالٌ صَعْبٌ حَقاً.

Actually, this is a really tricky **question**.

606. مشهد [n] *view*

كانُوا يَقُومُونَ بالتْقَاطِ مَشْهَدٍ آخَرَ مِنْ هَذَا الغَزْوِ الكَبِير.

They capture another **view** of this great invasion.

607. ما زلت [v] *I'm still* [part <- لا , زلت <- part]

ما زِلْتُ مُسْتَائَة لأنَّكَ أنْتَ وَأُمِّي لَسْتُمَا مَعاً.

I'm still upset that you and Mom aren't together.

608. مهم [adj] *important*

تَظَاهَرْتُ بِأنَّكَ لَسْتَ مُهِماً بالنِّسْبَةِ لي.

I just pretended that you weren't **important** to me.

609. انتظري [v] *wait*

سَبَقَ وَقلتُ لَكِ انْتَظِري حتَّى يَصِلَ الطَّبِيب.

I've already told you to **wait** until the doctor arrives.

610. يفضل [v] *prefer*

البَعْضُ مِنَّا يُفَضِّلُ التَّوَهُّمَ على اليَأْس.

Some of us **prefer** illusion to despair.

611. أربعة [n] *four*

لَدَيْنَا أَرْبَعَةُ شُهُودِ عِيَان وَأَرْبَعُ قِصَصٍ مُخْتَلِفَة.

We have **four** eyewitnesses and **four** different stories.

612. منكم [pl. part] *of you* [من <- prep, كم]

لَنْ يُغَادِرَ أَيٌّ مِنْكُمْ حَتَّى انْتِهَاءِ العَمَل.

None **of you** are leaving until the job's done.

613. أتعلمين [v] *do you know*

أَتَعْلَمِينَ أَسْعَدَ يَوْمٍ فِي حَيَاةِ وَالِدِي؟

Do you know the happiest day of my father's life?

614. مساعدة [n] *help*

شكراً لكِ، لَقَدْ قَدَّمْتِ مُسَاعَدَةً كَبِيرَةً اليَوْم.

Thank you, you've been a huge help today.

615. اسمه [n] *named*

أَلَمْ يَكُنْ عِنْدَكُمْ كَلْبٌ اسْمُهُ تَانْجِرِينْ؟

Did you not use to have a dog named Tangerine?

616. اتصال [n] *contact*

أَلَدَيْكَ رَقْمُ اتِّصَالٍ جَدِيد؟

Do you have a new contact number?

617. حقيقي [adj] *real*

كَانَ بُونُوكْيُو دُمْيَة وَأَرَادَ أَنْ يَكُونَ طِفْلاً حَقِيقِيّاً.

Pinocchio was a puppet that wanted to be a real boy.

618. عندما [adv] *when*

عِنْدَمَا ذَهَبَ زَوْجُهَا الثَّانِي إِلَى السِّجْنِ، صَنَعَتْ كَعْكاً بِالسُّكَّرِ.

When her second husband went to jail, she made sugar cookies.

619. حسن [n] *Hassan*

حَسَن طَالِبٌ مُجْتَهِدٌ.

Hassan is a diligent student.

620. النظر [n] *consideration*

سَوْفَ أَرْفَعُ اقْتِرَاحَكَ إِلَى اللَّجْنَة لِيُعِيدُوا **النَّظَرَ** فِي الأَمْر.

I'll submit your proposal to the committee for their **consideration** again.

621. المفترض [n] *presumably* prep, <- من -> المفترض <- من

كَانَ مِنَ **المُفْتَرَضِ** أَنْ تَكُونَ أَسْخَنَ وَأَرْطَب.

It was **presumably** warmer and wetter.

622. القليل [adj] *little*

كُلُّ مَايَحْتَاجُونَهُ هُوَ **القَلِيلُ** مِنَ الإِيمَانِ فَقَطْ.

All they need is just a **little** bit of faith.

623. فقدت [v] *lost*

حَاوَلْتِ التَّحَدُّثَ إِلَيَّ، وَأَنَا **فَقَدْتُ** أَعْصَابِي.

You tried to talk to me, and I **lost** my temper.

624. أسرع [adj] *faster*

لَقَدْ إعتَقَدتُ بِأَنَّك **أَسْرَعُ** مِنْ كُلّ هَؤُلاءِ الفِتْيان!

I thought you were **faster** than all the boys!

625. سأقوم [v] *I'm going to*

أَشْعُرُ بِالبَرْدِ، **سَأَقُومُ** بِتَشْغِيل المِدْفَئَة.

I'm so cold, **I'm going to** turn on the heater.

626. العمل [n] *work*

هَذَا **العَمَلُ** يَعْنِي لِيَ الكَّثِير.

This **work** means a lot to me.

627. البداية [n] *initially*

ظَنَنَّا فِي البِدَايَة أَنَّهَا الضَّحِيَّةُ الثَّانِيَة.

We **initially** thought that she was the second victim.

628. يريدون [pl. Masc. v] *they want*

سَوْفَ أَرَى مَنْ يَكُونُونَ وَمَاذَا يُرِيدُون.

I'll see who it is and what **they want**.

629. معهم [هم <- pl. pron, مع <- prep] *with them*

اسْمَحُوا لِي أَنْ أَتَفَاوَضَ مَعَهُمْ.

Let me negotiate **with them**.

630. يا رجل [رجل <- voc, يا <- n] *man*

يَا رَجُلْ، تَبْدُو بِحَالَة سَيِّئَة.

Man, but you look like you're in pretty rough shape.

631. مناسب [adj] *fitting*

إِنَّ هَذَا اليَوْمَ مُنَاسِبٌ لِهَذِه الجَلْسَة.

Today is a **fitting** day for such a meeting.

632. كن [v] *be*

كُنْ مَرِناً، كُنْ مُتَفَتِّحاً، اسْمَحْ لأفْضَلِ الأفْكَارِ بِالفُوْز.

Be flexible, **be** open-minded, let the best ideas win.

633. يتحدث [v] *speak*

جَاءَ وَطَلَبَ أَنْ يَتَحَدَّثَ مَعِي بِصُورَةٍ شَخْصِيَّة.

He came in and asked to **speak** to me personally.

634. أحد - أي [أي -> part, أحد -> n] *anyone*

طِبْقاً لِسِجِلَّاتِه، لا يُحِبُّ أَيَّ أَحَد.

According to his records, he didn't like **anyone**.

635. عشرة [n] *ten*

لَدَيْكَ عَشْرُ دَقَائِقَ لِكَيْ تَصِلَ هُنَا.

You have **ten** minutes to get down here.

636. جئْت [v] *I came*

جِئْتُ لِإعَادَتِكَ مَعِي إِلَى كَاليفُورْنِيَا.

I came to take you back to California with me.

637. مشاكل [n] *problems*

عِنْدَمَا هَرَبْتُ مِنْ القَرْيَة، وَاجَهَتْنِي مَشَاكِلُ كَثِيرَة.

When I ran away from the village, I had many **problems**.

638. الشمس [n] *the sun*

عِنْدَمَا تُشْرِقُ الشَّمْسُ، سَوْفَ تَغْرَقُ الأَنْفَاقُ فِي الضَّوْءِ.

When **the sun** comes up, the tunnels will flood with light.

639. يعود [v] *come back*

سَأَفْعَلُ مَا تُرِيدُ وَلَكِنَّهُ لَنْ يَعُود.

I'll do whatever you want, but he won't **come back**.

640. أبحث [v] *look for*

أَلَمْ تُفَكِّرِي فِي أَنِّي قَدْ أَبْحَثُ عَنْكِ؟

Did you not think I'd **look for** you?

641. بعيداً [adv] *away*

ضَعْ هَاتِفَكَ بَعِيداً، نَحْنُ فِي جَنَازَة.

Put your phone **away**, we're at a funeral.

642. تقصد [v] *you mean*

تَقْصِدُ السَّيِّدَةَ ذَاتَ الشَّعْرِ الطَّوِيلَ الذِي يُعْجِبُكَ كَثِيراً.

You mean the lady with the long hair that you admire so much.

643. بكثير [adv] *much*

رَأَيْتُ نِسَاءً يَلِدْنَ فِي حَالاتٍ أَسْوَأَ **بِكَثِير**.

I've seen women give birth in **much** worse conditions.

644. فكرت [v] *you thought about*

أَعْتَقِدُ أَنَّكَ **فَكَّرْتَ** بِخِيَارَاتِك.

I think **you thought about** your choices.

645. تبدين [تبدو -> v, ين -> fem. pron] *you look*

لِمَاذَا تَأْكُلِينَ السَّلَطَة؟ **تَبْدِينَ** نَحِيلَة جِداً!

Why are you eating a salad? **You look** so slim!

646. سأعود [v] *I'll be back*

حَسَناً، **سَأَعُودُ** بَعْدَ قَلِيل.

Well, **I'll be back** in a few hours.

647. تسجيل الدخول [تسجيل -> v, دخول -> n] *login*

تَمَّ الاتِّصَالُ وَتَسْجِيلُ **الدُّخُولِ** بِنَجَاح.

Connection and **login** to server success

648. الدم [n] *blood*

تَخَلَّصْ مِنْ هَذِهِ الأَسْلِحَةِ وَقُمْ بِتَنْظِيفِ الدّمِ.

Get rid of those guns and clean up the **blood**.

649. أطفال [n] *kids*

سَيَكُونُ هُنَاكَ أَطْفَالٌ آخَرِين لِتَلْعَبِي مَعَهُم.

There'll be other **kids** for you to play with.

650. مخدرات [n] *drug*

نَشُكُّ فِي أَنَّ سَبَبَ الوَفَاةِ جُرْعَةُ مُخَدِّرَات زَائِدَة.

We suspect that the cause of death could be a **drug** overdose.

651. المعلومات [n] *information*

هذِهِ مَعْلُومَاتٌ سِرِّيَّة.

This is confidential **information**.

652. تعد [v] *prepare*

سَتُعِدُّ أُمْسِيَتنا بِطَرِيقَة رائعة.

You will **prepare** our evening in exquisite detail.

653. جانب [adv] *side*

لا أَثِقُ بِرَجُلٍ لَدَيْهِ جَانِبٌ مُظْلِم.

I don't trust a guy with a dark **side**.

654. تحمل [v] *carry*

إِنَّهُ لَشَرَفٌ عَظِيمٌ أَنْ تَحْمِلَ لِوَاءَ عَائِلَة.

It's a great honor to **carry** your family sigil.

655. جريمة [n] *crime*

مَن ارْتَكَبَ هَذِهِ الجَرِيمَة؟

Who committed this **crime**?

656. أمس [adv] *yesterday*

غادرت أمّي أمس.

Mom left **yesterday**.

657. الآخرين [n] *other*

هُنَاكَ عَدَدٌ لا يُحْصَى مِنَ المُزَارِعين الآخَرِينَ هُنَا.

There are countless **other** farmers here.

658. محق [n] *right*

كنتَ مُحِقّاً، لا يُمْكِنُني الفَوْزُ أَمَامَك.

You were **right**. I couldn't win against you.

659. ترحيب [n] *welcome*

يَنْتَظِرُكَ تَرْحِيبٌ حَار لِلغَايَة.

A very warm **welcome** awaits you.

660. التالي [n] *next*

في اليَوْم التَّالِي، إصْطَحَبْتُهَا إلى المُنْتَزَّه.

The **next** day, I took her to the park.

661. كرة قدم [n] *soccer*

هَلْ لَعِبْتَ كُرَة القَدَم في المَدْرَسَة الثَّانَوية؟

Did you not play **soccer** in high school?

662. ترك [v] *leave*

لا أَسْتَطِيع تَرْكَ هَذِه الغُرْفَةِ حَتَّى أُنْهِيَ عَمَلِي.

I can't **leave** this room until I've done my job.

663. كلام [n] *speech*

هَذَا أَكْثَر كَلَامٍ قَاسٍ سَمِعْتُهُ مِنْكَ عَلَى الإِطْلاق.

Bravo. That's the most unforgiving **speech** you've ever made.

664. شكل [n] *form*

يُمَثِّل الوِيب المَعْلُومَات عَلَى شَكْلِ نُصُوص وَصُوَرٍ.

The Web puts information in the **form** of text and images.

665. الجزء [n] *section*

أُدْرِجَ جُزْءٌ جَدِيدٌ يَتَعَلَّقُ بِالمَعْلُومَاتِ وَالاتِّصَالات.

A new information and communications **section** is included.

666. الداخل [adj] *inside*

ذَهَبْنَا إلى الدَّاخِل وَكَانَتْ الغُرْفَةُ فَارِغَة.

We went **inside** and the room was empty.

667. جهاز [n] *device*

جِهَازٌ رَائِعٌ. لَقَدْ أَهْدَانِي إِيَّاهُ أَبْنَائِي.

An incredible **device**, it was a present from my children.

668. قتلت [n] *killed*

قُتِلَتْ إِمْرَأَةٌ قَبْلَ نِصْف سَاعَة قُرْبَ المَطَار.

A woman was **killed** half an hour ago, near the airport.

669. البحث [n] *search*

طَالَمَا يُوجَدُ بَلَاغٌ، فَيُمكِنُنَا البَحْثُ دُونَ أَمْرٍ قَضَائِي.

If there's a report, we can **search** without a warrant.

670. بضعة [adv] *a few*

سَأَلْقَاكِ هُنَاك، إِنَّمَا لَدَيَّ بِضْعَةُ أُمورٍ أُنْهِيهَا.

I'll meet you there. I just have **a few** things to clean up.

671. حلقة [n] *episode*

أَرَى أَنَّ هنَالك حَلْقَة أُخْرَى مِنْ بَرْنَامَج الغِنَاء هَذا.

I see there's a new **episode** of that singing show tonight.

672. عما [part] *about what*

لا زَال لَدَيْنَا بَعْضُ الأَسْئِلَة عَمَّا حَدَثَ بالأَمْس.

We still have a few questions **about what** happened last night.

673. واضح [adj] *clear*

كُلُّ شَئ وَاضِح.

It's **clear**.

674. جين [n] *Jane*

جين فَتَاة رَائِعَة.

Jane is an amazing girl.

675. مستعد [adv] *ready*

لا أَظُنُّ أَنَّهُ مُسْتَعِدٌّ لِيَقُومَ بِتِلْكَ التَّضْحِيَة.

I don't think he's **ready** to make that sacrifice.

676. أسوأ [adj] *worst*

هَذِه أَسْوَأ طَرِيقَة نَقَضِّي بِهَا لَيْلَة السَّبْتِ.

This is the **worst** way to spend a Saturday night.

677. القديمة [adj] *ancient*

تُثير اهْتِمَامي الحَضَارَات **القَديمَةُ**، وَ أَنْتِ تُحِبِّين المُغَامَرَات.

I'm fascinated with **ancient** culture and you love adventures.

678. الوصول [n] *access*

لا أسْتَطِيع **الوُصُولَ** لِمَصَادِرِ المُنَظَّمَة دُونَ مُوَافَقَتِه.

I can't **access** the organization's resources without his approval.

679. قط [adv] *never*

لَمْ أَسْمَعْ **قَطُّ** بِفَريق غَوْصٍ لَدَيْهِم طَائِرَتُهُمْ الخَاصَّة.

I **never** heard of a diving team having their own plane.

680. اسمي [n] *my name*

إسْمِي أَحْمَد.

My name is Ahmed.

681. ستة [n] *six*

لَدَيَّ سِتَّةُ إخْوَة.

I have **six** brothers.

682. يقولون [pl. masc. pron] -> v, ون <- يقول <- v] *they say*

يَقُولُون أَنَّها أَسْوَء عَاصِفَة صَيْفِيَّة مُنْذُ سَنَوَات.

They say it's the worst summer storm we've had in years.

683. مستشفى [n] *hospital*

سَوْفَ آخُذُكَ إِلَى أَكْبَر مُسْتَشْفَى فِي المَدِينَة.

I'll take you to the biggest **hospital** in the city.

684. توقفي [fem. pron <- ي <- v, توقف] *stop*

عُذْراً، لا يُمْكِنكِ الدُّخُولُ. تَوَقَّفِي.

Stop, excuse me, you can't go in there.

685. قطعة [n] *piece*

هَلْ يُمْكِنُكَ أَنْ تُعْطِيَني قِطْعَةً مِنْ الكَعْكَة؟

Could you give me a **piece** of cake?

686. لحظة [n] *moment*

النَّاسُ دَائِماً مَاكَانُوا فُضُولِيِّين حَوْلَ لَحْظَة المَوْتِ.

Folks have always been curious about that exact **moment** of death.

687. معاً [prep] *together*

أَنَا وهِيَ بَدَأْنَا العَمَلَ عَلَى عِدَّة قَضَايَا مَعاً.

She and I started working on a couple of cases **together**.

688. مختلف [n] *various*

شَارَكْتُ فِي مُخْتَلَفِ المُنظَّمَات النِّسَائِيَّة وَالمُؤَسَّسَات المُكَرِّسَةِ للفَنِّ.

I participated in **various** women's organizations and institutions dedicated to art.

689. صوت [n] *voice*

سَئِمْتُ مِنَ التَّحَدُّث مَعَ صَوْتٍ مَجْهُول عَبْرَ الهَاتِف.

I'm done talking to an anonymous **voice** over the phone.

690. كامل [adj] *full*

أَنَا فَقَطْ أُرِيدُ الحُصُولَ عَلَى نَوْمٍ **كَامِل** لِلَيْلَة وَاحِدَة.

I just want to get a **full** night's sleep for once.

691. فعلاً [adv] *actually*

لِمَ لا تَشْرَبِين مَا تَشْتَهِيه **فِعْلاً**؟

Why do you not drink what you're **actually** craving?

692. مضحك [adj] *funny*

النَّاسُ يُخْبِرُونَنِي أَنَّنِي رَجُلٌ **مُضْحِكٌ**.

People tell me I'm a **funny** guy.

693. منطقة [n] *region*

تَتَطَلَّبُ **مِنْطَقَةُ** المُحِيطِ الهَادِئ اهْتِمَاماً خَاصّاً.

The Pacific is a **region** that demands special attention.

694. نرى [v] *see*

سَوْفَ **نَرَى** بَعْضَنَا البَعْضَ في الإِجَازَاتِ الأُسْبُوعِيّة وَالعُطَلات.

We'll **see** each other on weekends and holidays.

695. صورة [n] *photo*

سَنَلْتَقِطُ **صُورَةً** أُخْرَى بَعْدَ وِلادَةِ الطِّفْل.

We'll go back and take another **photo** after birth.

696. خطر [adj] *risk*

لَقَدْ وَضَعْتِ القَضِيَّة وَنَفْسَكِ في **خَطَر** كَبِير.

You put the case, and yourself, at great **risk**.

697. أكره [v] *I hate*

أخبرتكِ بِأَنَّني أَكْرَهُ تَضْييعَ وَقْتي بِالأُمُور التَّافِهَة.

I think I told you that I **hate** wasting my time on useless things.

698. سماء [n] *sky*

أَلْوَانٌ جَدِيدَة في غَايَة الرَّوْعَة تَمْلأ سَمَاءِ مَسائِنَا.

Beautiful new colors fill our evening **sky**.

699. مركز [n] *center*

إنَّهُم يُرِيدُونَ بِنَاء مَرْكَز تَسْويقٍ كَبِير.

They want to build a big shopping **center**.

700. غداً [adv] *tomorrow*

اسْمي وَصُورَتي سَيُنْشَرَانِ في الصُّحف غَداً.

My name and my picture will be in the papers **tomorrow**.

701. مقابل [adv] *vs.*

طِبّ الأَسْنَانِ يتكَوَّنُ من 25.0 مِن الإنَاثِ مُقَابِل 75.0% من الذُّكُور.

Dentistry is 25% women **vs.** 75% men.

702. هواء [n] *air*

لَقَدْ إحْتَجَزوني لِ5 أَشْهُرٍ في غُرْفَة بِلا هَوَاء.

They kept me for five months in a room with no **air**.

703. تعيش [v] *live*

أَريدُ مِنْكَ أَنْ تَعِيشَ حَيَاةً جَدِيدَةً بِكُلّ سَعَادَة.

I want you to **live** this new life to the fullest.

109

704. أهتم [v] *care*

أَرَدْتُكِ أَنْ تَعْرِفِي أَنَّني لازِلْتُ أَهْتَمُّ بِكِ.

I want you to know I still **care** about you.

705. القائد [n] *commander*

حِينَ يُصبح **القَائِدُ** مَجنُوَنا، يَسْقُطُ حَقُّهُ في السِّيَادَة.

When a **commander** goes mad, he forfeits his right to supremacy.

706. طائرة [n] *aircraft*

تَخْضَعُ كُل سَفينة أَوْ **طَائِرَة** تَدْخُلُ الوِلايَاتِ للتَّفْتِيش.

Each vessel or **aircraft** entering the Federated States of Micronesia is subject to inspection.

707. كتاب [n] *book*

تُظنينَ بأنَّكِ سَتَجِدينَ مَعْنى لِلْحَيَاة في **كِتَاب**!

You think you can find the meaning of life in a **book**!

708. منتصف [n] *mid-*

نَحْنُ نَبْحَثُ عَنْ رَجُلٍ في **مُنْتَصَفِ** الخَمْسِينِات.

We're looking for a man in his **mid**-fifties.

709. شارع [n] *street*

أَعِيشُ بِنَفْس **شَارِع** وَالِدَيَّ.

I live on my parents' **street**.

710. عيد ميلاد [n] *birthday*

مَتَى **عِيدُ مِيلادِكَ**؟

When is your **birthday**?

110

711. تحميل [v] *download*

يُمْكِنُنِي **تَحْمِيلُ** التَّطْبِيقَات عَلَى هَاتِفِي إِذَا أَرَدتِ.

I can **download** the app on my phone if you want.

712. طالما [adv] *as long as*

دَاني لَنْ يَتْرُكَ هَؤُلَاء الأَطْفَال **طَالَمَا** بِهِ نَفَسٌ.

Danny will never leave those kids, **as long as** he is breathing.

713. رأيته [v] *I saw him*

كان الرَّجُلُ الصَّغِيرُ مُنْهَاراً فِي آخِرِ مَرَّة **رَأَيْتُه**.

The little man was cracking up the last time **I saw him**.

714. ممتاز [adj] *excellent*

تَكَلَّمْتُ مَعَ أَطِبَّائِكَ وَتَشْخِيصُكَ **مُمْتَاز**.

I've spoken with your doctors and your prognosis is **excellent**.

715. تقتل [v] *murder*

أَلا تَمْلِكُ قَلْباً؟ لِمَاذَا **تَقْتُلُ** الأَبْرِيَاء؟

Do you not have a heart? Why do you **murder** innocent people?

716. أجد [v] *I find*

لَنْ أَتَوقَّفَ حَتَّى **أَجِدَ** ذاكَ الرّجُلَ.

I will not stop until **I find** that guy.

717. مفهوم [n] *concept*

إِنَّ **مَفْهُومَ** عائِلَتِي عن الحبّ مُخْتَلِف.

My family's **concept** of love isn't what you think it is.

718. القادم [adv] *next*

أَحْضِر العَرُوسَ الأَسْبُوعَ القَادِمَ وَسَوْفَ نُلْقِي نَظْرَة.

Bring the bride **next** week and we'll take a look.

719. محتمل [n] *probable*

أَنَا لَنْ أُهَاجِمَ منزله دُونَ سَبَبٍ مُحْتَمَل.

I am not going to raid his house without a very **probable** cause.

720. بلدة [n] *town*

لَقَدْ سَافَرْنَا إِلَى كُلِّ مَدِينَة صَغِيرَة.

We have traveled to every small **town**.

721. شعور [n] *feeling*

يُرَاوِدُنَا شُعُور بالسَّعَادَة عِنْدَمَا نُغَنِّي أُغْنِيةً مَا.

We get a happy **feeling** when we're singing a song.

722. قسم [n] *department*

اسْتَلَمْتُ رِسَالَة نَصِّيَّةً مِنْ مَصْدَرِي دَاخِلَ قِسْمِ الشُّرْطَة.

I got a text message from my source inside the police **department**.

723. فيلم [n] *movie*

أَنْتَ تُشْبِهُ شَخْصِيَّة أَمَرِيكِيَّة فِي فِيلم إِنْجِلِيزيّ.

You're like an American character in an English **movie**.

724. جاهز [adv] *ready*

هَلْ تَعْتَقِد أَنَّني جَاهِز لِلإِنْتِقَال لِلمَبِيعَات؟

Do you think I'm **ready** to move into sales?

725. أحمق [adj] *fool*

أيُّ أَحْمَقٍ يَنبغي أَنْ يَعْرِفَ أَنَّ الإِنْتِقَامَ يُوَلِّدُ المَزيدَ مِنَ الأَلَمِ.

Huh, any **fool** should know that revenge only breeds more pain.

726. بشدة [adv] *strongly*

هَذِه امرأة حَاوَلَتْ بِشِدَّةٍ أَنْ تُغَازِلَ رَجُلاً مُتَزَوِّجاً.

This is a woman who **strongly** and forcefully tried to hit on a married man.

727. عرض [n] *display*

هَلْ تَوَدُّ الذَّهَابَ مَعي لِمُشَاهَدَةِ عَرْضِ الألعابِ النَّارِيَّةِ؟

Would you like to go with me to watch the fireworks **display**?

728. بعدها [adv] *then*

أخبرنَا بِمَكانِ شَقِيقَتِكَ وَبَعْدَهَا سَنُسَاعَدِكُ، اتَّفَقْنَا؟

Tell us where your sister is, **then** we'll help you, okay?

729. وجه [n] *face*

أَنْتَ أَوَّلُ وَجْهٍ لَطِيفٍ أَرَاه مُنْذُ أَشْهُر.

You're the first friendly **face** I've seen in months.

730. يعتبر [v] *consider*

الاتِّحَادُ الأورُوبي لا يَعْتَبِرُ التَّوَازُنَ الجُغْرَافِي مِعْيَاراً أَسَاسِيّاً.

The EU does not **consider** geographical balance to be an essential criterion.

731. أقسم [v] *I swear*

أقْسِمُ أنَّني سَأُعيدُ لَكَ المَالَ.

I swear I'll pay you back.

732. اسمعي [fem. pron → ي -> v, اسمع ← v] *listen*

اسْمَعي، إنْ كانَ يُزْعِجُكِ، يُمْكِنُني الإتصالُ بالأمْن.

Listen, if he's bothering you, we can just call security.

733. يعتقد [v] *believes*

يَعْتَقِدُ الهُنُود أنَّ الشَّيْطانَ نَفْسَهُ يَقْتَرِفُ الجَرَائِم.

The Indians **believe** that the devil himself is committing murders.

734. رحلة [n] *trip*

سَأذْهَبُ في رِحْلَةٍ، وسَأخْتَفِي قَليلاً.

I'm taking a **trip**, disappearing for a while.

735. عملي [adj] *practical*

أنْتَ أكْثَر شاب عَمَليٍّ عَرَفْتُه حَتَّى الآن!

You are the most **practical** young man I ever met!

736. شعرت [v] *I felt*

شَعُرْتُ بأني مُخْتَلِفٌ وأحْتَاج أنْ أشْعُرَ بِذَلِكَ مُجَدَّدا.

I felt different, and I needed to feel that way again.

737. دليل [n] *guide*

دَليل الغَذَاء القَديم كانَ بَسيطا وَوَاضِحا وَمَفْهوماً.

The old food **guide** was simple, bold, and understandable.

114

738. صور [n] *picture*

لَقَدْ أَحْضَرْتُ لَكَ كِتَابَ صُوَرٍ، أَظُنُّ أَنَّكَ تُرِيدُ قِرَائَتَه.

I bought a **picture** book I think you'll want to read.

739. تركت [v] *I left*

تَرَكْتُ له ملاحَظَة فَحْوَاهَا أن يَلْتَقِيَني عَلَى المَرْفَأ.

I **left** him a note to meet me on the dock.

740. وغد [adj] *bastard*

قلْتُ أَنَّك مَغْرُورٌ ووَغْدٌ.

What I said was, you're an arrogant **bastard**.

741. اخرج [v] *get out*

أَنْهِ تَحَرِّيَاتَكَ وَاخْرُجْ مِنْ بَلْدَتِي.

Finish your research and **get out** of my town.

742. تخرج [v] *graduated*

أَعْطَتْهُ أُمُّهُ تِلك السَّاعَةُ عِنْدَمَا تَخَرَّجَ مِن الثَّانَوِيَّة.

His mother gave him that watch when he **graduated** high school.

743. حاجة [n] *need*

يَقُولُ أن لَيْس هنالك حَاجَةٌ لِوُجُود المُهَرِّج في السِّيرْك.

He said that there's no **need** for clowns in a circus.

744. عدت [v] *I returned*

عُدْتُ على سَبِيل المُجَامَلَة لإعْطَائك كَلِمَة أَخِيرَة.

I **returned** as a matter of courtesy to give you the last word.

745. السيطرة [n] *control*

كُنْتُ أَقُودُ بِسُرعَة، فَفَقَدْتُ السَّيْطَرَة.

We were going too fast, and I lost **control**.

746. تعلمت [v] *I learned*

تِلْكَ هِي الدَّراجَة التي تَعَلَّمْتُ الرُّكُوبَ عَلَيْها.

This is the bike that **I learned** to ride on.

747. قهوة [n] *coffee*

وَهَذا هو ثَالِث استراحَة قَهْوَةٍ يَقُومُ بِها الطَّبِيبُ.

That is the third **coffee** break that doctor has had.

748. زوجي [n] *my husband*

أَنَا أَحْتَرِم زَوْجِي.

I respect **my husband**.

749. عربي [n] *Arabic*

أنتَ لا تَتَكَلَّمُ العَرَبِيّة.

You don't speak **Arabic**.

750. فرصة [n] *opportunity*

توجَدُ فُرْصَةٌ هُنَا للحُصُول عَلَى حيَاة أَفْضَل لِعَائِلَتِنا.

There is an **opportunity** here to make a better life for our family.

751. عميل [n] *customer*

أَنَا عَمِيلٌ وَأُحَاول بِبَسَاطَةٍ عَقْدَ صَفْقَة.

I'm simply a **customer** trying to conduct a transaction.

116

752. تملك [v] *owns*

لا **تَمْلِكُ** الحُكُومَةُ سِوَى مَحَطَّة تِلِفِزْيونِيَّة وَاحِدَة.

The government **owns** only one television channel.

753. المعذرة [n] *excuse me*

المَعْذِرَة. هَلَّا أَعْطيتِني دَقيقَة مِنْ فَضْلِكَ؟

Excuse me, could I have a minute, please?

754. قائمة [n] *list*

أَلمْ تَسْتَلِمُوا **قَائِمَة** الضُّيوفِ التي أَرْسَلْنَاهَا؟

Did you guys not get the guest **list** that we sent over?

755. أسفل [adv] *down*

في الخَارِج، **أَسْفَلَ** الجَبَل هناك مَدِينَة.

Outside, **down** the mountain, there's a town.

756. المساء [adv] *evening*

سَوْفَ نُقِيمُ حَفْلاً كَبِيراً هَذَا **المَسَاء.**

We'll have a grand party at our bungalow this **evening**.

757. هراء [n] *nonsense*

يَطْلُبون مِنّي أَنْ أَقُومَ بِهَذَا الإِخْتِبَارِ للتَّقْيِيم، لَكِنَّ هَذَا مُجَرَّدُ **هُرَاء.**

They demand that I do this test for evaluation, but this is just **nonsense**.

758. العثور [n] *found*

سَيَتِمُّ **العُثُورُ** عَلَى الطفل قَبْلَ حُلُول اللَّيْل سَيِّدِي.

The child will be **found** before nightfall, my Lord.

117

759. أطلق [v] *launch*

أَوَدُّ أَنْ أُطْلِقَ مُسَابَقَةً رَائِدَةً.

I wish to **launch** a groundbreaking competition.

760. قوة [n] *power*

لَقَدْ فَقَدْتُ كُلَّ مَا عِنْدِي مِنْ قُوَّةٍ.

I have lost all my **power**.

761. وراء [adv] *behind*

لا أَعْرِفُ أَيّاً مِنْ أَعْدَائِي وَرَاءَ هَذِه الجَرِيمَة.

I don't know which of my enemies is **behind** this crime.

762. خطة [n] *plan*

طَلَبْتُ حَلّاً، وَلَيْسَ خُطَّةَ هُرُوب.

I asked for a solution, not an escape **plan**.

763. حتى [prep] *even*

حَتَّى أَنَا لِيسَ لَدِيَّ الوَقْتُ لِكِي أَنْتَظِرِكَ حَتَّى تَتَفَرَّغ.

Even I don't have the time to wait until you're free.

764. تبدأ [v] *start*

بِمُجَرَّد أَنْ تَجْتَازَ الصَّدْمَة، سَوْفَ تَبْدَأ بِالتَّعَافِي.

Once she's over the shock, she'll **start** to recover.

765. بعيد [adv] *far*

مَاذا تُفَكِّر عَائِلَتُكَ وَأَنْتَ تَسْكُنُ بَعِيداً؟

What does your family think of you living so **far** away?

766. أخبر [v] *tell*

سَوْفَ أُخْبِرُ أَبَاكَ أَنَّكَ كُنْتَ بَطَلاً حَقِيقِياً.

I'll **tell** your father that you were a real hero.

767. ضع [v] *place*

ضَعِ المَفَاتِيح الخَاصَّة بِكَ تَحْتَ المَقْعَد.

Place your keys under the seat.

768. تحرك [v] *move*

لا تُحَرِّكُ سَاكِناً حَتَّى يَأْتِي اللُّوَرْد.

Don't **move** a finger until his lordship comes.

769. الأخبار [n] *news*

تَكَلَّمْنَا مَعَ الأمْنِ الدَّاخِلِي وَلَدَيْنَا أَخْبَارٌ رَائِعَة!

We spoke to Homeland Security, and we have good **news**!

770. لسوء الحظ [adj] [n] *unfortunately*

لِسُوءِ الحَظِّ، العَصْرُ الذَّهَبِي للنشر وَلَّى.

Unfortunately, the golden age of publishing is long gone.

771. قاتل [a.p.] *assassin*

لِمَاذَا لَمْ تُخْبِرْنِي أَنَّكَ قَاتِلٌ مَأْجُور؟

How could you not tell me you were an **assassin**?

772. عدا [part] *expect*

لَمْ أُخْبِرْهُم بِشيء عَدَا مُؤَهِّلاتِكَ للوَظِيفَة.

I've told them nothing about your history **except** your qualifications for the job.

773. مجدداً [n] *again*

رُبَّمَا لَنْ يَتَحَدَّثَ مَعِي مُجَدَّداً إذَا عَرِفَ مَاضِيَّ.

He may never speak to me **again** if he were to learn of my past.

774. رأسك [n] *your head*

رَأْسُكَ مَجْرُوح، وَأَنْتَ الآن بِالكَادِ تَسْتَطِيعُ الوُقُوف.

Your head is busted open, and now you can barely stand up.

775. السفينة [n] *ship*

لَقَدْ أَثْبَتَّ بَرَاعَتَكَ فِي قِيَادَة هَذِه السَّفِينَة.

You've proven yourself quite adept at piloting this **ship**.

776. نقطة [n] *point*

أَنْتِ مُحِقَّةٌ تَمَاماً وَلَقَدْ حَصَلْتِ عَلَى نُقْطَة.

You're exactly right, and you get a **point**.

777. قلبي [n] *my heart*

قَلْبِي تَخَطَّى كُلَّ حُدود السَّعَادَة.

My heart crossed all limits of happiness.

778. محاولة [n] *attempt*

لقد كَانَتْ مُحَاوَلَةً انْتِحَار.

It was obviously a suicide **attempt**.

779. أجلك [pron <- ك, part <- أجل] *for you*

لَدَيَّ أَمْرٌ فِي غَايَة الأَهَمِّيَّة مِنْ أَجْلِكَ لِتَقُومَ بِه.

I have a very important thing **for you** to do.

780. تمت [p.p] *done*

صَفْقَتِي التجَارية، **تَمَّتْ** وَسَوْفَ أَسْتَقِرُ في سُويسْرا.

My business deal is **done**, I'll settle down in Switzerland.

781. إيجاد [n] *find*

أَنَا وَاثِقٌ أَنّهُ بِإمْكَانِنَا **إيجادُ** طَرِيقَةٍ لِمُسَاعَدَةِ بَعْضِنَا.

I'm sure we can **find** a way to help each other.

782. البشر [n] *humans*

البَشَرُ أَقْوِيَاءُ لأَنَّ لَدَيْهِم القُدْرَة عَلَى تَغْيِير أَنْفُسِهِم.

Humans are strong because they can change themselves.

783. جيمس [n] *James*

جِيْمْسْ شَابٌّ وَسِيمٌ

James is an awesome man.

784. أملك [v] *I owned*

إذَا كُنْتُ **أَمْلِكُ** أَرْضاً هُنَا، لَنْ أَتَرَدَّدَ في بَيْعِهَا.

If **I owned** land here, I wouldn't hesitate to sell.

785. القيادة [n] *leadership*

لَدَيْنَا **القِيَادَةُ** وَالنِّظَامُ وَالوَعْدُ بِمُسْتَقْبَلٍ عَظِيم.

We have **leadership**, order, and the promise of a great future.

786. للأبد [n] *forever*

أُحِبُّكَ، وَيَجِبُ أَنْ نَبْقَى مَعاً **للأَبَد**.

I love you and we should be together **forever**.

787. غبي [adj] *stupid*

أَنْتَ غَبِيٌّ.

You are **stupid**.

788. عملك [عمل -> n, ك -> pron] *your business*

هل تريدين أن تستقيلي من **عملك**؟

Do you want to quit **your business**?

789. محكمة [n] *court*

جِئْتُ مِنْ **مَحْكَمَة** الكَفَالات للتَّوِّ.

I'm just coming from the bond **court**.

790. خائفة [adj] *scared*

أَتَعْرِف يَا بُروفِيسُور، إنَّني **خَائِفَة** مِنْك قَلِيلاً.

You know, Professor, I'm a little **scared** of you.

791. ولد [v] *born*

مَتَى وُلِدْتَ؟

When were you **born**?

792. يبدو [v] *It seems*

يبدو كأنه مُصَابٌ بالحمى لأنَّك خَائِفٌ جداً.

It seems like you are getting a fever because you are so frightened.

793. العاهرة [adj] *bitch*

لِمَاذَا لا تَذْهَبِين لِمُرَافَقَة **العَاهِرَة** الصَّغِيرَة؟

Why don't you go hang out with that little **bitch**?

794. خائف [adj] *afraid*

أَعْتَقِد بِأَنَّني خَائِفٌ مِنْ مُسْتَقْبَلي قَليلاً.

I guess I'm a little **afraid** of my future.

795. يستحق [v] *worth*

الأمْرُ يَسْتَحِقُّ التَّرَاجُعَ عَنْهُ.

It **worth** backing out of.

796. الحالة [n] *status*

ولا يبيّن التَّقْريرُ أَيْضاً الحَالَةَ الرَّاهِنَةَ للعَمَليَّة التَّأْديبِيَّة.

The report does not explain the current **status** of the disciplinary process.

797. أتى [v] *came*

لا نَعْرِف مَنْ أَتَى لإِنْقَاذ الأَميرَة.

We don't know who **came** to rescue the princess.

798. كلما [adv] *whenever*

لِمَاذَا تَسْتَبْعِدُني كُلَّمَا نَتَعَرَّضُ لِمُهمَّة خَطِرَة؟

Whenever we are given a dangerous mission, why do you always leave me out?

799. قريب [adj] *close*

أَنْتَ بِالوَاقِع قَرِيبٌ جِداً مِن مَكَان سَكَني السَّابِق.

You're actually pretty **close** to where I used to live.

800. ملابس [n] *clothing*

مَجْمُوعَةُ شَبَابٍ أَشْعَلُوا النَّارَ في مَحَلِّ مَلابِس.

Young people have set fire to a **clothing** store.

801. خيار [n] *option*

العَيْشُ وَحْدَكَ لَنْ يَكُونَ أَفْضَل خِيَارٍ لَكَ.

Living alone isn't going to be your best **option.**

802. ميل [n] *mile*

سَنَسِيرُ نِصْفَ مِيلٍ ثُمَّ سَنَتَنَاوَلُ الغَدَاءَ.

We've got about half a **mile**, then we'll have lunch.

803. أعلى [elat] *top*

نَحْنُ جَمِيعاً نُرِيدُ التُّفَّاحَةَ اللامِعَةَ فِي أَعِلى الشَّجَرَة.

We all want the shiny apple on **top** of the tree.

804. تغيير [n] *changing*

أَنتَ تعلَمُ أَنَّ تَغْيِيرَ رَأْيِ العَامَّة يَتَطَلَّبُ وَقْتاً.

You know better than most that **changing** public opinion takes time.

805. حفل [n] *ceremony*

فِي حَفْلِ التَّرْحِيبِ يَجِبُ ارْتِدَاء الزِّيِّ الرَّسْمِي.

At the welcome **ceremony**, you have to put on your uniform.

806. منطقة [n] *area*

وَضَعْنَا بَعْضَ الأَهْدَافِ الجَدِيدَة فِي مِنْطَقَة النِّفَايَات الصِّنَاعِيَّة.

We set some new targets in the **area** of industrial waste.

807. معنى [n] *meaning*

مَا مَعْنَى "رَائِع" بالإِنْجِلِيزِية؟

What is the **meaning** of "fantastic" in English?

808. يتعلق [v] *regarding*

كَمَا تَعْلَمِينَ، القَانُونُ صَارِمٌ جِداً بِمَا يَتَعَلَّقُ بِحُقُوق الوَالِدَيْن.

You know, the law is pretty strict **regarding** parental rights.

809. سبق [n] *already*

تُوجَدُ مِلَفَّاتٌ سَبَقَ كِتَابَتُهَا عَلَى هذَا القُرْص. أتُرِيدُ اسْتِيرَادَهَا؟

There are files **already** burned on this disc. Would you like to import them?

810. تحدثت [v] *I talked*

هَلْ تُمَانِعِين إِنْ تَحَدَّثْتُ إِلَى هَايْلِي لِلَحْظَة؟

Would you mind if **I talked** to Hayley for a second?

811. بجانب [adv] *next to*

جَلَسْنَا بِجَانِب بَعْضِنَا البَعْض فِي مَأْدُبَة الجَوَائِز.

We sat **next to** each other at an awards banquet.

812. السابقة [adv] *previous*

أَأَنْتِ مُدْرِكَة لِمَا حَلَّ بِشَرِيكَتِي السَّابِقَة؟

Are you aware of what happened to my **previous** partner?

813. يهتم [n] *care about*

لا يَبْدُو أَنَّ أَحَداً يَهْتَمُ لِمَا أُرِيدُه.

No one seems to **care about** what I like.

814. ودود [n] *friendly*

أَنَا وَاثِقٌ بِأَنَّكَ وَدُودٌ لِلْغَايَة مَعَ كُلِّ النِّسَاء.

I'm sure you're very **friendly** with all the ladies.

815. موسيقى [n] *music*

مَا نَوْعُ **المُوسِيقَى** التي تُحِبِّينَ؟

Which type of **music** do you love?

816. حمام [n] *bathroom*

لَدَيْنَا **حَمَّامٌ** وَاحِدٌ فَقَطْ.

We only have one **bathroom**.

817. الأكثر [elat] *the most*

سَوْفَ نَسْتَهْدِفُ المَنَازِلَ **الأكثر** تَزْيِيناً.

We target all the houses with **the most** decorations.

818. الطابق [n] *floor*

لَدَيْهِم كَامِيرَات خَارِجَ المَصَاعِد في كُلّ **طَابق**.

They've got cameras outside the elevators on every **floor**.

819. صندوق [n] *fund*

صُنْدُوق نَقْدِ الأَطْفَال قَدْ إِزْدَهَر تَحْتَ قِيَادَة العُمْدَة.

The children's **fund** has thrived under the Mayor's leadership.

820. برنامج [n] *program*

هَذا المَرِيضُ لَمْ يَعُدْ مُشَارِكا في **بَرْنَامَج** بَحْثِنَا.

This patient is no longer a participant in our research **program**.

821. أشخاص [n] *people*

نَحْنُ خَمْسَةُ **أَشْخَاصٍ** نَعِيشُ في مَنْزِل لأَرْبَعَة أَشْخَاصٍ.

We're five **people** living in a four-person house.

822. مضى [v] *before*

يُوجَدُ شَرٌّ مِنْ حَوْلِنَا أَكْثَرُ مِمَّا وَاجَهْتُهُ في أَيِّ وَقْتٍ مَضَى.

There is more evil around us here than I have ever encountered **before**.

823. قدم [n] *foot*

القَدَم أَحَد أَعْضَاءِ الجِسْمِ.

The **foot** is one portion of our body.

824. يديك [n] *your hand*

أَنْتَ مَحْظُوظٌ. بِالكادِ لَدَيْكَ تَجَاعيد في يَدَيْكَ.

You're lucky. You barely have wrinkles on **your hand**.

825. خط [n] *line*

خَطُّ الإسْتِوَاءِ هُوَ خَطٌّ تَخَيُّلِي يَفْصِلُ شَمَالَ وَجَنُوبَ الكُرَة الأَرْضِيَّة.

The equator is that imaginary **line** that separates the Earth into the northern and the southern hemisphere.

826. لمن [prep] *for those*

لا تَعْتَذِرْ لي. وَفِّر هَذَا لِمَنْ يَحْتَاجُونَهُ.

Don't apologize to me, save it **for those** that need it.

827. اللعينة [n] *damned*

أُريدُ أَنْ أَذْهَبَ بَعيداً عَنْ هَذِه الجَزيرَةِ اللَّعينَة.

I want to go far away from this **damned** island.

828. مكانك [n] *your place*

هنَاكَ طَابُور مِنَ الفَتَيَات يَنْتَظِرنَ لِيَأْخُذْنَ مَكَانَكِ.

There's a line of girls just waiting to take **your place**.

829. تقريباً [adv] *almost*

أَفْكَارُكِ حِيَالَ زَوْجِكِ **تَقْرِيباً** سَلْبِيَّةٌ كُلِّياً، صَحِيحٌ؟

Your thoughts about your husband are **almost** entirely negative, aren't they?

830. بالكاد [adv] *barely*

هُوَ مَرِيضٌ لِلغَايَة، الآنَ **بِالكَادِ** يُمْكِنُهُ رَفْعُ رَأْسِه.

He's so sick; he can **barely** hold up his head.

831. الأخير [adv] *last*

سَأَحَاوِلُ أَنْ أَجْعَلَ يَوْمَكَ **الأخيرَ** هُنَا مُرِيحاً قَدْرَ المُسْتَطَاع.

I'll try to make your **last** day here as comfortable as possible.

832. أخبرتني [pron ني <- , v أخبرت <-] *she told me*

أَخْبَرَتْنِي بِقِصَّةٍ مَجْنُونَة عَنْ عَائِلَتِهَا!

She told me the craziest story about her family!

833. وظيفة [n] *function*

أَعْتَقِدُ أَنَّ الحَرَكَةَ هِيَ أَهَمُ وَظِيفَةٍ لِلدِّمَاغ.

I believe movement is the most important **function** of the brain.

834. ظهر [n] *back*

مُنْذُ مَتَى وَظَهْرُكَ يُؤْلِمُكَ؟

How long has your **back** been hurting you?

835. ابتعد [v] *stay away*

كَيْفَ لِي أَنْ **أَبْتَعِدَ** عَنْكِ الآن؟

How can I **stay away** from you?

836. تقل [elat] *less than*

يَجِبُ أَلَا **تَقِلَّ** الرَّاحَةُ الْأُسْبُوعِيَّةُ لِلْعُمَّال عَنْ أَرْبَعٍ وَعِشْرِينَ سَاعَة.

The weekly rest period may not be **less than** 24 hours.

837. يجدر [v] *you should*

يَجْدُرُ أَنْ تَعْرِفِي أَنَّ أَبْنَائِي هُمْ أَبْنَاؤُك.

You should know that my kids are your kids.

838. هدية [n] *gift*

هَلْ اشْتَرَيْتَ **هَدِيَّةً** لِأُخْتِكَ فِي عِيدِ مِيلَادِهَا؟

Did you buy a **gift** for your sister on her birthday?

839. السلاح [n] *arms*

السَّلَامُ الْمَفْرُوضُ بِقوة **السِّلاح** مَآلُهُ الْفَشَلُ.

Peace imposed by force of **arms** is always doomed to failure.

840. لاحقا [adv] *later*

حَسَنٌ، لِنَتَحَدَّثْ **لاحِقاً** الْيَوْم.

Okay, let's talk **later** today.

841. غريبة [n] *strange*

عِنْدَمَا تَبْتَعِدُ عَنِّي، كُلُّ لَحْظَة تَبْدُو **غَرِيبَة**.

When you're away from me, every moment seems **strange**.

842. جعل [v] *make*

أَعْتَزِم **جَعْلَ** هَذَا الْفَوْجِ الْأَفْضَلَ عَلَى الْحُدُود.

I intend to **make** this regiment the finest on the frontier.

843. سلاح [n] *weapon*

البُندُقِيَّة لَيْسَت أَكْثَر سِلاحٍ يُمْكِنُ الإعْتِمَادُ عَلَيْه.

The musket isn't the most reliable **weapon**.

844. الخلف [adv] *behind*

خَلْفَ تِلْكَ الأَشْجَارِ، يُوجَدُ مَسَارٌ يُؤَدِّي مُبَاشَرَةً إلَى القَصْرِ.

Behind those trees, there's a path that goes straight to the castle.

845. قريبا [adv] *soon*

سَيَتِمُّ افْتِتَاحُ المَعْرِض قَرِيباً.

The exhibition will open **soon**.

846. قطع [v] *cut*

لا أَسْتَطِيعُ الحَرَكَة. أَعْتَقِدُ أَنَّهُ قَطَعَ الوَتْرَ.

I can't move. I think he **cut** my tendon.

847. أميركا [n] *America*

هَلْ سَافَرْتَ إلَى أَمْرِيكَا؟

Have you traveled to **America**?

848. كفاية [n] *enough*

في بَعْضِ الدُّوَلِ، أَنَا كَبِيرَة كِفَايَة لأَتَزَوَّجَ.

In some countries, I'm old **enough** to marry.

849. الأمن [n] *security*

تَكلمْنَا مَعَ الأَمْنِ الدَّاخِلي وَلَدَيْنَا أَخْبار رائعة!

We spoke to Homeland **Security**, and we have good news!

850. خرجت [v] *came out*

خَرَجَتْ إمرأة مِنَ المَنْزِل تَحْمِلُ طِفْلَة وَتُمْسِكُ أُخرى بِيَدِهَا.

A woman **came out** of the house, carrying a girl and holding another by the hand.

851. وإلا [part] *otherwise*

أَحْسِنِي التَّصَرُّفَ **وَإلَّا** لا يُمْكِنُكِ البَقَاءُ فِي الفِرْقَة.

Lighten up. **Otherwise**, you can't stay in the choir.

852. مريض [n] *patient*

لَدَيَّ **مَرِيضٌ** يَجِبُ عَلَيَّ الاهْتِمَامُ بِه.

I have a **patient** that I should look at.

853. الصوت [n] *sound*

مَاهَذَا **الصَّوْتُ** الغَرِيبُ الذِي تُصْدِرُه؟

What is that strange **sound** you're making?

854. المتحدة [n] *United*

لَقَدْ أَرْسَلْتُ رِسَالَةً للقُوَّاتِ **المُتَّحِدَة.** سَيَأْتُونَ قَرِيباً.

I sent word to the **United** Forces, they will be here soon.

855. عادة [adv] *usually*

أُحِبُّ **عَادَةً** طَرْحَ الأَسْئِلَة قَبْلَ تَلَقِّي الأَجْوِبَة.

I **usually** like to ask the questions before I get the answers.

856. طريقي [n] *my way*

فِي **طَرِيقِي** إلى المَدِينَة الكَبِيرَة فِي رِحْلَةِ عَمَلٍ.

I'm on **my way** to the big city for a business trip.

857. سأتصل [v] *I'll call*

سَأَتَّصِلُ بِكُمْ عِنْدَمَا أَكُونُ قَادِراً عَلَى التَّحَدُّث.

I'll **call** you when I can speak.

858. أخشى [n] *be afraid of*

أُرِيدُ أَنْ أَكُونَ جَرِيئَةً وَلا أَخْشَى شيئاً.

I want to be bold, and not to **be afraid of** anything.

859. أراد [v] *he wanted*

سَيَكُونُ غَرِيباً إِنْ أَرَادَ تَكْوِينَ عَائِلَةٍ مَعَكِ.

It would be weird if **he wanted** to have a family with you.

860. معظم [adj] *most of*

مُعْظَمُ المَالِ الذِي يَجْنِيه يَذْهَبُ إِلَى الفُقَرَاء.

Most of the money he makes goes to the poor.

861. الكرة [n] *ball*

لَمْ أَعْرِفْ شَخْصاً يُحِبُّ الكُرَةَ مِثلك.

I never knew anyone who loved **ball** as much as you.

862. تعامل [n] *dealings*

هَلْ لَدِيهِ أَيُّ تَعَامُلٍ سِرِّي مَعَ الإِمْبَرَاطُور؟

Does he have any secret **dealings** with the emperor?

863. سماع [n] *hear*

اخْرُجْ مِنَ المَاء. أَسْتَطِيعُ سَمَاعَ صَرِيرَ أَسْنَانِكَ مِنْ هُنَا!

Out of the water! I can **hear** your teeth chattering from here!

864. رائحة [n] *smell*

لا أَسْتَطِيعُ إِزَالَةَ رَائِحَةِ الطّينِ مِنْ مَلابِسي.

I can't get the **smell** of slurry out of my clothes.

865. العجوز [n] *old*

الكُمْبيوتَر مَوجودٌ تَحْتَ مَكْتَبِ تِلْكَ السَّيِّدَةِ العَجوزِ اللَّطيفَة.

The computer is underneath that sweet **old** lady's desk.

866. السرير [n] *bed*

يُمكنك الاستلقاء عَلَى السَّريرِ وَالاسْتمتَاع بنَوْمٍ هَانئٍ.

You can slide into **bed** and get a good night's sleep.

867. درجة [n] *degree*

لَمَاذَا تُريدينَ دَرَجَةً عِلْمِيَّةً وَأَنْتِ بالفعل لديكِ وظيفَة؟

Why do you need a **degree** when you already have a job?

868. سهل [adj] *easy*

مَا يَأتِي بِسُهولَة، يَذْهَبُ بِسُهولَة.

Easy come, **easy** go.

869. تصل [v] *up*

أَنْتَ غَارِقٌ في دُيونٍ تَصِل حَتَّى أُذُنَيْكَ.

You're in debt **up** to your ears.

870. بالمناسبة [n] *by the way*

بالمُنَاسَبَة، هُنَالِكَ طِفْلٌ صَغيرٌ تَحْتَ مَكْتَبِكَ.

By the way, there's a small boy under your desk.

871. مبنى [n] *building*

إنَّهُ أَطْوَلُ مَبْنًى في المَدِينَة.

It's the tallest **building** in the city.

872. مستقبل [n] *future*

أتظنّين أنَّ لِهَذا العَالَم أَيُّ مُسْتَقْبَل؟

Do you think there's any **future** for this world?

873. ما هذا [part] [dem. Pron] *what is this*

مَا هَذا؟ - خَاتَمُ تَخَرُّجِي مِنَ الثَّانَوِيَّة.

What is this? - My high school graduation ring.

874. عملت [v] *I've worked*

عَمِلْتُ لِفَتْرَة طَويلَةٍ لِإسْتِعَادَةِ السَّيْطَرَة عَلَى شركَةِ عَائِلَتِي.

I've worked long and hard to regain control of my family's company.

875. فجأة [adv] *suddenly*

لِمَاذَا شَحُبَ لَوْنُهَا فَجْأةً؟

Why did she **suddenly** get faint?

876. تناول [v] *eat*

ليسَتْ لَدَيَّ الرَّغْبَةُ في تَنَاوُلِ الوَجَبَاتِ السَّرِيعَة.

I have no desire to **eat** any of that fast food right now.

877. المسيح [n] *Christ*

مَاذَا تَعْرِفُ عَن المَسِيح؟

What do you know about **Christ**?

134

878. أَتَرى [v <- ترى -> part, أ <-] *do you see*

أَتَرَى مَا يَحدثُ عندَمَا تسمِّمُ عُقُولَ الآخَرينَ بالأَفْكَارِ؟

Do you see what happens when you poison other people's minds with ideas?

879. حسب [n] *according to*

إنْ كُنْتَ تُريدُ اسْتِجْوَابِي، افْعَلْ ذَلِكَ حَسَبَ القَوَاعِد.

If you want to interrogate me, do it **according to** the rules.

880. مهمة [n] *task*

لَمْ أَكُنْ أَعْرفُ أَنَّ سَكْبَ الشَّاي مَهَمَّةٌ صَعْبَةٌ!

I didn't realize pouring tea was such a difficult **task**!

881. موجودة [adj] *present*

أُريدُكِ أَنْ تَكُونِي مَوْجُودَةً عِنْدَمَا أَسْتَلِمُ الجَائِزَة.

I want you to be **present** when I receive this award.

882. أمزح [v] *kidding*

أَنَا لَا أَمْزَح، لَقَدْ قَرَّرْتُ الزَّوَاجَ مِنْكِ.

I am not **kidding**, I've decided to marry you.

883. ربما [n] *maybe*

رُبَّمَا وَالدُكِ مُحِقٌّ. نَحْتَاجُ جَمِيعُنَا لِبِدَايَةٍ جَدِيدَة.

Maybe your dad's right, we all need a fresh start.

884. سخيف [adj] *silly*

هَذَا سُؤَالٌ سَخِيفٌ بالنسْبَة لِفَتَاةٍ مِثْلك.

That's a **silly** question for a girl like you.

135

885. وصل [v] *arrived*

عِندَما **وَصَلَ** المُحَقِّقُون وَجَدُوا البَابَ الخَلْفِي مَفْتُوحاً.

When the detectives **arrived**, they found the back door propped open.

886. السلامة [n] *safety*

أَكمَلْتُ دَوْرَةً كامِلَة عَلى تَدْرِيبَات **السَّلامَةِ** بالمُخْتَبَرَات.

I've completed a full course of lab **safety** training.

887. موسم [n] *season*

الخَرِيفُ **مَوْسِمٌ** جَمِيلٌ.

Autumn is a beautiful **season**.

888. مذهل [adj] *stunning*

لَيْلَى، هَذَا فُسْتَانٌ **مُذْهِلٌ**.

Lily, that is a **stunning** dress.

889. اللعب [n] *playing*

سَئِمْتُ مِن **اللَّعِبِ** مَعَكِ.

I'm tired of **playing** with you.

890. رغم [n] *despite*

رَغْمَ صِغَرِ سِنِّه، عَمِلَ بِنَصِيحَتِي.

Despite his young age, he listened to my advice.

891. الرقص [n] *dancing*

أَخَافُ مِنَ **الرَّقْصِ** عَلَى المَسْرَح أَمَامَ الجُمْهُورِ.

I am afraid of **dancing** on stage in front of an audience.

892. أعتذر [v] *apologize*

لَسْتِ بِحَاجَةٍ لِإِخْبَارِي، كَيْفَ أَعْتَذِرُ لِلنَّاس.

You don't need to tell me how to **apologize** to people.

893. القبض [n] *capture*

هَربَ في مُنْتَصَفِ الليْل لِيتَجَنَّب إلقَاءَ القَبْضِ عَلَيْه.

He had fled in the middle of the night to avoid **capture**.

894. يقدر [v] *estimate*

في 2008، شَهِدَت الوِلايَاتُ المُتَّحِدَة مَا يُقَدَّرُ بـ16 مليون مَرَضٍ قَلْبِيٍّ وِعَائي و5,8 مليون سَكْتَة.

In 2008, the **estimate** for the US was 16 million cases of atherosclerotic heart disease and 5.8 million strokes.

895. هاتف [n] *phone*

لا توجَدُ خَدمَات هَاتِفٍ أو إنترنَتْ بالمَدِينَة.

There's no **phone** service and no internet in town.

896. شعر [n] *poetry*

هَلْ تَكْتُبُ الشِّعْر؟

Do you write **poetry**?

897. أختك [n] *your sister*

كم عُمُرَ أُخْتِكَ؟

How old is **your sister**?

898. محقق [n] *detective*

بِصِفَتِي مُحَققاً، تَمَّ حَلُّ هَذِه الجَرِيمَة.

Everyone, as a **detective**, I've solved this crime.

137

899. يظهر [v] *shows*

عِنْدَما يُظْهِرُ الأَطْفَالُ إِهْتِماماً بِشَيء، عَلَيْكَ تَنْشِئَتُه.

If a kid **shows** interest in something, you have to foster it.

900. مجنونة [adj] *crazy*

إنكِ تبالغين بِرَدةِ فعلك كِامرأةٍ مجنونة.

You are overreacting like a **crazy** woman.

901. يجعلك [v] *makes you*

يجِبُ أَنْ تَذْهَبُ وَتَعْثُرَ علَى مَا يَجْعَلُكَ سَعِيداً.

You need to go and find what **makes you** really happy.

902. من المهم [n] *it is important*

مِنَ المُهِم التفريقُ بَيْنَ تَحْلِيل المُشْكِلَة وَصُنْعِ القَرَار.

It is important to differentiate between problem analysis and decision-making.

903. ابنتي [n] *my daughter*

كنت في طريقي إلى شيكاغو لرؤية ابنتي.

I was on my way to Chicago to visit **my daughter**.

904. طاقة [n] *energy*

لدينا طَاقَةٌ نَظِيفَةٌ ومتَجَدِّدَةٌ وغذاء يكْفِى لإِطْعَامِ الكَوْكَب.

We have renewable, clean **energy,** and enough food to feed the planet.

905. الغداء [n] *lunch*

يريد أن يأخُذَنَا جَمِيعاً إلى الغَداء للاِحْتِفَال بعيد مِيلادِي.

He wants to take us all out to **lunch** to celebrate my birthday.

906. لندن [n] *London*

هَلْ سبقَ وَأَنْ زُرْتَ لَنْدُن؟

Have you ever been to **London**?

907. اثنين [n] *two*

يمْكِنُكَ تعلم شيء أو **اثْنَيْنِ** عندَمَا تَتْرُك عَرِينَكَ.

You can learn a thing or two when you leave your **lair**.

908. ظلام [n] *darkness*

إنَّها لَيْلَة غَيْرُ مُقْمِرَة، **ظلامٌ** وَصَمْتٌ مُطْبِقٌ.

It's a moonless night, **darkness** and silence reign.

909. القاضي [n] *judge*

هَلْ تُخْبِرُ فَخَامَة **القَاضِي** عَنْ مَاهية القَضِيَّةُ؟

Will you inform the honorable **judge** of what the case is about?

910. لديه [n] *has*

كُلُّ شَخْصٍ **لَدَيْهِ** إدْمَانُه الخَاصُّ.

Everyone **has** their special addiction.

911. سمحت [v] *allowed*

هل يمكِنُ أن تُخْبِرَني لِمَاذَا **سَمَحْتَ** لَهُ بالهُرُوب؟

Can you tell me why you **allowed** him to escape?

912. إلى جانب [prep] [adv] *besides*

هَلْ هناك أَشْيَاء أُخْرَى **إلى جَانِب** كرة السَّلَّة تَجِدُ نَفْسَكَ بها؟

Are there other areas **besides** basketball where you find yourself able to perform?

913. إحدى [n] *one*

مَهْلاً، إحْدَى الذِّراعَين أقْصَرُ مِنْ الأُخْرَى.

Wait a minute, **one** arm is shorter than the other.

914. جنون [adj] *mad*

قَاتلوا مَعاً للتَّغلُّب عَلَى جُنُون المَلِك.

They fought together to overcome the **mad** King.

915. الولايات المتحدة [n] *U.S.*

التحق بجيشِ الوِلايَاتِ المُتَّحِدَة حَيْثُ تَلَقَّى تَدْرِيباً عَسْكَرياً.

He joined the **U.S.** Army, where he received military training.

916. قررت [v] *I decided to*

قَرَّرْتُ البَقَاءَ مَعَكِ للأَبَد.

I decided to stay with you forever.

917. رؤية [n -> prep, ل -> لرؤية] *to see*

أَنَا لَنْ أُرسِلَكَ هُنَاك لِرُؤْيَة أَيِّ شَخْصٍ.

I wouldn't send you out there **to see** anyone.

918. ضوء [n] *light*

أنا شُعَاعُ ضَوْءٍ في هَذا العَالَم المُظْلِم.

I am a **light** in this dark world.

919. عملية [n] *operation*

أنا أعْتَقَلك كمُتآمِر في عَمَلِيَّة تَزْوِير.

I'm arresting you as an accomplice in a counterfeiting **operation**.

920. بطاقة [n] *card*

لَقَدْ أَعْطَيْتُكَ **بِطَاقَة** ائْتِمَانِى لتدفعِى ثَمَن المَشْرُوبَات.

I gave you my credit **card** to pay for drinks.

921. تلفاز [n] *TV*

لا **تِلْفَاز** حَتى تنتهِي من وَاجبَاتِكَ المَدْرَسِيَّة.

No **TV** till you do your homework.

922. يبقى [v] *remain*

يَبْقَى الأَطْفَالُ أَشَدَّ المُسْتَضْعَفين في الصِّراعَات، وَهُمْ دائما أَكْثر المُعَانِين.

Children **remain** most vulnerable in conflicts; they always suffer the most.

923. الشعر [n] *hair*

إنَّكَ مُعْجَبٌ فِعْلاً بالفَتَيَات ذوَات **الشَّعْر** الأَسْوَدِ الطَّويل.

You do like the girls with long, dark **hair**.

924. إن [part] *if*

سَوْفَ تُتَّهَمِينَ بمُسَانَدَةِ الإِرْهَاب **إنْ** لَمْ تَتَعَاوَنِي مَعَنَا.

You'll be charged with supporting terrorism **if** you do not cooperate with us immediately.

925. الأعلى [elat] *the top*

نَحْنُ في الطَّابَق الأَعْلَى.

We're on **the top** floor.

926. إلى -> prep, ﻪ -> pron] إليه [*to him*

لَقَدْ تَحَدَّثْتُ **إليهِ** عِدَّة مَرَّات حَوْلَ اسْتِخْدَام الحِمَايَة.

I've talked **to him** so many times about using protection.

927. الرسالة [n] *message*

خُذْ هَذِهِ الرِّسَالَةَ للقروين بِأَسْرَعِ مَا يُمْكِنُ.

Take this **message** to the village as fast as you can.

928. واثق [a.p.] *confident*

أَنْتَ شَابٌّ وَاثِقٌ جِدّاً.

You are a very **confident** young man.

929. دفع [n] *payment*

لَمْ أَعْتَقِدْ أَنَّكِ قَادِرَة عَلى دَفْعِ أَمْوَالِكِ.

I didn't think that you were going to be able to make your **payment**.

930. حكومة [n] *government*

هَلْ سَبَق لكَ أن عَمِلْتَ كَحَارِسٍ لِأَيَّة حُكُومَة رَسْمِيَّة؟

Have you ever served as a guard for any **government** official?

931. ساعدني [pron] -> v, ي <- [ساعد] -> *help me*

سَاعِدْنِي أو سَتَذْهَبُ للسِّجْنِ مَعَ بَقِيَّتِهم.

Help me or you're going to jail with the rest of them.

932. تغيير [v] *change*

فقط تقدم بدلاً من الاستمرار في الأمور التي لا يُمْكِنُنَا تَغْيِيرُهَا.

Just move forward instead of holding on to things we can't **change**.

933. القتال [n] *fighting*

العَالِمُ مَكَانٌ جَمِيلٌ وَيَسْتَحِقُّ القِتَالَ مِنْ أَجْلِه.

The world is a fine place and worth **fighting** for.

934. الرغم [n] *although*

لا أَفْهَمُ، لِمَاذَا يَكُونُ اسمُ الاثْنَيْنِ والتِر رَغْمَ أَنَّهُمْ اخْوَة!

What I don't understand is why they're both called Walter, **although** they're brothers!

935. فندق [n] *hotel*

إِنَّهُ فُنْدُقٌ جَميل معَ حَانَةٍ رَائِعَة.

It's a charming **hotel** with a quiet bar.

936. طيب [n] *okay*

طَيِّبٌ، هَلّا فَتَحْت الحقيبَة، رَجَاءً؟

Okay, could you open the back for me, please?

937. الرقم [n] *number*

إن كَانَت لَدَيْكَ شَكْوَى، فَقَطْ اتَّصِلْ بِهَذَا الرَّقْم.

If you have a consumer complaint, just call this **number**.

938. بسيط [adj] *simple*

العَمَلُ بَسِيطٌ جداً وَلَكِنَّهُ مُمْتِعٌ حَقاً.

The job is very **simple**, but it's really fun.

939. قطار [n] *train*

سَأرى غَداً إذَا كَانَ هُنَالك قِطارٌ لإيطَاليَا.

Tomorrow I'll see if there's a **train** for Italy.

940. تشعرين [v] *feel*

جَعَلَكِ تَشْعُرِينَ حَقاً وَكَأَنكِ كُنْتِ مَرْكَزَ العَالَم.

He really made you **feel** like you were the center of the world.

143

941. الأسئلة [n] *questions*

أخبروني إذا كانَ لَدَيْكُم أيّةُ أَسْئِلَة.

Look around, and let me know if you have any **questions**.

942. يدعى [v] *called*

هل نسيتِ شَيْئاً صَغيراً يُدْعَى عَقْد أمْضَينا عَلَيْه بالأَمْسِ؟

Did you forget a little thing **called** a contract that we signed yesterday?

943. آمن [adj] *safe*

انا رتّبتُ لها مكاناً آمناً لِتَبْقَى بهِ.

I've arranged a **safe** place for her to stay.

944.يمكنهم [يمكن -> v, هم <- pl. pron] *they can*

يُسْعِدُني أن أعرف أنّهم يُمْكِنُهُم رُؤْيَتي كل يوم.

It's nice to know **they can** see me every day.

945. شخصية [adj] *personal*

مُشْكِلَتي مَعَه ليسَت في العَمَل انّما مَسَألَة شَخْصِيَّة.

My issues with him are not professional, they are **personal**.

946. غابة [n] *jungle*

يَجِبُ عَلَى المَرْء أنْ يَعْرِفَ أنّنا نَعيشُ في غَابَة.

You should also know that we live in a **jungle**.

947. المدير [n] *director*

يُمكنني مَعْرِفَة تَاريخ المُكَالَمَات وَالرَّسَائل بَيْنَكِ وبين المُدير.

I can figure out your history of calls and texts between you and the **director**.

948. استخدم [v] *use*

أَمَلِي الوَحِيد كَانَ إيجَادُ تَوْأَم يَسْتَطِيعُ اسْتِخْدَامَ تِلْكَ الأَحْجَار.

My only hope was to find other twins who could **use** the stones.

949. العمر [n] *age*

رَجَاءً، لا حَاجَةَ للشَّكْلِيات، نَحْنُ فِي نَفْسِ العُمُر.

Please, no need for formality, we are the same **age**.

950. رائع [adj] *wonderful*

أُسْبوعَيْن فِي طُوكْيُو، سَنَحْظَى بِوَقْت رَائِع.

Two weeks in Tokyo. We'd have a **wonderful** time.

951. خاطئ [adj] *wrong*

سَأَدَعُكِ تَخْرُجِين عِنْدَما تُدْرِكين بأَنَّ التَّجَسُّسَ عَلَى الأَشْخَاصِ أَمْرٌ خَاطِئ.

I'll let you out when you realize that spying on people is **wrong**.

952. شراب [n] *drink*

أَنْزِلُوا حَقَائِبَكُمْ وَقَابِلِني فِي البِرْكَة لِنَشْرَبَ شَرَاباً لَطِيفاً.

Put your bags down and meet me at the pool for a nice **drink**.

953. مسألة [n] *issue*

أُرِيدُ أَنْ آخُذَ دَقِيقَةً لِمُنَاقَشَةِ مَسْأَلَةٍ أَمْنِيَّة.

I want to take a minute to address an **issue** of security.

954. موافقة [n] *approval*

سَيَتَطَلَّبُ كل كتيب مُوَافَقَة الفريقِ العَامِل.

Each handbook will require the **approval** of the Working Group.

955. أُدخل [v] *enter*

أَدْخِل هَذه الرمُوز عَلَى وحدَة التَّحكمِ أمامَكَ.

Enter these symbols on the control console in front of you.

956. تتعلق [v] *related to*

وفي كُلِّ عَام تُسْتَنْبَطُ تِقَنِيَّاتٌ نَوَوِيَّةٌ جَدِيدَة **تتعلَق** بصحة الإنسان.

With each year, new nuclear techniques **related to** human health are developed.

957. خط [n] *line*

كِلَا أَعْضَاء الفَريق عَلَيْه أَنْ يُعَبِرُ **خَطَّ** النِّهَايَة للفَوْز.

Both members of a team have to cross the finish **line** to win.

958. فكر [v] *think*

تَعَال مَعِي، **فَكِّرْ** فيمَا يُمْكِنُنَا تَحْقِيقُه مَعاً.

Come with me, **think** of what we could achieve together.

959. خدمة [n] *service*

خِدْمَةُ الغُرْفَة لَمْ تَكُنْ جَيِّدَةً كَمَا تَوقَّعْتُهَا.

The room **service** isn't as good as I expected.

960. سرقة [n] *theft*

حَقَّقَ ثَرْوَةً كَبِيرَةً مِنْ **سَرِقَة** الهُوِيَّة.

He made a fortune off of identity **theft**.

961. باريس [n] *Paris*

لَقَدْ تَعَرَّفْتُ عَلى شَابٌ في **بَاريس** مُنْذُ سَنَوَاتٍ عَدِيدَة.

In **Paris**, many years ago, she knew a young man.

962. قمر [n] *moon*

إنكِ جَمِيلَةٌ كالقَمَر.

You are as beautiful as the **moon**.

963. تاريخ [n] *date*

يُمْكِنُكَ تَغْيِيرُ اسْمِك لكن ليسَ تَارِيخَ مِيلادِك.

You can change your name, but not your birth **date**.

964. أراهن [v] *I bet*

أُرَاهِنُ أَنَّها تَعِبَتْ جِداً من تَحْدِيق النَّاس لَهَا طَوال الوَقْتِ.

I bet she's pretty tired of people staring at her all the time.

965. أبقى [v] *kept*

أَبْقَى وَالِدِي مَشَاعِرَهُ المُعَبَّأَةَ في زُجَاجَاتٍ لِسَنَوات وَبَعْدَهَا انْفَجَرَت.

My dad **kept** his feelings bottled up for years, and then he exploded.

966. سجادة [n] *carpet*

سَتَجِدُ مِفْتَاح ذَلكَ البَابَ تَحْتَ سَجَّادَة الدَرَج.

You'll find the key to this door under the stair **carpet**.

967. ثمن [n] *price*

سَوْفَ يَدْفَعُ ابني أَيَّ ثَمَنٍ لِأَجْلِ وَالِدَتِه وَزَوْجَتِه.

My son will pay any **price** for his mother and his wife.

968. دفاع [n] *defense*

الحُكُومَةُ لَدَيْهَا بَرْنَامَجُ دِفَاعٌ سِرِّي بِخُصُوص الصَّوَارِيخ.

The government has a secret **defense** program about missiles.

969. سيء [adj] *bad*

قُمْتُ بِفِعْلٍ سَيِء أَحْتَاجُ لِلإعْتِراف لَكَ بِه.

I did something **bad** I need to tell you about.

970. عد [v] *counting*

إنَّهُ مَشْغُولٌ قَلِيلاً فِي عَدِّ نُقُودِهِ فَحَسْبُ.

He's just a little too busy **counting** his money.

971. المفضل [p.p] *favorite*

لا أَتَذَكَّرُ إخبارَكَ أَنّ الأُرْجُوَانِي لَوْنِيَ المُفَضَّل.

I don't remember telling you lavender was my **favorite** color.

972. بالإضافة [n] *in addition*

بالإضَافَة لِلرَّقْصِ هِيَ أَيْضاً مُهْتَمَّة بِتَغَيُّر المَنَاخِ وَرِّوَايَات جنيفر واينر.

In addition to dancing, she is also interested in climate change and Jennifer Weiner novels.

973. الكنيسة [n] *church*

هذا صَكُّ تَحْوِيل مِلْكِيَّة الكنيسَة وَالأرْضِ كَمَا إتَّفَقْنَا.

That's a deed of transfer for your **church** and land, as agreed upon.

974. البلاد [n] *country*

تَرَبَّيْتُ فِي جِبَال وصحاري هَذِه البِلاد.

I've grown up in the mountains and the deserts of this **country**.

975. قوي [adj] *strong*

كُلُّ مَا تَحْتَاجُه قَلْبٌ قَوِيٌّ وَأعْصَابٌ مِنْ حَدِيدٍ.

All you need is a **strong** heart and a nerve of steel.

976. أهلا [n] *welcome*

أَهْلاً مُجَدداً في البيْت الأبيض، إنَّه مَكان رَائِع.

Welcome back to the White House. Wonderful to be here.

977. حماية [n] *protection*

لَيْسَ لِهَذِهِ الأَقْفَالِ **حِمَايَةٌ** كَهْرَبَائِيَّة، أيّ أنَّه يُمْكِنُكَ إبطالُها.

Those locks don't have power **protection**, which means you can overwrite them.

978. الصف [n] *class*

لاحَظْتُ شيئاً من عَمَلِك في **الصَّفِّ**.

I saw some of your stuff in **class**.

979. التالية [adj] *the following*

لَنْ تَتَجاوَزْنا حَتَّى تُجاوِب عَلَى الأسْئِلة **التَّالِيَة**.

You may not pass until you answer the following **questions**.

980. كلمات [n] *words*

يُمْكِنُني إعْطَاؤُكَ الوَصَايَا العَشْر في عَشْرِ **كَلِمَات**.

I can give you the ten commandments in ten **words**.

981. حالما [adv] *as soon as*

أَنَا سَأُخبِرُها اللَّيلة **حَالَمَا** تَصِلُ إلى البَيْتِ.

I'll tell her tonight **as soon as** she gets home.

982. تسير [v] *going*

حَياتُنا لَنْ **تَسِيرَ** عَلَى نَفْسِ النَّهْجِ هَذا.

Our lives are never **going** to be the same again.

149

983. الشاحنة [n] *truck*

يَجِبُ أَنْ نَتْرُكَ هَذِهِ الشَّاحِنَة هُنَا لِفَتْرَة.

We have to leave this **truck** here for a while.

984. بمجرد [n] *once*

سَأَعْلَمُ المَزِيدُ بِشَأْنِ الأَمْرِ بِمُجَرَّدِ عَوْدَتِي إلى المُخْتَبَرِ.

I'll know more **once** I'm back at the lab.

985. شخص ما [n] *someone*

لَكَيْ تَعْرِفِي شَخْصاً مَا جَيِّداً، تَحْتَاجِينَ لِقَضَاءِ الوَقْتِ سَوِيَّة.

To know **someone** well you need to spend time together.

986. أبيض [adj] *white*

أَعْتَقِدُ بِأَنَّنِي سَأَطْلُبُ مَلْبَساً أَبْيَضَ بالأَشْرِطَة الحَمْرَاء.

I think I'll order a **white** dress with red stripes.

987. السرعة [n] *speed*

لَمْ أَتَجَاوَزْ أَبَداً السُّرْعَةَ المَسْمُوحَة أَوْ غَششت في ضَرَائِبِي.

I never went over the **speed** limit or cheated on my taxes.

988. أحيان [adv] *often*

أُرِيدُ مِنْكَ المَجِيء وَمَفَاجَأَتِي في أَحْيَانٍ كَثِيرَة.

I want you to come and surprise me more **often**.

989. السادة [n] *gentlemen*

لِمَاذَا لا تَسْمَح لِهَؤُلَاء السَّادَة بِإِيصَالِك لِلمَنْزِل؟

Why don't you let these nice **gentlemen** take you home?

990. تدخل [n] *intervention*

هَدَأَ القِتَال بِسَبَبِ تَدَخُّلِ شُيُوخِ العَشَائِر.

The fighting has subsided due to the **intervention** of clan elders.

991. لله [n] *God*

مَا أُرِيدُه هُوَ الحُبُّ المُطْلَقُ والإخْلاص التَّامُّ لله.

What I want is absolute love and total devotion to **God.**

992. اعتقدت [v] *I thought*

اعْتَقَدْتُ بِأَنَّني لَنْ أَرَاكِ إلَّا بَعْدَ الإجَازَة.

I thought I wouldn't see you until after the holidays.

993. الجلوس [n] *sitting*

أشعر بالغَرَابَة في الجُلُوسِ هُنَا وَتَنَاوُلِ القَهْوَة مَعَك.

It's strange, **sitting** here and drinking coffee with you.

994. كابتن [n] *captain*

كابْتِن، السَّفِينَةُ لا تَظْهَرُ عَلَى الشَّاشَة.

Captain, the ship no longer appears on our scopes.

995. الثانوية [n] *secondary*

هَذَا أَقْصَى مَا يُمْكِنُنَا فِعْلُهُ بِالخِدْمَة الثَّانَوِيَّة.

It's the best we could do with **secondary** service.

996. طبيعي [adj] *normal*

لَقَدْ أَطْعَمْتُهَا مُنْذُ سَاعَتَيْنِ وَكُلُّ شَيء كَانَ طَبِيعِيّاً.

I just fed her two hours ago and everything was **normal.**

997. زوج [n] *pair*

كُلُّ زَوْجٍ سَيُرَافِقُهُم حَارِسٌ خِلَالَ هَذِهِ الزِّيَارَة.

Each **pair** must be accompanied by a guard during your visit here.

998. صفقة [n] *deal*

عِنْدَمَا التقيْتُ بالحَاكِم، قَدَّم لِي صَفْقَةً.

When I met with the Governor, he offered me a **deal**.

999. مناسب [adj] *suitable*

نَحْتَاجُ إلى عِقَابٍ مُنَاسِبٌ لِهَؤُلاء الذِينَ يَنْشُرُونَ القِيلَ وَالقَالَ عَن افْتِرَاء.

We need a **suitable** punishment for those who spread slanderous gossip.

1000. مشغول [adj] *busy*

كُنْتُ أُحِبُّ مُشَاهَدَةَ المُبَارَيَات لَكِنَّنِي مَشْغُولٌ جِدّاً هَذِه الأَيَّام.

I used to like watching soccer, but I'm too **busy** these days.

1001. كهذه [ك <- هذه] dem. pron, prep <- ك] *such a*

لماذا قد العب هَذِهِ اللُّعْبَةَ المُمِلَّة؟

Why would I want to play **such a** boring game?

1002. صنع [v] *making*

نَسْتَطِيع بسهولَة صُنْعَ طاولة بإستخدام بعض الصناديق.

We could easily **make** a table out of some of the cases.

1003. نوع من [n] *a kind*

هَلْ هَذَا نَوْعٌ مِنَ المُزَاح؟

Is this **a kind** of joke?

1004. المسدس [n] *pistol*

أَبْعِدْ يَدَيْكَ عَن المُسَدَّس.

Get your hand off that **pistol**.

1005. صحيح [adj] *true*

هَلْ صَحِيحٌ أَنَّكِ عائِدَة إلى الثَّانَوِيَّة؟

Is it **true** that you're going back to high school?

1006. فرقة [n] *band*

مَا هِي فِرْقَتُكَ المُفَضَّلَة؟

What's your favorite **band**?

1007. بالقرب [adv] *near*

سَأَشْتَري شُقَّة بالقُرْبِ من السَّاحِل.

I'll buy an apartment **near** the coast.

1008. إبن [n] *son*

لدَيْنَا ابنٌ وَسِيمٌ وَجَميلٌ.

We have a bright and beautiful **son**.

1009. الأسود [adj] *black*

سَأَشْتَري قَميصاً أَسْوَدَ.

I'll buy a **black** shirt.

1010. الرئيسي [adj] *main*

يُعْتَبَر المُسَخَّن طَبَقا رَئيسِيّاً نَشَأ في جنين ومنطقة طُولكرم في شَمَال الضِّفَّة الغَرْبِية.

Musakhan is a common **main** dish that originated in the Jenin and Tulkarm areas of the northern West Bank.

153

1011. النجدة [adv] *rescue*

لَقَدِ اتَّصَلْتُ بِالنَّجْدَة، لَكِنَّهَا قَدْ تَسْتَغْرِقُ سَاعَاتٍ.

I radioed for **rescue**, but it could be hours.

1012. الحقيقة [adj] *real*

أمي تقول أنه يستخدم الفكاهة لإخفاء مشاعره **الحقيقة**.

Mom says he just uses humor to hide his **real** feelings.

1013. أحسنت [adj] *well done*

أَحْسَنْتَ، قُمْتَ بِعَمَلٍ رَائِع!

Well done, you did a great job!

1014. اتفقنا [pron <- v, نا <- اتفق <- v] *we agreed*

سَآتِي لِأَصْطَحِبَكَ يَوْمَ الأَحَدِ السَّاعَةَ الثَّامِنَةَ كَمَا اتَّفَقْنَا.

I'll come to get you Sunday at 8:00, as **we agreed**.

1015. يكذب [v] *lie*

إِنَّهَا غَلْطَتِي، أَنَا مَنْ جعلته يَكْذِبُ عَلَيْكِ.

It's my fault. I made him **lie** to you.

1016. بقية [n] *the rest of*

مَاذَا لَو بقينَا وَشَاهَدْنَا بَقِيَّةً عَرْضِك؟

How about we stay and watch **the rest of** your show?

1017. دخل [n] *income*

والدتها اسْتَكْمَلَتْ دَخْلَ الأُسْرَة مِنْ خِلَالِ العَمَل كَمُصَمِّمَة.

His mother had to supplement the family **income** by working as a designer.

154

1018. أمل [n] *hope*

لتجعَلْ **أَمَلَكَ**، وَلَيسْ أَلَمَكَ، مَنْ يحدِّدُ مُسْتَقْبَلَكَ.

Let your **hope**, not your hurt, shape your future.

1019. وداعاً [n] *goodbye*

وداعاً، ألقاك غداً.

Goodbye, I'll see you tomorrow.

1020. أقدر [v] *I appreciate*

أُقَدِّرُ قُدُومَكَ هُنَا، وَلَكن أَنَا بِخَيْرٍ.

I appreciate your coming down here, but I'm fine.

1021. قادر [a.p.] *capable*

مَا الذي أَنْتَ **قَادِرٌ** عَلَيْهِ بِالضَّبْطِ؟

What exactly are you **capable** of?

1022. عميل [n] *client*

أَليسَ لديكِ **عميل** قَادِم على السَّاعَة السَّادسَة؟

Do you not have a **client** coming in at 6:00?

1023. تلعب [v] *play*

كان من اللطيف مِنْكَ أَنْ **تَلْعَبَ** مَعَهَا الأَوْرَاق.

That was awfully sweet of you to **play** cards with her.

1024. تقدم [v] *offer*

فَكَّرتُ في أَنَّ أُخْتَنَا الجَدِيدَةَ سَوْفَ **تُقَدِّمُ** دُعَاء اليَوْم.

I thought that maybe our new sister could **offer** today's blessing.

1025. استمع [v] *listen*

اسْتَرْخِ واسْتَمِع إلى المُوسِيقَى.

Relax and **listen** to music.

1026. شراء [n] *buy*

هَلْ تَوَدّ شِرَاء بَعْضَ البسكويت اللَّذِيذ؟

Would you like to **buy** some delicious cookies?

1027. رحلة [n] *flight*

كَانَتْ رحلتِي على المِّرِّيخ أَكْثَر إنجَازَاتِي فَخْراً.

My Mars **flight** was my proudest accomplishment.

1028. جميعاً [n] *all of us*

نَحْنُ جَميعاً نُرِيدُ أَنْ نَكُونَ سُعَدَاء.

All of us want to be happy.

1029. تطلب [v] *call for*

إنّه دَوْرُكَ لكي تَطْلُبَ البيتزَا يَا رَجُلْ.

It's your turn to **call for** pizza, man.

1030. أقرب [elat] *nearest*

هَلْ يُمكنكَ أَن تُخْبِرَنِي أَيْنَ أَقْرَبُ مَكْتَبة؟

Can you tell me where the **nearest** library is?

1031. نادي [n] *club*

هَلْ ذَهَبْتَ للنَّادِي بالأمْس؟

Did you go to the **club** yesterday?

1032. سلام [n] *peace*

يُمْكِنُكَ أَنْ تَتْرُكَني في سَلام لأَسْتَمْتِعَ بِشَرَابي.

You could leave me in **peace** to enjoy my drink.

1033. خطر [adj] *dangerous*

لا يُمْكِنُكِ التَّوَاجُدُ هُنَا. إِنَّه خَطِر.

You know you can't be here; it's **dangerous**.

1034. طول [adj] *length of*

هَلْ تَعْتَقِدِينَ أَنَّ طُولَ هَذَا الفُسْتَان مُنَاسِبٌ؟

Do you think the **length of** this dress is flattering?

1035. أتعتقد [v] *do you think*

أَتَعْتَقِد أَنَّهُمْ عَرِفُوا كَيْفِيَّة قِراءَة الكِتَاب؟

Do you think they figured out how to read the book?

1036. سيدات [pl. fem. n.] *ladies*

أَنتن سَيِّدَات رائعاتٌ من الطَّبقَة العُلوية.

You're great and top-shelf **ladies**.

1037. قرأت [v] *I read*

قَرَأت بمجَلَّة أَنَّ الطَّعامَ الأَبْيَضَ يَجْعَلُكِ سَمِينَة.

I read in a magazine that white food makes you fat.

1038. زفاف [n] *wedding*

سَيكُون هُنالك زَفَافٌ وَنَحْنُ الوَالَدانِ السَّعيدَان.

There's going to be a **wedding** and we're happy parents.

1039. عطلة [n] *holiday*

شَخْصِياً، أَنَا دَائِما أَشْعُر بِالرَّاحَة عِنْدَمَا أَكُونُ في عُطْلَة عَلَى البَحْر.

Personally, I always feel very relaxed when I'm on **holiday** in a sea resort.

1040. فيل [n] *elephant*

لَدَيْنَا أُنْثَى فِيل في حَدِيقَة الحَيَوَان.

We have a female **elephant** in the zoo.

1041. الملازم [n] *lieutenant*

لايهُمُّ مَنْ كَانَ في مَنْصِبِ المُلازِم حِينَهَا.

It doesn't matter who was in the **lieutenant**'s position.

1042. أتوقع [v] *expect*

أَتَوقَّعُ منك التَّصَرُّفَ جَيِّداً حَتى قدوم مَوْعِد الزَّوَاج.

I **expect** you to keep things smooth until the wedding.

1043. مجال [n] *field*

لِمَاذا لا تَعْمَل في نَفْسِ مَجَال تَخَصُّصِ دِرَاسَتِكَ؟

Why don't you work in the same **field** as you are studying?

1044. باب [n] *door*

أَغْلِق البَابَ إذا سَمَحْت.

Close the **door**, please.

1045. خروج [n] *out*

مَاذَا عَنْ خُروج لليْلَة رومَانِسِيَّة بالمَدِينَة؟

What about a romantic night **out** in the city?

1046. جو [n] *air*

هُناك رَائِحَة عِطْرٍ جَميلَة في الجَوِّ.

There is a beautiful scent in the **air**.

1047. يتوجب [v] *must*

يَتَوَجَّبُ عَلَيْكَ حُضُور الاجْتِمَاع.

You **must** attend the meeting.

1048. للحظة [adv] *for a moment*

هَل يمكنُكَ الاسْتِمَاعُ إليَّ لِلَحْظَة؟

Can you listen to me **for a moment**?

1049. نافذة [n] *window*

افْتَح النَّافِذَة، لَوْ سَمَحت.

Open the **window**, please.

1050. عمي [n] *my uncle*

سَأقُومُ بِزِيَارَة عَمِّي الأسبوعَ المُقْبِل.

I'll visit **my uncle** next week.

1051. ضغط [n] *pressure*

هَلْ تَعْمَلُ جيداً تَحْتَ الضَّغْط؟

Do you work well under the **pressure**?

1052. ثلج [n] *ice*

نَاوِلْني كَأساً بِه ثَلْج.

Give me a glass of **ice**.

1053. ابقي [v] *stay*

هَذا تَحْذِيرِكِ الأخير. ابقي بَعِيدَة عَن طَرِيقي!

This is your last warning, **stay** out of my way!

1054. شك [v] *doubt*

لا يُسَاوِرُني شَكٌّ في أَنَّ العَدَالة سَتَسُودُ في نِهايَة الَمَطاف.

I have no **doubt** justice will eventually prevail.

1055. موضوع [n] *topic*

التَّعَاطُف هُو مَوْضوع بَحْثي الرَّئِيسي حَالِياً.

Empathy is my main **topic** of research at the moment.

1056. تعالى [adj] *almighty*

أَنَا أُومن بِإرادَة الله تعالى.

I believe in the will of the **Almighty** God.

1057. محظوظ [adj] *lucky*

أَنَا مَحْظُوظ لأَنَّ لَدَيَّ ابن أخٍ مُتَفَهِّم.

I'm **lucky** to have such an understanding nephew.

1058. تقرير [n] *report*

أُريدُ تقْريراً كامِلاً عَن المُمْتلِكَات عَلَى مَكْتَبي غداً.

I want a full **report** on all remaining assets on my desk by tomorrow morning.

1059. لا داعي [n] *needless*

لا دَاعِي لأَقُولَ أَنَّني لَمْ أَكُنْ مَدْعُواً لِلزِّفَاف.

Needless to say, I wasn't invited to the wedding.

1060. الأحمر [adj] *red*

شَريطُك الأحمَرُ جَميل وَجَذّابٌ جداً.

Your **red** ribbon is so beautiful and attractive.

1061. قديم [adj] *old*

إنَّهُ بَيْتٌ **قَديمٌ** وَجَميل، لَكِنَّ الجُدرانَ رَقيقَة.

It's a nice **old** house, but the walls are thin.

1062. موقع [n] *site*

أَهُنَاك أَحَدٌ لَيْسَ لَدَيه **مَوْقِعٌ** للمُعْجَبِين؟

Is there anyone that doesn't have a fan **site**?

1063. طاولة [n] *table*

هلْ تَذْكُرين عِنْدَمَا صَنَعْتُ **طَاوِلَة** الطَّعَام؟

Do you remember when I built our dining room **table**?

1064. النجوم [n] *stars*

النُّجُوم زَيَّنَت السَّمَاء.

Stars adorned the sky.

1065. أسألك [v] *I ask you*

لَوْ كَانَتْ لَدَيّ أَسْئِلَة، فَسَوْفَ **أَسْأَلُك** لاحِقاً.

If I have any questions, **I'll ask you** later.

1066. وقعت [v] *signed*

بَعْدَ مُرُور عَام **وَقَّعَتْ** الجُمْهُورِيَتَان سَلاماً.

A year later, the Republics **signed** a peace treaty.

1067. فضاء [n] *space*

مَا هُوَ شُعُورُكَ عِنَدما مَرَرْتَ عَبْرَ فَضَاءِ المَجرّة؟

What were your feelings when you passed through galactic **space**?

1068. الخوف [adj] *fear*

يَجِبُ أَلَّا يَمْنَعَنَا الفَشل مِنَ الخَوْف من المُحَاوَلَة.

You can't let the **fear** of failure keep you from trying.

1069. سوية [n] *together*

أَنَا سَعيد لأَّنَّنا نَمْضِي يَومَ الحُبِّ سَوِيَّة.

I'm so happy we're spending Valentine's Day **together**.

1070. ببساطة [adv] *simply*

كُنْتُ أحاول ببساطة استخْدَامَ لُغَتِكَ العَامِّيَّة لِتَوْصِيل فِكْرَة.

I was **simply** attempting to use your vernacular to convey an idea.

1071. قيمة [adj] *value*

كُرَةُ الثَّلْجِ التي لَهَا قِيمَةٌ عَاطِفِيَّة عَظِيمَة.

The snow globe that you said had great sentimental **value**.

1072. تأكيد [n] *confirm*

نَحْنُ لا نَسْتَطِيعُ تَأْكيدَ ذَلِكَ في هَذَا الوَقتِ.

We can't **confirm** that at this time.

1073. القدر [n] *destiny*

القَدَرُ يحاول أَن يَجعَلَكِ مَشْهُورَة وَأَنْتِ تَرْفُضِين.

Destiny is trying to make you famous but you're refusing.

162

1074. الحدود [n] *border*

سَوفَ أَعَبِّر **الحُدودَ** بَاكراً في الصَّباح.

I will cross the **border** in the morning.

1075. ذكر [n] *male*

لَقَدْ تَمَّ تَحْدِيدُ جِنْسَ الطِّفْل، إنَّهُ **ذَكَر.**

The baby's gender has been determined; it is **male**.

1076. بدا [v] *it seemed*

بدتْ وَكَأَنها تُقَاوِم هذَا الزَّواجَ مُنْذُ الأَمَد.

It seemed she'd been fighting for this marriage forever.

1077. تحقيق [n] *investigation*

هَلْ سَأْحْتَاجُ لفتْحِ **تَحْقِيقٍ** حوْل كَيفية حُصُولِكَ عَلَى التَّسْجِيل؟

Do I need to open an **investigation** into how you obtained this recording?

1078. محطة [n] *station*

عِنْدَمَا غَادرتُ **مَحطَّة** القِطَار، رَأَيْتُ بيتر.

When I left the train **station**, I saw Peter.

1079. الجامعة [n] *university*

هَلْ لَدَيْكَ أَيُّ أَصْدِقاء في **الجَامِعَة**؟

Have you got any friends at **university**?

1080. حادث [n] *accident*

إنَّهُ مُسْتَاء جِدّاً مُنْذُ **حَادِث** انهِيَار الجِسر.

He's been a bit disturbed since the bridge **accident**.

1081. فتح [v] *open*

هَلْ يُمْكِنُكَ **فَتْحُ** النَّافِذَة؟

Could you **open** the window?

1082. شاي [n] *tea*

هَلْ تُحِبُّ **الشَّاي**؟

Do you like **tea**?

1083. الداخلية [n] *interior*

وزير **الدَّاخِلِيَّة** يُهَنِّئُكُمْ عَلَى هَذِه النّجَاحَات الكَبِيرة.

The Minister of the **Interior** congratulates you on your great successes.

1084. ضابط [a.p.] *officer*

لا تَسْتَفْسِر عَنْ قَرَارَاتِي أَمَامَ **ضَابِط** آخَر.

Don't ever question my orders in front of another **officer**.

1085. علامة [n] *mark*

هَل حَصَلْتَ عَلَى **علامَتِكَ** في حِصَّة المُدَاوَاة؟

Did you get the **mark** on your therapy work?

1086. المطبخ [n] *the kitchen*

هِيَ في **المَطْبَخِ** تُعِدُّ لَنَا العَشَاءَ جَمِيعاً.

She's in **the kitchen**, making us all dinner.

1087. تستخدم [v] *use*

لا **تَسْتَخْدِم** هَذا الهَاتِف حَتَّى أُهَاتِفكَ عَلَيْه.

Don't **use** this phone until I call you on it.

1088. استوديو [n] *studio*

أُرِيدُ أَنْ أُلْقَى نَظرة عَلَى الأُسْتُوديو خَاصَّتِكَ.

I'd like to take a little peep at your **studio**.

1089. مفاجأة [n] *surprise*

أَعْتَقِد أَنَّهُ من الرَّائِع الاسْتِمْرار في مُفَاجَأة بَعْضِنَا البَعْض.

I think it's great that we can still **surprise** each other.

1090. الجثة [n] *the body*

لِنَدَعْ الجُثَّة تَرْقُد بِسَلام.

Let **the body** rest in peace.

1091. الأول [n] *first*

حَصَلْتُ عَلَى المَرْكَز الأَوَّلِ في مُسَابقة العُلُوم.

I got **first** place in the science fair.

1092. فمك [م -> فم < ك -> n, ك -> pron] *your mouth*

أَغْلِق فَمَك!

Shut **your mouth**!

1093. الحالي [adj] *current*

لَنْ أَطْرَح أَيَّ أَسْئِلَة تَخُصُّ مَنْصِبَك الحَالِيَّ.

I will not ask any questions about your **current** position.

1094. كلهم [pron] *all of them*

أَنَا مُتَأَكِّدَةٌ أَنَّكِ كُنْتِ تُحِبِّينَهُم كُلَّهُم بِجُنُون.

I'm sure you were madly in love with **all of them**.

1095. خطوة [n] *step*

هَذِه أَوَّلُ خُطْوَة نحْوَ كَوْنِكَ طَبيباً حَقِيقِياً.

That's the first **step** to being a real doctor.

1096. حركة [n] *movement*

تَحَقَّقَا إذا كانَ هناكَ أَيَّةُ حَرَكةٍ دَاخِل المَنْزِل.

See if there's any **movement** in the house.

1097. انظر [v] *look*

انْظُر، يَا لَهُ مِنْ قَوْسِ قزَح جميل!

Look, what a beautiful rainbow!

1098. مكالمة [n] *call*

هُنَالِكَ مُكَالَمَةٌ أُخْرَى أُريدُ أَنْ أَسْأَلَكِ عَنْها.

There's another **call** I want to ask you about.

1099. محادثة [n] *conversation*

هَلْ يُمْكِنُني إِجْرَاء مُحَادَثَةٍ وَاحِدَةٍ عَلَى حِدَه؟

Okay, could I just have one **conversation** at a time?

1100. حي [n] *district*

في كُلِّ حَي وَمِنْطَقَة هُنَاك قَائِد وَاحِدٌ للتَّنْظِيم.

In every **district** and area, there is one organization leader.

1101. كتب [v] *wrote*

مَنْ كَتَبَ هَذِه الرّسَالَة؟

Who **wrote** this letter?

1102. مَضَتْ [v] *ago*

منذ لَحْظَة مَضَتْ، كُنْتُ أَشْعُرُ بالسُّوء.

I was feeling pretty pathetic just about a minute **ago**.

1103. قصيرة [adj] *short*

لَقَدْ كَتَبْتُ قِصَّةً قَصِيرَة تُدْعَى الأَمَل.

I wrote a **short** story called "The Hope".

1104. علاج [n] *treatment*

تَمَّتْ مُعَالَجَتُهُم الآن، عِلاج جيُد جداً، المُمَرِّضَات كنّ لَطِيفَات.

All fixed now, perfectly good **treatment**, the nurses were lovely.

1105. آلة [n] *machine*

هَلْ تَعْتَقِدُ أَنَّ آلَة الزَّمَن مجَرَّدُ وَهْمٍ؟

Do you think that a time **machine** is mere fantasy?

1106. الصيف [n] *summer*

هَلْ تُحِبُّ فَصْلَ الصَّيْف؟

Do you like **summer**?

1107. ترتدي [v] *dressed*

ترتَدِي إليسَا دَائماً ثياباً مثلَ الأَميرَات.

Alisa is always **dressed** like a princess.

1108. حقيبة [n] *bag*

لَدَيْكَ حَقِيبة زرْقَاءُ جَميلَة.

You have a beautiful blue **bag**.

1109. فوضى [n] *chaos*

لَقَدْ تَسَبَّبَ هَؤُلاء الأَطْفَال بِالكَثِير مِنَ الفَوْضَى.

These children have caused much **chaos**.

1110. المراقبة [n] *surveillance*

لَيْسَتْ كُلُّ كَامِيرَاتِ المُرَاقَبَة مُجَهَّزَةً لِلرُؤْيَة اللَّيْلِيَّة.

Not all **surveillance** cameras are outfitted with night vision.

1111. نبيذ [n] *wine*

هَلْ سَبَقَ لَكَ أَنْ تَذَوَّقْتَ النَبِيذ؟

Have you ever tasted **wine**?

1112. قف [v] *stand*

إذا سَقَطْتَ، قِفْ وَتَابِع.

If you fall down, **stand** up and continue.

1113. النهر [n] *river*

هَلْ سَبق وَرَأيتَ نَهْرَ المسيسيبي؟

Have you ever seen the Mississippi **River**?

1114. رواتب [n] *salary*

المبْلَغُ المُطَالَبُ به هُوَ تَعْوِيض رَوَاتِب سِتَّة أَشْهُر.

The amount claimed is **salary** for six months.

1115. الجزيرة [n] *island*

أَسْتَطِيعُ رُؤْيَة كَامِل الجَزِيرَة مِن هُنَا.

From up here, I can see the whole **island**.

1116. أكل [v] *eat*

لا أُسْتَطِيعُ **أَكْلَ** أَيَّ شَئ مُنْذُ البَارِحَة.

I haven't been able to **eat** a thing since yesterday.

1117. تدفع [v] *pay*

هَلْ أَخْبَرْتَهَا أَنَّكَ لَنْ **تَدْفَعَ** رُسوم كُلِّيَّتِهَا؟

Did you tell her you weren't going to **pay** for college?

1118. بأكمله [n <- أكمله, prep <- بِ] *the entire*

لَقَدْ قَضَّيْتُ اللَّيْلَ **بِأَكْمَلِه** مَعَ سِتَّة أَشْخَاص.

I've spent the **entire** evening with six guys.

1119. جدي [adj] *serious*

إذَا كُنْتَ **جَدِّي فِعْلاً**، سَأَكُونُ مُلْزَماً بِعَمَل شَيء بِشَأْن ذَلِك.

If you're **serious**, I would be obligated to do something.

1120. لمعرفة [n <- معرفة, prep <- لِ] *to find out*

نَحْتَاج **لِمَعْرِفَةٍ** مَا كَانَ يَفْعَلُه في ذَاكَ الطَّريق اللَّيْلَةَ المَاضِية.

We need **to find out** what he was doing on that road last night.

1121. مر [adj] *over*

هَذَا دَرْسٌ تَعَلَّمْتُه عَلى مَرِّ السِّنِين.

This is a lesson I have learned **over** the years.

1122. يعجبني [v] *I like*

يُعْجِبُني الشَّخْصُ الذِي يَعْتَمِد عَلَى نَفْسِه.

I like the one who counts on themselves.

1123. ذكي [adj] *clever*

أَنْتَ فَتىً **ذَكي**، اكْتَشِف ذَلكَ بِنَفْسِك.

You're a **clever** boy, you figure that one out.

1124. الشكل [n] *figure*

لِمَاذَا يَجِبُ أَنْ أُكَافِحَ لإِصْلَاح هَذَا **الشَّكْل**؟

Why should I struggle to maintain this **figure**?

1125. بسهولة [adv] *easily*

يُمْكِنُنَا أَنْ نَصِلَ لأَسْوَار القَلْعَة **بِسُهُولَة** بالجِسْر.

We can reach the walls of the castle **easily** with a bridge.

1126. حقير [adj] *despicable*

لا تَكُنْ شَخْصاً **حَقيراً**.

Don't be a **despicable** person.

1127. موقع [n] *position*

أَتَمَنَّى لَوْ كُنَّا في **مَوْقِعٍ** يسَمَحُ لَنَا بمسَاعَدَتِك.

I wish we were in a better **position** to offer more.

1128. البحرية [n] *marine*

يَهْدِفُ النظَام إِلَى تَعْزِيز السَّلَامَة وَالحِمَايَة للبيئَة **البَحْريَّة**.

The objective is to enhance safety and the protection of the **marine** environment.

1129. أفترض [v] *I suppose*

أَمَامِي سَاعَة، **أَفْتَرِضُ** أَنَّهُ يُمْكِنُنَا تَنَاوُلُ الغَدَاء.

I have an hour; **I suppose** we could still grab lunch.

170

1130. أغلق [v] *closed*

أُغْلِقَ المَطْعَمُ الشَّهْرَ المَاضِي. لا يُوجَدُ عُنْوَان مُتَوَفِّر.

The restaurant **closed** a month ago and there was no forwarding address.

1131. مدة [adv] *long*

لَقَدْ انْتَظَرْنَا **مُدَّةً** كافِية. عَلَيْنَا أَنْ نَنْطَلِق.

We've waited **long** enough, we need to go in.

1132. ملايين [n] *millions*

سَأَكْتُبُ لَكَ شيكاً بـ10 **ملايين**.

I'll write you a check for ten **million** right here.

1133. يحمل [v] *hold*

مَاذَا **يَحْمِلُ** المُسْتَقْبَلُ لِهَؤُلاء الأَطْفَال؟

What does the future **hold** for these children?

1134. كاميرا [n] *camera*

اسْتِخْدَام **كامِيرَا** الفِيدِيُو لِتَسْجِيل التَّدْرِيبَات مُفيدٌ جِدّاً.

Using the video **camera** to record the practices is really helpful.

1135. بيض [coll. n] *eggs*

أَنْتَ مَجْنُون، هَذا أَفْضَلُ **بَيْضٍ** تَنَاوَلْتُه!

You're crazy, these are the best **eggs** I've ever eaten!

1136. قضيت [v] *I spent*

لَمْ أَسْتَطِعِ النَّوْمَ، لِهَذا، **قَضَّيْتُ** وَقْتِي عِنْدَ الشَّاطِىء.

I couldn't sleep so **I spent** my time at the seashore.

1137. الوجه [n] *face*

أَيَّتُها الأَمِيرَةُ الصَّغِيرَة ذَات الوَجْهِ المُبْتَسِم، هَذِه لَكِ.

Little princess smiling **face**, this one is for you.

1138. الكون [n] *universe*

أَطْلِقْ لِنَفْسِكَ العِنَان وَسِرْ مَعَ التَّيَّارِ إِلَى حَيْثُ يَأْخُذُك الكَوْنُ.

Open yourself up and go with the flow wherever the **universe** takes you.

1139. سفينة [n] *ship*

هَلْ سبَق وَسَافَرْتَ عَلَى مَتْنِ سَفِينَة؟

Have you ever been on a **ship**?

1140. عضو [n] *member*

أَنَا عُضْوٌ في هَذَا الفَرِيق الرَّائِع.

I'm a **member** of this great team.

1141. أغنية [n] *song*

يُمْكِنُك أَنْ تُغَنِّيَ مَعَها أَيَّ أُغْنِية تُرِيد.

You can sing any **song** you want with her.

1142. بطل [adj] *champion*

أَنْتَ بَطَلٌ حَقِيقِيٌّ.

You're a real **champion**.

1143. أضع [v] *I put*

لَمْ أَضَعْ أَشْيَاء شَخْصِيَّةً كَثِيرَةً في هَذِهِ المُذَكِّرَة.

I didn't **put** so much personal stuff in this memo.

1144. أطول [elat] *longer*

ابقيْ لِوَقْتٍ أَطْوَل وَعَلِّمي مِيلي كَيْفِيَّة التَّصَرُّفِ.

Do stay **longer**, and teach Millie how to behave.

1145. عقلك [عقل -> pron, ك -> n <- pron] *your mind*

أَغْلِقْ عَيْنَيْكَ وَاحْتَفِظْ بِذَلِكَ الهَدَفِ في عَقْلِكِ.

Close your eyes and hold that goal in **your mind**.

1146. جدتي [n] *my grandmother*

كَانَتْ جَدَّتي تَحْكي لي قِصَصاً عَنِ الأَيَّام القَدِيمَة.

My grandmother used to tell me stories about the old days.

1147. روح [n] *spirit*

أُقَدِّرُ تَطَوُّعَكَ، فَقَدْ أَظْهَرْتَ رُوحاً عَالِيَة وَرَائِعَةً.

I appreciate your volunteering, you showed mighty fine **spirit**.

1148. أمزح [v] *joking*

أَمْزَحُ. إِنَّهُ دَوْرِي في الدَّفْع اليَوْم.

I'm **joking**, it's my turn to pay tonight.

1149. الفيديو [n] *video*

آمُلُ أَنَّهُ الوَقْتُ المُنَاسِبُ لعَرْضِ الفِيدْيُو.

I hope this is an opportune time to show the **video**.

1150. لوحة [n] *board*

هَلْ اشْتَرَى لكِ والدكِ لوْحَة أَمْوَاج أَثَرِيَّة؟

Did your daddy buy you an antique surf**board**?

173

1151. قابلت [v] *I met*

أَخِيراً **قَابَلْتُ** شَخْصاً سَوْفَ يُحَقِّقُ أَحْلامِي.

Finally, **I met** a person who can achieve my dreams.

1152. كذبت [v] *lied*

عَلى الأرجح أَنَّ الفَتَاةَ **كَذِبَتْ** عليكِ لِتَحْمِي وَالِدَهَا.

Probably the girl **lied** to you to protect her father.

1153. عقد [n] *contract*

الزَّوَاجُ **عَقْدٌ** يَجِبُ ألا تَسْتَهِينُوا بِه.

Marriage is a **contract** that should not be taken lightly.

1154. أنزل [adv] *down*

أَخْبِرْهَا بِأَنْ تَنْتَظِر، سَأَنْزِلُ بَعْدَ خَمْسِ دَقَائِقَ.

Tell her to wait, I'll be **down** in 5 minutes.

1155. اسم [n] *name*

مَا أسْمُكَ؟

What's your **name**?

1156. مرض [n] *disease*

فَشِلْتُ في إيجَادِ تَشْخِيصٍ لِأَنَّهُ لَمْ يَكُنْ هُنَالِكَ مَرَضٌ.

I failed to find a diagnosis because there was no **disease**.

1157. حتى [part] *until*

حَتَّى نُنْهِيَ الكِتَابَ، أَوْ **حَتَّى** يُنْهِيَنَا الكِتَابُ!

Until we finish the book, or **until** the book finishes us!

1158. في أرجاء [prep] [n] *around*

هل غَنَّيْتَ مِنْ قَبْل في أَرْجَاءِ المَنْزِل؟

Do you ever sing **around** the house?

1159. غادر [a.p.] *left*

لَقَدْ مَرَّتْ بِضْعُ سَاعَاتٍ فَقَطْ مُنْذُ أَنْ غَادَرَ المَطَار.

It's only been a few hours since he **left** the airport.

1160. سأحضر [v] *I'll get*

أنتظري هُنَا يَا حبيبتي، سَأُحْضِر الحَقِيبَة.

You wait right here, honey. **I'll get** the bag.

1161. يشبه [v] *look like*

إنّهَ لا يُشْبِهُ الطَّرِيقَة التي وَصَفْتَه بها.

He doesn't **look like** how you described him.

1162. متجر [n] *shop*

الرَّجُلُ الذي يُدِير أَفْضَلَ مَتْجَرٍ يَحْصُلُ عَلَى أَكْبَر عَدَد مِنَ الزَّبَائن.

The guy who runs the best **shop** has the most customers.

1163. انتهيت [v] *I finished*

حَسَناً، انتَهَيْتُ مِنَ البَرْنَامَج التَّلِفِزْيُونِي.

Well, **I finished** with the TV show.

1164. يسمح [v] *allow*

يَجِبُ أَلَّا يَسْمَحَ لِنَفْسِه بِأَنْ يُقَادَ إلى الضَّلال.

He must not **allow** himself to be led astray.

175

1165. مصدر [n] *source*

لا يُمْكِنُني الذَّهَابُ للإدَارَة مَعَ مَصْدَر مَجْهُولٍ.

I can't go to the administration with an anonymous **source**.

1166. رأيتك [v] *I saw you*

أَعْلَمُ أَنِّي وَقَعْتُ في غَرَامِكَ في اللَّحْظَة التي رَأَيْتُكَ بِهَا.

I knew I was in love with you the moment **I saw you**.

1167. ممتع [adj] *fun*

اعْتَقَدَ أنَّ البقاء في البَيْت مَعَ الأَطْفَال مُمْتِعٌ.

I think it's **fun** to stay home with the kids.

1168. أعطني [v] *give me*

أَعْطِني فُرْصَة، دَعْني أَنْظُرْ في الأَمْر.

Give me a chance, let me look into it.

1169. فظيع [adj] *terrible*

إنَّه لإحْسَاسٌ فَظِيع أَنْ تَخُونَ شَخْصاً تُحبُّه.

It's a **terrible** feeling, betraying someone you love.

1170. أصدرت [v] *released*

أُصْدِرَت اللُّعْبة أَوَّلاً في اليَابَان في 27 أفريل 1990.

The game was originally **released** in Japan on April 27, 1990.

1171. مسرح [n] *theater*

عُرِضَتْ الأَفْلام الرُّوسِيَّة الأُولَى في مَسْرَح مُوسْكُو كورش للفنان فُلادِيمِير ساشين.

The first Russian movies were shown in the Moscow Korsh **Theatre** by artist Vladimir Sashin.

176

1172. الفائدة [n] *utility*

هَلْ يَنْبَغِي لَنَا أَنْ نَفْعَلَ ذَلِكَ مِن أَجْلِ الرِّبْح أم من أَجْلِ الفَائِدَة؟

Should we do it for profit or for **utility**?

1173. قاعدة [n] *base*

دَخَلَتْ هَذِهِ القَاعِدَة الحجْرَ الصِحِيَّ.

This **base** is now under quarantine.

1174. وحدي [adj] *alone*

أَعْتَقِدُ أَنَّني لَسْتُ مُعْتَاداً أَنْ أَكُونَ وَحْدِي.

I think I'm just not used to being **alone**.

1175. بعيدة [adj] *distance*

كَمْ هِي بعيدة هَذِهِ النُّجُوم.

How **distant** are the stars!

1176. السبت [n] *Saturday*

لَيْلَةَ السَّبْت، سَوْفَ تَأْتُونَ إِلَى مَنْزِلي لِلْعَشَاءِ.

Saturday night, you are coming to my place for dinner.

1177. تحضر [v] *attend*

لِمَاذَا لَمْ تَحْضُر المُحَاضَرَة؟

Why didn't you **attend** the lecture?

1178. أحدكم [pron] *one of you* -> أحد] -> كم n, أحد

أَتَمَنَّى لَوْ أَنَّهَا تَتْرُكُ أَحَدَكُمْ يَحْمِلُ الطِّفْلَة.

I wish she'd let **one of you** just hold the baby.

1179. علاقة [n] *relationship*

التواصل هو المفتاح الأساسي لأي **علاقة** ناجحة.

Communication is the key to any successful **relationship**.

1180. القرار [n] *resolution*

هَذَا تحدٍ كبير وَأَسَاسِيٌّ أَمَامَ تَنْفِيذ **القَرَار**.

This is a major and fundamental challenge to the implementation of the **resolution**.

1181. المحيط [n] *ocean*

أنتَ تشعُرُ بِأَنَّكَ جُزْءٌ مِن الشَّاطِئ وَمِن **المُحِيط**.

Feels like you're part of the beach and **ocean**.

1182. تثق [v] *trust*

عَلِّميها أَنْ تَكُونَ قَوِيّة وَأَنْ **تَثِقَ** في نَفْسِهَا.

Teach her to be strong, to **trust** in herself.

1183. ينجح [v] *succeed*

أَحْيَاناً، كُلُّ مَا يَحْتَاجُه الطِّفْلُ لِكَيْ **يَنْجَحَ** هُوَ الحُبُّ.

Sometimes all a child needs to **succeed** is love.

1184. جولة [n] *tour*

ظَنَنْتُ أَنَّ حُلْمَهَا هُوَ أَنْ تَذْهَبَ في **جَوْلَة** مُوسِيقِيَّة.

I thought her dream was to go on a musical **tour**.

1185. لا يصدق [part] [v] *incredible*

هَذَا اسْتُديو عَظِيمٌ يَحْمل تَارِيخاً **لا يُصَدَّقُ**.

It's a great studio with an **incredible** history.

1186. تجربة [n] *experience*

قَد تَكُونُ هَذِهِ الرِّحْلَةُ أَفْضَلَ تَجْرِبَةٍ تَعْلِيمِيَّةٍ لَهُمْ.

That trip could have been the best learning **experience** for them.

1187. أدرك [v] *realized*

لَمْ أُدْرِك أَبَداً مَدَى رَوْعَة هَذِهِ الأَشْيَاء اللامِعَة.

I've never **realized** how pretty all this shiny stuff is.

1188. بصراحة [adv] *frankly*

بِصَرَاحَة، تَسَاءَلْنَا مَا تَنْوِينَ فِعْلَهُ مَعَ طِفلكِ.

Frankly, we wondered what you intend to do with your baby.

1189. مريضة [adj] *sick*

كَانَتْ مَرِيضَةً جِداً، فَقَضَّتْ أُسْبُوعَيْن فِي العِنَايَة المُرَكَّزَة.

She was quite **sick**, she'd been in the ICU for two weeks.

1190. تفضلي [v] *go ahead*

تَفَضَّلِي، أَعْرِفُ بِأَنَّكِ تَتَلَهِفِينَ لِقَوْلِ شَيءٍ مَا.

Go ahead, I know you're itching to say something.

1191. نعتقد [v] *we believe*

نَعْتَقِدُ بِأَنَّ الالْتِزَامَ بِهَذِهِ الدَّعْوَة فِكْرَة جَيِّدَة.

We believe it's a good idea to comply with this subpoena.

1192. الجمعة [n] *Friday*

حَسَناً، سَأَرَاك يَوْمَ الجُمُعَة.

Good. I'll see you on **Friday**.

1193. نقل [v] *transfer*

أَيُمْكِنُكَ **نَقْلُ** مِلَفَّاتِي كَي أَسْتَطِيعَ استِخْدَامَهَا فِي المَنْزِل؟

Can you **transfer** my files, so I can use them at home?

1194. الطرق [n] *roads*

هُنَالِكَ الكَثِيرُ مِنَ **الطُّرُق** التي يجِبُ أَنْ نَعْبُرَهَا.

There are still a lot of **roads** ahead.

1195. حادثة [n] *incident*

كَانَتْ مُجَرَّدَ **حَادِثَةٍ** مُفَاجِئَةٍ لا يمكِنُ لِأَحد تَصَوُّرُهَا.

It was a sudden **incident**; nobody could imagine it.

1196. ضمن [n] *within*

مِنَ الأَفْضَلِ أَنْ تَجْعَلَ طُمُوحَكَ **ضِمْنَ** إِمْكَانِيَّاتِك.

It's best to set your aspirations **within** your limits.

1197. قادرة [a.p.] *capable*

أَعْرِفُ أن دِيَانَا **قَادِرَةٌ** عَلَى الإِعْتِنَاء بِنَفْسِهَا.

We all know Diana is **capable** of taking care of herself.

1198. قارب [n] *boat*

أَنَا أَعْمَلُ فِي **قَارِب** الصَّيْد. لا آتِي إِلَى المَدِينَةِ كَثِيراً.

I work on a fishing **boat**, I don't get into town much.

1199. وسيلة [n] *means*

يَجِبُ القَضَاء عَلَى المَرَض بِأَيَّة **وَسِيلَةٍ** مُمْكِنَة.

The illness must be eradicated by any **means** necessary.

1200. النوم [n] *sleep*

أَنَا لَا أَسْتَطِيعُ **النَّوْمَ** عَلَى السَّرِيرِ الصَّغِيرِ!

Come on! I'm not getting any **sleep** in the little bed!

1201. قائمة طعام [n] *menu*

يَجِبُ أَنْ أَقُومَ بِتَغْيِيرِ **قَائِمَةِ الطَّعَامِ** اللَّيْلَة.

I have to make a change to the **menu** tonight.

1202. انقاذ [n] *rescue*

إِنْ اسْتَخْدَمْنَا ذَلِكَ بِحِكْمَةٍ، يُمْكِنُنَا **إِنْقَاذُ** الفَتَى.

If we use this time wisely, we can **rescue** the boy.

1203. استمر [v] *continue*

أُحِبُّ أَنْ **أَسْتَمِرَّ** فِي ذَلِكَ لَكِن حَانَ وَقْتُ الفَطُور.

I would love to **continue** this, but it's time for breakfast.

1204. وحش [n] *monster*

سَتَرَى كُلَّ **وَحْشٍ** يَقُومُ بِمَا يَتَخَصَّصُ فِيه.

You're going to see every **monster** do his specialty.

1205. أدنى [adj] *lowest*

المَدْرَسَةُ الَّتِي تُسَجِّلُ **أَدْنَى** نِقَاطٍ سَتُغْلِقُ لِلْأَبَد.

Whichever school scores the **lowest** will be closed forever.

1206. أثر [n] *impact*

لِلفَقْرِ **أَثَرٌ** مُدَمِّرٌ عَلَى صِحَّةِ الأَطْفَال وَرَفَاهِهِم.

Poverty has a devastating **impact** on children's health and welfare.

1207. بدعة [n] *fad*

لا تُحَاوِل أَنْ تُقَارِنَنَا بِبِدْعَة أُخْرَى صَغِيَرة.

Don't try to compare us to another bad little **fad.**

1208. احتفظ [v] *keep*

يمكنك أن **تحتفِظ** بالخَاتِم.

You may **keep** the ring.

1209. لوحة [n] *panel*

سَيِّدِي، أَتَرَى **لَوْحَة** التَّحَكُّمِ الرِّئِيسِيَّة؟

Sir, do you see the maintenance **panel?**

1210. عَزْبَاء [adj] *single*

إِنَّها أُمٌّ **عَزْبَاءٌ** لِثَلاثَة أَطْفَال.

She's a **single** mother with three kids.

1211. الفرق [n] *the difference*

المنهَجُ هُوَ **الفرق** الوَحِيد.

The only **difference,** however, appears to be in the approach.

1212. لِ [adv] *toward*

أَتْرُكِي هَذَا المَكَان. إنَّهُ مُهِين لِلنِّسَاء.

Leave this place; it's degrading **toward** women.

1213. يسبق [v] *preceded by*

يَسْبَقُ اجْتِمَاعَاتَ المَجْلِس يَوْمَين مِنَ المُشَاوَرَات.

Meetings of the Board are **preceded by** two days of consultations.

1214. أسود [adj] *black*

لَدَيْنَا كَلْبَانِ؛ أَحَدُهُمَا أَسْوَدُ وَالآخَرُ أَبْيَضُ.

We have two dogs; one is **black** and the other is white.

1215. للغاية [adv] *very*

هَذَا الوَضْعُ خَطِيرٌ لِلْغَايَة.

This is a **very** serious situation.

1216. معجبين [n] *fan*

أَنْشَأَ شَخْصٌ مَا صَفْحَةَ مُعْجَبِينَ صَغِيرَةً لِي.

Someone created a little **fan** page for me.

1217. بيع [n] *selling*

أَعْرِفُ أَنَّهُ كَانَ مِنَ الصَّعْبِ عَلَيْكَ بَيْعُ الجِذَاء، لَكِنَّكَ قُمْتَ بِالأَمْرِ الصَّحِيح.

I know it was hard **selling** that shoe, but you did the right thing.

1218. كافية [adj] *sufficient*

أَعْتَقِدُ بِأَنَّ كَلِمَةَ "كَلَّا" كَانَتْ كَافِيَةً.

I believe his "no" was **sufficient**.

1219. اخرس [v] *shut up*

يَا رَجُل، اخْرَسْ مِن فَضْلِك!

Man, **shut up**, please!

1220. ضوء [n] *light*

أَنَا شُعَاعُ ضَوْءٍ فِي هَذَا العَالَم المُظْلِم.

I am a **light** in this dark world.

1221. الفوز [n] *winning*

الفَوْزُ بِهَذِهِ المُسَابَقَة سَيَكُونُ بِدَايَةً أَشْيَاءٍ عَظِيمَةٍ لَنَا.

Winning this pageant's going to be the beginning of great things for us.

1222. كتب [n] *books*

أُحِبُّ **كُتُبَ** الخَيَال لأني أَعْتَقِدُ أَنَّهَا تَأْخُذُكَ إِلَى عَالَمٍ مُخْتَلِف.

I like fiction **books** because I think it takes you to a different world.

1223. حظ [n] *fortune*

أَرَدْتُ فَقَطْ أَنْ أَتَمَنَّى لَكَ وِلِشَعْبِكَ **حَظّاً** طَيِّباً.

I just wanted to wish you and your people good **fortune**.

1224. بعدما [adv] *after*

غَادَرَتْ قَبْلَ عَشْرِ دَقَائِقِ **بَعْدَما** تَلَقَّتْ إِتِّصَالاً آخَرَ.

She left about 10 minutes ago, **after** she got another call.

1225. عالية [adj] *high*

لَدَيْهِ مَعَايِيرٌ أَخْلاقِيَّةٌ **عَالِيَة**، وَأَنَا كَذَلِك.

He has **high** ethical standards, and so do I.

1226. عنوان [n] *title*

هَلْ لَدَيْكَ **عُنْوَانٌ** لِكِتَابِكَ الجَدِيد؟

Do you have a **title** for your new book?

1227. حلم [n] *dream*

كَانَ لَدَيْهَا **حُلْمٌ** أَنْ تُصْبِحَ مُهَنْدِسَةً كَهْرَبَائِيَّة.

She had a **dream** of becoming an electrical engineer.

1228. أصل [adj] *out of*

يَجِبُ أَنْ تَرْبَحِي ثَلَاثَ جَولاتٍ مِنْ أَصْلِ خَمْسٍ.

You have to win three **out of** five games.

1229. أحياناً [adv] *sometimes*

يَجِبُ أَحْيَاناً أَنْ نَتَعَايَشَ مَعَ عَوَاقِبِ اخْتِيَارَاتِنَا.

Sometimes we have to live with the choices we make.

1230. مليئة [adj] *full of*

الحَيَاةُ لا تَزَال مَلِيئَة بِالسَّعَادَة.

Life is already **full of** happiness.

1231. نسخة [n] *version*

لِنُحَاوِلْ أَنْ نَكُونَ أَفْضَلَ نُسْخَةٍ مِنْ أَنْفُسِنَا هَذَا اليَوْم.

Let's try to be the best **version** of ourselves out there today.

1232. ابني [n] *my son*

هَلا عَذَرْتِنَا؟ أُرِيدُ لَحْظَةً مَعَ ابني.

If you'll excuse me, I need a moment with **my son**.

1233. عرف [n] *custom*

فِي الرِّيف، تَمَّ تَنْظِيم المِهَن حَسَبَ العُرْفِ وَلَيْسَ القَوَانِين.

In the countryside, professions were regulated by **custom** rather than laws.

1234. فوراً [n] *immediately*

عَلَيْكَ أَنْ تُغَادِرَ فَوْراً.

You have to leave **immediately**.

1235. الرقيب [n] *sergeant*

هذا صَحيحٌ، حَتَّى الرَّقيبُ كَانَ في صَفِّي.

That's right, even the **sergeant** is on my side.

1236. محامي [n] *lawyer*

لِمَاذَا تَتَهَرَّبُ دَائِماً مِنْ مُقَابَلَة مُحَامِي التَّبَنِّي؟

Why are you dragging your feet to see the adoption **lawyer**?

1237. أرض [n] *land of*

لَنْ تَسْقُطَ أَرْضُ شَعْبِي بَيْنَ أَيْدِي العَدُو.

Never again will the **land of** my people fall into enemy hands.

1238. يرغب [v] *wishes*

يَرْغَبُ الأَميرُ بِمُقَابَلَة جَميع الفَتَيَات الصَّغيرَات في هَذَا البَيْت.

The Prince **wishes** to meet all the young maidens of this house.

1239. وكالة [n] *agency*

كُنْتُ أَعْمَلُ لَدَى وَكَالَة حِمَايَة البيئَة في السَّنوَاتِ الثَّلَاثِ الأَخِيرَة.

For the last three years, I worked at the Environmental Protection **Agency**.

1240. نشرت [v] *posted*

لَقَدْ نَشَرْتُ بَعْضَ الصُّوَر، تَسْتَطِيع مُشَاهَدَتَهَا.

I have **posted** some photos, you can see them.

1241. النهائية [adj] *ultimate*

مَن الذي سَيَقْبَلُ تَحَمُّلَ المَسْؤُولِيَّةَ النِّهَائِيَّةَ عَنْ هَذِه القَرَارَات؟

Who will accept **ultimate** responsibility for these decisions?

186

1242. الأكبر [elat] *the largest*

تُسَاهِمُ السِّيَاحَة بِالنَّصِيبِ **الأكبَر** مِنْ قِطَاعِ الخَدَمَاتِ.

Tourism accounts for **the largest** share of the services sector.

1243. تسمعني [v] [pron] *hear me*

لا، لَنْ أُغَادِر حَتَّى **تَسْمَعَنِي**.

No, I am not leaving until you **hear me**.

1244. ضرب [v] *hit*

رُبَّمَا **ضَرَبَ** الرَجُلُ رَأْسَهُ حِينَ قَفَزَ.

This man might have **hit** his head when he jumped.

1245. رحل [v] *is gone*

نَنْتَظِرُ عِدَّةَ دَقَائِقَ حَتَّى نَتَأَكَّدَ أَنَّهُ **رَحَلَ**.

Let's wait a few minutes, so we know that he **is gone**.

1246. كوكب [n] *planet*

المِرِّيخُ **كَوْكَبٌ** شَبِيهٌ إِلَى حَدٍّ مَا بِالأَرْضِ، ولَكِنَّهُ أَصْغَر بِقَلِيلٍ مِنَ الأَرْضِ.

Mars is a **planet** somewhat similar to Earth. It's a little bit smaller.

1247. مثله [n] [pron] *like him*

سَيَكُونُ وَالِدُهَا سَعِيداً لِمَعْرِفَة أَنَّ بِجَانِبِهَا رَجُلٌ **مِثْلَهُ**.

Her father would be glad to know she's got a guy **like him** around.

1248. أجلس [v] *sit*

أَأَنْتَ تُرِيدُنِي حَقاً أَنْ **أَجْلِسَ** مَعَ عَائِلَتِكَ؟

Do you really want me to **sit** with your family?

1249. تفاصيل [n] *details*

لَا أُحِبُّ إِعْطَاءَ **تَفَاصِيلَ** غَيْرَ جَوْهَرِيَّة.

I don't like to give extraneous **details**.

1250. وجهة نظرك [n] *your point*

آسِفَة. أَنَا لَازِلْتُ لَمْ أَسْتَوْعِبْ **وِجْهَةَ نَظَرِكَ**.

Sorry, I still don't get what **your point** is.

1251. صديقتك [pron <- ك ,n <- صديقة] *your girlfriend*

تَفَقَّدْ هَذَا. زَوْجَتُكَ السَّابِقَة تَجْلِسُ بِجَانِبِ **صَدِيقَتِكَ**.

Check it out, your ex-wife is sitting next to **your girlfriend**.

1252. مصاب [a.p.] *infected*

لَا أَحَدَ مَرِيضٌ أَوْ **مُصَابٌ** هُنَا.

No one is sick or **infected** here.

1253. مدهش [adj] *amazing*

هَذَا **مُدْهِشٌ**. لَقَدْ دُعِينَا إِلَى حَفْلَةٍ رَائِعَة.

This is **amazing**, we have been invited to a cool party.

1254. تستخدم [v] *use*

هَلْ **تَسْتَخْدِمُ** جِهَازَ كُمْبِيوتَر فِي العَمَل؟

Do you **use** a computer at work?

1255. أرجو [v] *I hope*

إِنَّه يَافِعٌ. **أَرْجُو** أَنَّهُ يَعْرِفُ مَا يَفْعَل.

He's so young, **I hope** he knows what to do.

1256. الملكة [n] *Queen*

فَخَامَة المَلِك وَالمَلِكَة. ابنْتُكُم غَطَّتْ في نَوْمٍ عَميقٍ.

My dearest King and **Queen**, your child falls asleep.

1257. هرب [v] *fled*

هَرَبَ أَغْلَبُ السُّكَّان عِنْدَمَا بَدَأَتْ المَعْرَكَة.

Most of the residents **fled** as soon as the battle started.

1258. الحلوى [n] *candy*

كُنْتُ دَائماً الفَتَاةَ التي تَتَحَدَّثُ مَعَ الغُرَبَاء وَتَأْخُذُ الحَلْوَى مِنَ العَجَائِز.

I was always the kid that talked to strangers and took **candy** from old men.

1259. الهاتف [n] *telephone*

عُذراً يَا سَيِّدِي. هَلْ يُمْكِنُني اسْتِخْدَامُ الهَاتِف؟

Excuse me, sir. Could I please use the **telephone**?

1260. البوابة [n] *the gate*

كُنْتُ أَطْرُقُ الجَرَسَ عِنْدَما غَادَرُوا من خِلَالِ البَوَّابَة.

I was ringing the bell when they drove through **the gate**.

1261. قيادة [n] *command*

نَحْنُ في حَاجَةٍ لِسِلْسِلَةِ قِيَادَة وَاضِحَة هُنَا.

We really need a clearer chain of **command** around here.

1262. الحد [n] *limit*

عِدْني بَألا تَتَجَاوَزَ الحَدَّ الأَقْصَى للسُّرْعَة.

Promise me you won't break the speed **limit**.

1263. الحانة [n] *pub*

آسِف، أَعْتَقِدُ أَنَّني سَأَبْقَى في تلْكَ **الحَانَةِ** في النَّهَايَةِ.

Sorry, I just think I might stay in that **pub** after all.

1264. التحقيقات [pl. n] *investigations*

هُنَالِكَ قَدْرٌ كَبيرٌ من **التَّحْقيقَات** يَجِبُ اتمَامُهُ.

There's a huge amount of **investigations** left to be done.

1265. يرتدي [v] *wearing*

إنَّها صُورَة رَجُلٍ بَرِيدٍ **يَرْتَدي** قُبَّعَةَ رَاعِي أَبْقَارٍ.

It's a picture of a mailman **wearing** a cowboy hat.

1266. جيف [masc. n] *Jeff*

لَقَدْ تَكَلَّمْتُ مَعَ **جيف** بالأَمْسِ.

I spoke to **Jeff** yesterday.

1267. الطيران [n] *aviation*

يَقَعُ مَتْحَفُ **الطَّيَران** الفِنْلَنْديُّ بالقُرْبِ مِن المَطَار.

The **Aviation** Museum of Central Finland is located near the airport.

1268. مفتاح [n] *key*

التَّسْويَةُ هُي مِفْتَاحُ نجَاح الْعِلاقَاتِ طَويلَةِ الْمَدَى.

Compromise is the **key** to any long-term relationship success.

1269. بداخل [adv] *inside*

سَنَجِدُ مَا تَحْتَاجُ إِلَيْهِ بِدَاخِلِ نَفْسِكَ.

Dig down deep **inside** yourself, you'll find out what you need.

1270. جيل [n] *generation*

لا يَعْرِفُ الجِيلُ الحَاضِرُ كَيْفَ يَأكُل.

The **generation** of these days doesn't know how to eat.

1271. عنا [prep] *about us*

أنتَ بِبَسَاطَة تَعْرِفُ عَنَّا أكْثَر مِنَ اللازِم.

You simply know too much **about us**.

1272. بدلاً [n] *instead*

لِمَاذَا تُصَدِّقُ الشَّخْصَ الذِي تَخَلِّي عَنْكَ بَدَلاً مِنِّي؟

Why would you believe the person who gave up on you **instead** of me?

1273. قنبلة [n] *bomb*

إذا تَأكَّدْنَا مِنْ وُجُودِ قُنْبُلَةٍ، سَأتَوَلَّى المَسْؤوليّة.

If we confirm that there's a **bomb**, I'll take command.

1274. العامة [adj] *general*

بِإمْكَاننا أَنْ نَعْرِضَ فِكْرَةً عَامَّةً.

We can only afford one **general** idea.

1275. شريط [n] *tape*

أتُمَانِعِين إذَا اسْتَمَعْتِ لِكِتَابِي عَلَى الشَّرِيط؟

Would you mind if I listen to my book on **tape**?

191

1276. كالفورنيا [n] *California*

احْزِمْ مَاتَحْتَاجُ وَاذْهَبْ مُبَاشَرَةً إلى "**كالِفُورْنْيَا**".

Pack up what you need and go straight to **California**.

1277. ممارسة [n] *exercise*

يحقُّ للأُمِّ مُمَارَسَةُ الرِّعَايَة الأَبَوِيَّة.

The mother is entitled to **exercise** parental custody.

1278. النهار [n] *day*

تدور الأَرْضُ حَوْلَ نَفْسِهَا، مِمَّا يُكَوِّن **النَّهَارَ** وَاللَّيْلَ.

Earth rotates around itself, which creates **day** and night.

1279. فحص [n] *examination*

لكِنْ لَدَيْنَا بِضْعُ أُنَاسٍ هُنَا يَوَدُّونَ إجْرَاءَ **فَحْصٍ** آخَرَ.

We do have a few people here who would like a further **examination**.

1280. تصديق [v] *ratification*

يَجِبُ **تَصْدِيقُ** تِلْكَ الاتِّفَاقَات في البَرْلَمَانَات الوَطَنِيَّةِ.

The **ratification** of those agreements had to be made in the national parliaments.

1281. الثمن [n] *price*

كَانوا يَبِيعُونَ شَطَائِرَهُمْ بِنِصْفِ **الثَّمَنِ** في نِهَايَة اليَوْم.

They sell off their sandwiches half **price** at the end of the day.

1282. لا تنسى [part] [v] *memorable*

لَقَدْ مَرَرْنَا بِتَجْرُبَةٍ فَرِيدَةٍ **لا تُنْسَى**.

We had a unique and most **memorable** experience.

192

1283. تقديم [v] *provide*

كَانَ **تَقْدِيمُ** مَلابِسَ مُنْخَفِضَة الثَّمَنِ جيِّداً.

Which was a very good thing, **providing** low-cost clothing.

1284. يعتمد على [v] [prep] *depend on*

الحُبُّ لا يَعْتَمِدُ عَلَى الطُّولِ أَوْ الوَزْنِ أَو اللَّوْن.

Love doesn't **depend on** height, weight, or color.

1285. الصفقة [n] *deal*

حَسَناً. أَنَا سَعِيدٌ بِمُسَاعَدَتِكَ وَسَوْفَ أُعْطِيكَ صَفْقَةً جَيِّدَة.

Well, I'm happy to help, I'll give you a good **deal**.

1286. المسؤول [n] *in charge*

لا أَفْهَم. مَنْ هُوَ المَسْؤُولُ هُنَا؟

I don't understand, who's **in charge** here?

1287. تعالوا [v] *come*

هَيَّا يَا شَبَاب. **تَعَالَوا**. حَانَ وَقْتُ التَّأْبِين.

Ok, guys, **come** on, eulogy time.

1288. واشنطن [n] *Washington*

هَا نَحْنُ هُنَا فِي **وَاشِنْطُن**، قَلْبَ الدِّيمُقْرَاطِيَّة.

Here we are, **Washington** D.C., the heart of democracy.

1289. تحقيق [v] *achieving*

مَنْ فِي اعْتِقَادِكِ يَمْنَعُكِ عَنْ **تَحْقِيقِ** أَهْدَافِك؟

Who do you think is keeping you from **achieving** these goals?

1290. معركة [n] *battle*

المعركة الحقيقية هي إبقَاءُ شُكُوكِكَ مَكْتُومَةً.

The real **battle** is the one within yourself, to keep your doubts at bay.

1291. راحة [n] *rest*

حَالِيَاً، لابُدَّ أَنْ تَسْتَرِيحَ رَاحَة تَامَّةً.

In the meantime, she must have complete **rest**.

1292. الوظيفة [n] *position*

لَقَدْ عَرَّضْتُ حيَاتي للخَطَرِ لإعْطَائِكَ هَذه **الوَظِيفَة**، فافْعَلْ مَا في وِسْعِكَ.

I stuck my neck out trying to get you this **position**, so do your best.

1293. المفضلة [p.p.] *favorite*

الشّكُولاتة الأَلْمَانِيَّة هيَ واحداةٌ مِنْ نَكْهَاتي **المُفَضَّلَة**.

German chocolate is one of my **favorite** flavors.

1294. هيئة [n] *body*

مَجْلِسُ الأَمْنِ لَيْسَ **هَيْئَةً** تدَاوُلِيَّةً؛ بَلْ **هَيْئة** تَنْفِيذِيَّة.

The Security Council is not a deliberative **body**; it is essentially an executive **body**.

1295. اللون [n] *color*

اللَّوْنُ الأَبْيَضُ هُوَ رَمْزُ الحِكْمَة والتَّعَلُّم والنَّظَافة.

The white **color** is a symbol of wisdom, learning, and cleanliness.

1296. الحرية [n] *freedom*

أؤمِنُ بِإعطَاءِ الأَطْفَالِ **الحُرِّيَّةَ** لِيَفْعَلُوا مَا يَشَاؤُونَ.

I believe in giving children the **freedom** to do what they desire.

1297. معروف [p.p.] *known*

أَنَا **مَعْرُوفٌ** لَدَى الجَمِيعِ فِي مَدْرَسَتِي.

My name is **known** to everybody in my school.

1298. في الحقيقة [prep] [n] *in fact*

فِي الحَقِيقَة، أَنْتِ تَعْنِينَ لِي الكَثِير.

In fact, you mean so much to me.

1299. ولاية [n] *state of*

تُعْتَبَر وِلاية ألاسكا مُنْتِجاً وَمُسْتَهْلِكاً للغَازِ الطَّبيعِي.

The **state of** Alaska is both a producer and consumer of natural gas.

1300. بجد [adv] *hard*

ذَاكِر **بِجِدٍّ** وَسَتَكُونُ شَخْصاً مُفِيداً فِي المُسْتَقْبَل.

Study **hard** and be a useful person in the future.

1301. تأجيل [v] *delayed*

انتباه. تَمَّ **تَأْجِيلُ** الرَّحَلاتِ التَّالِية.

Attention, all passengers, the following flights have been **delayed**.

1302. لاحظت [v] *I noticed*

لاحَظْتُ أَنَّكَ تَمْلِكُ بَشَرَةً نَاعِمَةً.

I noticed you have very smooth skin.

1303. الحافلة [n] *bus*

مِنَ المُمْكِنِ أَنْ أَنْتَظِرَ حَتَّى تَأْتِي الحَافِلَة.

Maybe I should wait with you till the **bus** comes.

1304. جديد [adj] *new*

عُمرك أَرْبَعُونَ سَنَةً، وَلا تَسْتَطِيعِينَ تَجْرِبَة أَيَّ شَيئ جَدِيدٍ!

You're 40 and you can't try something **new**!

1305. دع [imp] *let*

دَعِ القَمَرَ المُكْتَمِلَ يضِئ الظَّلام الذِي بِدَاخِلِكَ.

Let the waxing moon alight the darkness within you.

1306. المباحث [n] *detective*

أنا مُحَقِقُ مَدِينَة نيويُورك.

I'm a **detective** for the New York City Police Department.

1307. استطعت [v] *I was able*

هَذَا رَائِع. أَنَا سَعِيدٌ أَنَّنِي اسْتَطَعْتُ أَنْ أُسَاعِدَك يَارَجُلْ.

That's great. I'm glad **I was able** to help you, man.

1308. أسأل [v] *ask*

آسِفَة، أَسْأَلُ الكَثِيرَ مِنَ الأَسْئِلَةِ عِنْدَمَا أَكُونُ مُتَوَتِّرَة.

Sorry, I **ask** a lot of questions when I'm nervous.

1309. رُحّل [v] *deported*

رُحّلَ الرَّجُلُ الذِي صَنَعَ الأَوْرَاقَ المُزَوَّرَة.

The guy who made the fake papers got **deported**.

1310. السطح [n] *surface*

هَذَا السَّطْحُ مُغبَّر.

This **surface** is dusty.

1311. جلبت [v] *brought*

جَلَبْتُ لَكِ بَعْضاً من كَعْكِ الشُّكُولاتَة لِمُسَاعَدَتِكِ عَلى التَّحَسُّن.

I **brought** you some chocolate cake to make you feel better.

1312. قوات [coll. n] *troop*

الأُرْدُنُ هوَ ثَانِي أَكْبَر الدُّوَلِ المُسَاهِمَةِ في قُوَّاتِ حِفْظِ السَّلام.

Jordan today is the second-largest **troop** contributor to peacekeeping operations.

1313. لقد وجدت [part] [v] *I've found*

لَقَدْ وَجَدْتُ عَمَلاً رائعاً مؤخراً.

I've **found** a great job recently.

1314. نووي [adj] *nuclear*

إنَّها مُفَاعِلٌ نَوَوِيٌّ عِمْلاقٌ كَغَيْرِهَا مِن النُّجوم.

Like all stars, it's basically a giant **nuclear** reactor.

1315. وجبة [n] *meal*

الإِفْطَارُ هُوَ أَهَمُّ وَجْبَةٍ في اليَوْم.

Breakfast is the day's most important **meal**.

1316. الحرارة [n] *heat*

دَعنَا لَا نُحَاوِلْ تَسَلُّقَ التَّلِّ في هَذِهِ الحَرَارَةِ الرَّهيبَة.

Let's not try to climb that hill in this dreadful **heat**.

1317. حاضِر [n] *present*

يُمَثِّلُ الأَطْفَالُ حَاضِرَ مُجْتَمَعِنَا وَمُسْتَقْبَلَهُ.

Children represent the **present** and the future of our society.

1318. حِساب [n] *account*

لَمْ أَسْتَثْمِرِ المَالَ، بل احْتَفَظْتُ بِهِ في حِسَابِ التَّوْفِيرِ.

I never invested the money, I just kept it in my savings **account**.

1319. خطاب [n] *speech*

هَلْ سَتُلْقِي خِطَابَ الاحْتِفَال؟

Are you going to give the celebration **speech**?

1320. شديد [adj] *severe*

إِنَّ الاقْتِصَادَ العَالَمِيَّ يَبْدُو الآنَ وَكَأَنَّهُ يَتَّجِهُ في مُنْحَدَرٍ شَدِيدٍ.

The global economy now appears to be headed for a **severe** downturn.

1321. طيلة [adv] *throughout*

كَانَتْ رِسَالَتُهُ مَصْدَرَ إِلْهَامٍ لَنَا طِيلَةَ هَذِهِ الدَّوْرَةِ.

His message has been an inspiration to us **throughout** this session.

1322. النظرة [n] *outlook*

إِنَّ النَّظْرَةَ العَامَّةَ للاقتِصَادِ العَالَمِيَّ تَتَحَسَّنُ.

The global economic **outlook** is improving.

1323. سر [n] *secret*

كَيْفَ سَأَتَزَوَّجُ شَخْصاً وَبِحَوْزَتِي سِرٌّ عِمْلاقٌ عَمَّنْ أَكُونُ؟

How do I marry someone when I have this giant **secret** about who I am?

1324. تراجع [v] *decline*

حَدَثَ **تَرَاجُعٌ** في العَمَالَةِ الزِّرَاعِيَّةِ عَلَى الصَّعِيد العَالَمِيِّ.

Globally, there has been a **decline** in agricultural labor.

1325. خطة [n] *plain*

سَأَلْتُ عَنْ حَلٍّ، وَلَيْسَ عَنْ **خُطَّةِ** هُرُوبٍ.

I asked for a solution, not an escape **plan**.

1326. الفصل [n] *chapter*

افتَحُوا كُتُبَكُمْ عَلَى **الفَصْلِ** الثَّالِث وَابْدَؤُوا القِرَاءَة.

Turn your books to **chapter** three, please, and start reading.

1327. مثالي [adj] *ideal*

وَضْعُنَا بالكَاد **مِثَالي**، لَكِنْ نَعَمْ، نحنُ سُعَدَاءُ جِدّاً مَعاً.

Our situation is hardly **ideal**, but yes; we're very happy together.

1328. رأيي [رأي <- n, ي <- pron] *my opinion*

لَقَدْ اتَّخَذْتِ قرارَكِ، فَلِمَاذَا تَسْأَلِينَني عَنْ رَأْيِي؟

You've made your decision, why are you asking me for **my opinion**?

1329. سمك [n] *fish*

إنهم يُعِدُّون حَسَاءَ سَمَكٍ سَتُحِبِّينَهُ كَثيراً!

They make a **fish** soup that'll drive you crazy!

1330. جائع [a.p.] *hungry*

بصراحة، لَقَدْ حَانَ وَقْتُ الغَدَاءِ وَأَنَا جَائِعٌ.

Honestly, it's almost lunchtime, and I'm **hungry**.

1331. المرور [n] *traffic*

لا أُرِيدُكِ أَنْ تَعْلَقِي فِي حَرَكَةِ المُرُور.

I don't want you to get stuck in **traffic**.

1332. المجيء [n] *coming*

أُحِبُّ المَجِيء إِلَى الدَّوْحَة. إِنَّها مَكَانٌ عَالَمِي.

I love **coming** to Doha; it's such an international place.

1333. أتعلم [v] *learn*

يَجِبُ أَنْ أَتَعَلَّمَ طَرِيقَةَ العَمَل معَ الآخَرِين.

I need to **learn** how to work with other people.

1334. السفر [n] *travel*

مازلتُ أَحَاوِلُ فَهْمَ فِكْرَة السَّفَرِ عَبْرَ الزَّمَنِ بِرُمَّتِها.

I'm still trying to wrap my head around this whole idea of time **travel**.

1335. مباراة [n] *match*

تَذَكَّرْ أَنَّها مُبَارَاةٌ وِدِّيَّةٌ، هَيَّا.

Remember, it's a friendly **match**, so go on.

1336. من فضلكم [prep] [n] [pron] *please*

حَسَناً أَيُّهَا الآبَاءُ وَالأَبْنَاءُ، خُذُوا مَقَاعِدَكُمْ **مِنْ فَضْلِكُمْ**.

All right, parents and students, **please** take your seats.

1337. عبارة [n] *word*

ثَمَّةَ **عِبَارَةٌ** سِحْرِيَّةٌ في المُفَاوَضَات الدُّوَلِيَّةِ وهي التَّوَازُنُ.

There is a magic **word** in international negotiations, which is balance.

1338. هدف [n] *goal*

مَا هُوَ هَدَفُكَ؟

What is your **goal**?

1339. تطلق [v] *launches*

نَاسَا **تُطْلِقُ** مِسْبَارَ مَافِنْ إلى المِرِّيخ - 2013.

2013 - NASA **launches** the Maven probe to Mars.

1340. أؤمن [v] *I believe in*

إنَّني أَهْتَمُ بِأَمْرِ وَالِدِكِ - وَأَنَا **أُؤْمِنُ** بِه.

I care about your father, and **I believe in** him.

1341. نخب [n] *toast*

افْتَقَدْنَاكَ هُنَا في **نَخْبٍ** مَاقَبْلَ الحَفْلَة.

We did miss having you here for the pre-party **toast**.

1342. سريع [adj] *rapid*

إنَّنَا نَعِيشُ مَرْحَلَةً تَغَيُّرٍ تَارِيخِي **سَرِيع**.

We are living through a phase of **rapid** historical change.

1343. الخلفي [adj] *rear*

الطَّابَقُ **الخَلْفِي**، أَلَمْ يَقُولُوا أَنَّهُ سيُعادُ تَأهِيلُه؟

The **rear** deck, did they not say that would be refinished?

1344. الجنود [n] *soldiers*

ثَلاث **جُنُودٍ** صِغَارٍ يَمْشُونَ في حَدِيقَةِ الحَيَوَان.

Three little **soldiers** walking in the zoo.

1345. رد [n] *reply*

لَمْ أَتَلَقَّ أَيَّ **رَدٍّ** عَلَى رِسَالَتِي.

I received no **reply** to my letter.

1346. لذلك نتيجة [n] *as a result*

هَذِه البَعْثَةُ قَيْدَ التَّصْفِيَة حَالِياً، وَ**نَتِيجَة لِذَلِكَ**، تَمَّ سَحْبُ المُوَظَّفِين.

The mission is now being disbanded, **as a result**, the staff has been withdrawn.

1347. تصرف [v] *behave*

تَصَرَّفْ بِلُطْفٍ، فَنَحْنُ سَنُقَابِل سَيِّدَةً مُحْتَرَمَةً.

Behave gently, we are meeting a decent lady.

1348. العدالة [n] *justice*

يَجِبُ تَحْقِيقُ **العَدَالَةِ**.

Justice must be served.

1349. سندات [n] *securities*

يَجُوزُ لِلشَّرِكَةِ أَيْضاً إِصْدَارُ السَّنَدَاتِ، وَهِيَ **سَنَدَاتُ** الدُّيُون.

A company may also issue bonds, which are debt **securities**.

1350. كسر [v] *breaking*

أَعْتَقِدُ أَنَّنِي أَدَّيْتُ عَمَلاً رَائِعاً في **كَسْرِ** القَوَاعِد.

I think I've done a pretty good job of **breaking** the rules.

1351. يمر [v] *passes*

لا أَعْرِفُ كَيْفَ **يَمُرُّ** الوَقْتُ هَذِه الأَيّام.

I don't realize how the time **passes** these days.

1352. أهتم [v] *care*

أَنَا آسِفٌ، وَلَكِنَّنِي لا **أَهْتَمُّ** بِشَأْنِ هؤُلاءِ الرِّجَال.

I'm sorry, but I don't **care** about these men.

1353. سجل [n] *record*

هَذَا **سِجِلُّ** حُضُور الطُّلابِ الذِينَ يَضَعُونَ عَلامَةً بِأَنْفُسِهِم.

This is a **record** of attendance, the students sign themselves in.

1354. تجري [v] *conduct*

وظِيفَتُكَ هِي أَنْ **تُجْرِيَ** المُقَابَلاتِ الأَوَّلِيَّة الخَاصَّة بالشَّكَاوَى.

Your job is to **conduct** preliminary interviews with the complainant.

1355. الجنون [adj] *madness*

ذَهَبَ للكَلامِ مَعَهَا ومُحَاوَلَة وَضْعِ حدٍّ لِهَذَا **الجُنُون**.

He went to talk to her to try and put an end to this **madness**.

1356. يدور [v] *spin*

مَا يُمْكِنُكِ إيجَادُهُ عَلَى الإِنْتَرْنِت قَدْ يجْعَلُ عَقْلَكِ **يَدُور**.

What you can find on the Internet would make your head **spin**.

1357. النصر [n] *victory*

لَنْ يُوقِفَنَا أَحَدٌ في سَعْينَا لاسْتِعَادَة النَّصْرِ.

No one will stop us in our quest to reclaim **victory**.

1358. حدثت [v] *occurred*

حَدَثَتْ مُشْكِلَةٌ في صَفْحَةِ الوِيبِ هَذِهِ، لِذَا تَمَّتْ إعَادَةُ تَحْمِيلِهَا.

A problem **occurred** with this webpage so it was reloaded.

1359. هربت [v] *ran away*

لَقَدْ هَرَبَتْ مِنَ البَيْتِ وَاتَّصَلَتْ بِي.

She **ran away** from home and called me.

1360. مقرف [adj] *nasty*

يُوجَدُ شيءٌ مُقْرِفٌ في شَعْرِكِ.

There's something really **nasty** stuck in your hair.

1361. مشروع [n] *project*

أنتِ مَشْرُوعٌ مُشَوِّقٌ وَأَنَا أَتَمَتَّعُ بِمُشَاهَدَة تَقَدُّمِكِ.

You're an interesting **project**, and I enjoy watching your progress.

1362. قراءة [n] *reading*

أَتَطَلَّعُ إلَى قِرَاءَةِ مَقَالاتِكُم الشَّخْصِيَّة.

I look forward to **reading** your personal essays.

1363. فرنسا [n] *France*

فَرَنْسَا سَتُنقِذُ نَفْسَهَا بِمُرَاقَبَة المَعَايِير الأعلَى للإنْضِبَاطِ.

France will save herself by observing the highest standards of discipline.

1364. شجرة [n] *tree*

سَنَذْهَبُ لِمُشَاهَدَة أَكْبَرِ شَجَرَةٍ معمرة في العَالَم.

We're on our way to see the world's largest banyan **tree**.

1365. تلقيت [v] *I received*

لَقَدْ تَلَقَّيْتُ شيئاً خَاصاً مِنْ وَالِدِي.

I received something rather special from my father.

1366. المغادرة [n] *departure*

مُضِيفَاتُ الرِّحْلَة، إلتزمْنَ مَقَاعِدَكُنَّ. نَحْنُ عَلَى وَشْكِ المُغَادَرَة.

Flight attendants, take your seats for **departure**.

1367. مرحلة [n] *stage*

لَقَدْ اجْتَزْتَ أَوَّلَ مَرحْلَةٍ مِنْ الاخْتِبَار.

You have passed the first **stage** of the test.

1368. قرن [n] *century*

وَسَيَدْخُلَ القَرْنُ العِشْرُونَ التَّارِيخَ بِوَصْفِهِ قَرْنَ المُتَنَاقِضَات.

The twentieth **century** will go down in history as a **century** of contradictions.

1369. ذكية [adj] *smart*

أَعْرِفُ أَنَّكِ فَتَاةٌ ذَكِيَّةٌ، لِذَا، سَأَثِقُ بِكِ.

I know you're a **smart** kid, so I'll trust you.

1370. إدارة [n] *management*

أَنْتَ تَفْتَقِرُ إِلَى مَهارَاتِ إِدَارَةِ الوَقْتِ.

You lack time **management**.

1371. الوقت الحالي [n] [adj] *the meantime*

فِي الوَقْتِ الحَالِي، اهْتَمِّي بِنَفْسِك.

In **the meantime**, take care of yourself.

1372. السعادة [n] *happiness*

قَلْبِي تخَطَّى كُلَّ حُدُودِ السَّعَادَة.

My heart has crossed all limits of **happiness**.

1373. أمسك [v] *hold*

أَرجوك أَمْسِك الطِّفْلَ، يَجِبُ أَنْ أَذهَبَ إلَى هُنَاك.

Please **hold** the baby, I have to go in there.

1374. أدلة [n] *evidence*

لَدَيْنَا أَدِلَّةٌ تُثْبِتُ أَنَّكِ كُنْتِ في حفْلِ زَفَافٍ.

We have **evidence** proving that you were present at a wedding.

1375. مهتم [a.p.] *interested*

أَنَا مُهْتَمٌّ للْغَايَة بِكُلِّ مَا سَتَقُولِينَهُ.

I am very **interested** in everything that you have to say.

1376. بوجود [prep] {n) *the existence of*

هَلْ تُؤْمِنين بِوُجُود مَصَّاصِي الدِّمَاء؟

Do you believe in **the existence of** vampires?

1377. مزحة [n] *joke*

إذَا كَانَتْ هَذِه مَزْحَة، فَإنَّهَا غَيْرُ مُضْحِكَة!

If this was a **joke** then it really wasn't funny!

1378. يتصرف [v] *act*

هَلْ رَأَيْتَ هَذَا الفَتَى **يَتَصَرَّفُ** بِمَسْؤُولِيَّةٍ؟

Have you ever seen that kid **act** reasonably?

1379. الجنرال [n] *General*

أَخْرِجُوا **الجنرال** رِيتْشَارْد وامْرَأَتَهُ خَارِجَ المَدِينَة وَدَعُوهُمَا يَذْهَبَا.

Take **General** Richard and his wife outside the city and let them go.

1380. أجمل [elat] *the most beautiful*

لَقَدْ كَانَ هَذَا **أَجْمَلَ** يَوْمٍ حَظِيتُ بِهِ.

This was **the most beautiful** day I've ever had.

1381. ضخم [adj] *huge*

إِنَّهُ حُلْمٌ **ضَخْمٌ** لَيْسَ بِإِمْكَانِكِ تَحْقِيقُهُ بِمُفْرَدِكِ.

It's a **huge** dream, and you can't do it alone.

1382. بهدوء [adv] *quietly*

فِي يوم تَارِيخِي كَهَذَا، أَوَدُّ أَنْ أَبْقَى بالمَنْزِل **بِهُدُوء**.

On a momentous day like today, I would like to stay **quietly** at home.

1383. الهند [n] *India*

كَيْفَ جِئْتَ مِنَ الهِنْدِ إِلَى أَمْرِيكَا؟

How did you come from **India** to the U.S.A.?

1384. عم [n] *uncle*

هَذَا الطِّفْلُ سَيَحْظَى بِعَمٍّ رَائِعٍ.

This kid's going to have a great **uncle**.

1385. شقة [n] *apartment*

لا أَحَدَ يَشْتَري شُقَّةً قَبْلَ أَنْ يَبِيعَ شُقَّتَهُ.

Nobody buys an **apartment** nowadays before they sell their own.

1386. الفدرالية [n] *federal*

بَذَلَ مُوَكِّلي كُلَّ جُهْدِه لِلإِمْتِثَالِ لِلقَوَانِينِ الفِدِرَالِيَّةِ.

My client made every effort to comply with **federal** regulations.

1387. يترأّس [v] *leads*

قُمتُ بِتَعْيينِ مُحْتَرِفٍ لِكَيْ يَقُودَ هَذِه النَّدْوَةَ

I've hired a professional to **lead** the seminar.

1388. بيانات [n] *data*

أعطِ مثالاً مِنَ البَيَانَات أَوْ الرّسْمِ البَيَاني لِدَعْمِ رَأْيِكَ.

Give an example from the **data** or graph to support your thinking.

1389. معقول [adj] *reasonable*

يجِبُ أَنْ نَتَعَرَّفَ عَنْ بَعْضِنَا البَعْضِ لِوَقْتٍ مَعْقُولٍ.

We should know each other for a **reasonable** time.

1390. مسرور [adj] *delighted*

مَسْرُورٌ لِمُقَابَلَتِكَ. تَعَالَ، دَعْنَا نَجْلِسْ هُنَا.

Delighted to meet you. Come, let's sit down here.

1391. التخلص [v] *eliminate*

عَلَيْنَا التَّخَلُّص مِنَ الأفْكَار السَّلْبِيَّة.

We must **eliminate** negative ideas.

1392. أسهل [elat] *easier*

رُبَّمَا يَجِبُ عَلَيْكُمُ البَحْثُ عن وَظَائِفَ أَسْهَل.

Well, maybe you guys should look for **easier** jobs.

1393. الأوقات [pl. n] *time*

كَانَتْ أَسْعَدُ الأَوْقَاتِ في حَيَاتِي عِنْدَمَا كُنْتُ مُفْلِساً.

The happiest **time** of my life was when I was broke.

1394. التدريب [n] *training*

بَعْدَ تِسْعَةِ أَشْهُرٍ مِنَ التَّدْرِيبِ، سَنَكُونُ المُخْتَارِين.

After 9 months of **training**, we will be the chosen ones!

1395. بالتحديد [prep] [v] *specifically*

كَيْفَ عَرَفْتَ بِالتَّحْدِيدِ أَنَّهَا كَانَتْ رِحْلَةَ صَيْدٍ؟

How did you know it was **specifically** a fishing trip?

1396. بحلول [adv] *by*

أَقْتَرِحُ أَنْ تَذْهَبَ بِحُلُولِ الصَّبَاحِ.

I suggest that you be gone **by** morning.

1397. زاك [n] *Zak*

زاك هُوَ مُدَرِّبِي المُفَضَّل.

Zak is my favorite coach.

1398. السُلطة [n] *power*

لا تُحِبَّ أَحَداً يُحِبُّ السُّلْطَةَ أَكْثَرَ مِنَ الحَيَاة.

Don't love anyone who loves **power** more than life.

1399. تعرض [v] *exposure*

يُعْتَبَر تَعَرُّضَ الجَنِين للكُحُول السَّبَبَ الرَّئِيسِيَّ لِلإِعَاقَة الذِّهْنِيَّة.

Fetal **exposure** to alcohol is a major reason for mental disability.

1400. أبيض [adj] *white*

لَقَدْ تَحَدَّثْتُ إِلَى وَالِدِكِ. اذْهَبِي لِانتِقَاءِ فُسْتَان أَبْيَضَ.

I talked to your dad, go pick out a **white** dress.

1401. قادمة [a.p.] *coming*

صَدِيقَتِي المُفَضَّلَة قَادِمَة لِزِيَارَتِي اليَوْم.

My best friend is **coming** to visit me today.

1402. برفقة [n] *accompanied by*

كَانَ بِرِفْقَةِ صَدِيقَتِه وابنَ عَمِّهِ وَصَدِيقٍ آخَرَ.

He was **accompanied by** his girlfriend, his cousin, and a friend.

1403. حسب [v] *according to*

حَسَبَ مَا سَمِعْتُ، سَيُغْلَقُ المَحَلُّ غَداً.

According to what I heard, the shop will be closed tomorrow.

1404. المهمة [n] *task*

هَلْ هَذِه المَهَمَّةُ صَعْبَةٌ عَلَيْك؟

Is this **task** difficult for you?

1405. تحذير [v] *warning*

بِأمرٍ مِن المَحْكَمَة، هَذَا آخِرُ تَحْذِير.

By order of the court, this is your final **warning**.

1406. ال (التعريف) [part] *the*

انتَظِري لَحْظَةً، أَنَا أَتَحَدَّثُ عَلَى الهَاتِفِ.

Wait a moment, I'm on **the** phone.

1407. موجودة [n] *present*

كُلُّ العَائِلَةِ كَانَتْ مَوْجُودَةً.

The whole family was **present**.

1408. نحصل [v] *we get*

نَحْنُ **نَحْصُلُ** عَلَى بعْضِ البَسْكَوِيت عِنْدَ تنْظِيفِ المَنْزِل.

We get some cookies when we clean the house.

1409. أحمد [n] *Ahmed*

أَحْمَدُ هُوَ أَخِي.

Ahmed is my brother.

1410. غطاء [n] *cover*

سَأشْتَري **غِطَاءً** لِهَاتِفِي.

I'll buy a **cover** for my phone.

1411. ربما [adv] *maybe*

رُبَّمَا يَجِبُ أَنْ نَبْدَأ مُجَدَّداً.

Maybe we should start again.

1412. خزانة [n] *closet*

وَضَعْتُ المَلَابِسَ في **الخِزَانَة**.

I put the clothes in the **closet**.

1413. فطيرة [n] *pie*

كُوني كَرِيمَةً وَاتْرُكِي لِي قِطْعَةً مِنَ الْفَطِيرَةِ.

Be a good girl and save me a piece of the **pie**.

1414. يفعل [v] *do*

مَاذَا يَفْعَلُ؟

What does he **do**?

1415. غرفة النوم [n] *bedroom*

أَحْضَرْتُ فُسْتَاناً مِنْ غُرْفَةِ النَّوْمِ الْخَاصَّةِ بِكِ.

I brought a dress from your **bedroom**.

1416. وصل [v] *arrived in*

نَعَمْ، وَصَلَ إِلى لَنْدُنْ فِي وَقْتٍ لاحِقٍ مِنْ ذَلِكَ الْيَوْم.

Yes, he **arrived in** London later that day.

1417. السلامة [n] *safety*

لِلسَّلامَة، نُوصِيكَ بِارْتِدَاءِ حِزَام الأَمَانِ أَثْنَاءَ الرِّحْلَة.

For **safety**, we recommend that you keep your seat belt on during the flight.

1418. الحمد [n] *praise*

الحَمْدُ لِلرَّبِ الذِي نَثِقُ بِهِ.

Praise be to the Lord in whom we trust.

1419. الموسم [n] *season*

يبدأ مَوْسِمُ كُرَةِ القَدَم فِي أُغُسْطُسْ.

The soccer **season** begins in August.

1420. مذهل [adj] *stunning*

يَا لَهُ مِنْ فُسْتَانٍ مُذْهِلٍ!

What a **stunning** dress!

1421. نعود [v] *Go back*

يُمْكِنُنَا دَائِماً أَنْ نَعُودَ إِلَى الْخُطَّةِ الْأَصْلِيَّة.

We can always **go back** to the original plan.

1422. يأخذ [v] *takes*

إِنَّهُ يَأْخُذُ مسْؤولِيَّتَهُ عَلَى مَحْمَلِ الجِدِّ

He **takes** his responsibility very seriously.

1423. العب [v] *playing*

كُنْتُ أَلْعَبُ كُرَةَ القَدَمِ مَعَ أَصْدِقَائِي.

I was **playing** soccer with my friends.

1424. قال [v] *he said*

قَالَ إِنَّ بِيلْ قَدْ وَصَلَ يَوْمَ السَّبْتِ.

He **said** that Bill had arrived on Saturday.

1425. تتحدثين [v] *talking*

سَمِعْتُكِ وَأَنتِ تَتَحَدَّثِينَ وَظَنَنْتُ أَنَّهُ اسْتَيْقَظَ.

l overheard you **talking** and l thought he might be awake.

1426. رغم [n] *despite*

مَا زِلْتُ أَسْتَمْتِعُ بالأَسْبُوعِ عَلَى الرَّغْمِ مِنَ الطَّقْسِ السَيء.

I still enjoyed the week **despite** the bad weather.

1427. انتظار [v] *wait*

هلْ يُمْكِنُكَ الانْتِظَارُ لَوْ سَمَحْت؟

Can you **wait**, please?

1428. ايمكنك [v] *can*

أَيُمْكِنُكَ القِيَادَة؟

Can you drive?

1429. الرقص [n] *dancing*

أَنَا أُحِبُّ الرَّقْصَ.

I love **dancing**.

1430. محق [adv] *rightly*

إِنَّهُ قَلِقٌ للغَايَة بِشَأْنِ الوَضْعِ وهُوَ مُحِقٌّ في ذَلِكَ.

He is very concerned about the situation and **rightly** so.

1431. أعتذر [v] I apologize

يَجِبُ عَلَي أَنْ أَعْتَذِرَ مِنْ وَالِدَتِي.

I have to **apologize** to my mother.

1432. القبض [n] *capture*

اثنَانِ مِنَ الجُنُود اسْتَطَاعَا الهَرَب، وَالبَاقِي تَمَّ القَبْضُ عَلَيْهِم.

Two of the soldiers managed to escape and the rest were **captured**.

1433. بنفس سرعة [adv] as far as

يُمْكِنُنِي الرَّكْضُ بِنَفْسِ سُرْعَةِ صَدِيقِي.

I ran **as far as** my friend.

1434. تتكلم [v] *speak*

هَلْ تَسْتَطِيعُ أَنْ **تَتَكَلَّم** دُونَ أَنْ تَتَوَتَّرَ؟

Can you **speak** without being nervous?

1435. هاتف [n] *phone*

أَعْطِنِي **الهَاتِفَ** لَوْ سَمَحْت.

Give me the **phone**, please.

1436. تصرخ [v] *screaming*

كَانَتْ تُكَلِّمُنِي عَلَى الهَاتِفِ وَبَدَأَتْ **تَصْرُخُ**.

While she was on the phone, she started **screaming**.

1437. بطاطا [n] *potatoes*

أَحْضِرْ مَعَكَ اثنين كيلُو مِنَ **البَطَاطَا**.

Bring two kilos of **potatoes** with you.

1438. والتي [dem. pron] *which*

لَقَدْ أَضَعْتُ سَاعَتِي **التي** كَانَتْ على الطَّاوِلَة.

I lost my watch, **which** was on the table.

1439. يخرج [v] *out*

يُحِبُّ أَنْ **يَخْرُجَ** مِنْ فَتْرَةٍ إِلَى أُخْرَى وَيَسْتَمْتِعَ.

He likes to go **out** and have fun.

1440. أختي [n] *my sister*

عُمُرُ **أُخْتِي** خَمْسُ سَنَوَاتٍ.

My sister is 5 years old.

1441. أظهر [v] *shows*

أَظْهَرَ عُمَرُ تَعَاطُفَهُ مَعَ الأَطْفَال.

Omar **shows** his empathy toward kids.

1442. محقق [n] *detective*

جَاءَ مُحَقِّقٌ إِلَى بَيْتِنَا الْيَوْم.

The **detective** came to our house today.

1443. شرير [adj] *wicked*

يَا لَكَ مِنْ شِرِّير.

You are so **wicked.**

1444. تجرؤ [v] *dare*

كيفَ تَجْرُؤْ!

How **dare** you!

1445. يهتم [v] *cares about*

هُوَ يَهْتَمُّ بِي.

He **cares about** me.

1446. ودود [adj] *friendly*

صَدِيقِي المُفَضَّل وَدُودٌ.

My best friend is **friendly.**

1447. ديك [n] *rooster*

أَيُّ دِيكٍ تُرِيدُ؟

Which **rooster** do you want?

1448. بالمقابل [n] *by contrast*

وَقْفُ أَعْمَالِ العُنْفِ، بِالمُقَابِلِ، لَيْسَ مَسْأَلَة يجْري التَّفَاوُضُ عَلَيْهَا أَوْ طرحها أَوْ سَحْبِهَا سَاعَةً يَشَاؤُون.

Cessation of violence, **by contrast**, is not a matter to be negotiated or to be switched on and off at will.

1449. المكتبة [n] *library*

أَنَا ذَاهِبٌ إِلَى المَكْتَبة.

I am going to the **library**.

1450. وزن [n] *weight*

كَمْ وَزْنُك؟

What is your **weight**?

1451. ستعمل [v] *would work*

هَلْ سَتَعْمَلُ مَعِي ثَانِيَة؟

Would you **work** with me again.

1452. فعلتها [v] *I did it*

فَعَلْتُهَا. لَقَدْ نَجَحْتُ فِي الاخْتِبَارَات.

I did it! I passed the tests.

1453. صوفيا [n] *Sofia*

صُوفِيَا هِيَ صَدِيقَتِي المُقَرَّبَة.

Sofia is my close friend.

1454. بريء [adj] *innocent*

إِنَّهُ بَرِي.

He's **innocent**.

1455. أبناء [n] *sons*

أَيْنَ هُمْ أَبْنَاؤُكَ؟

Where are your **sons**?

1456. إليك [adv] *here*

إِلَيْكَ المَالَ الذِي أَدِينُ لَكَ بِهِ.

Here's the money I owe you.

1457. يفسر [v] *explain*

هَلْ لِأَحَدِكُمْ أَنْ يُفَسِّرَ لِي مَا حَدَثَ لِلتّوِّ؟

Can somebody please **explain** to me what just happened?

1458. الاهتمام [n] *interesting*

مُثِيرٌ لِلِاهْتِمَام!

It's **interesting**!

1459. خزانة [n] *treasury*

عَلَى حَسَب عِلمِي، أَنْتِ مُجَرَّدُ خِزَانَة سَنَدَاتٍ عَابِرَة.

As far as I'm concerned, you're just a walking **treasury** bond.

1460. متألق [adj] *outstanding*

أَنْتَ شَخْصٌ مُتَأَلِّقٌ.

You are an **outstanding** person.

1461. قلم [n] *pen*

هَلْ يُمْكِنُ أَنْ أَسْتَعِيرَ مِنْكِ قَلَماً.

Do you have a **pen** I could borrow?

1462. متأخر [v] *late*

أَنْتَ مُتَأَخِّرٌ عَنْ مَوْعِدِكَ.

You are **late** for your appointment

1463. مصابة [a.p.] *infected*

تَعَالَ غَداً، دَعْنِي أُلْقِي نَظْرَةً لِلتَّأَكُّدِ أَنَّهَا غَيْرُ مُصَابَة.

Come by tomorrow, let me take a look, make sure she's not **infected**.

1464. مشترك [p.p.] *joint*

أَوَدُّ أَنْ أَقُولَ بِالتَّأْكِيد كُلُّ هَذَا جُهْدٌ مُشْتَرَكٌ.

I'd definitely say all of this is a **joint** effort.

1465. استعار [v] *borrowed*

مَنْ اسْتَعَارَ سَيَّارِتِي الأُسْبوعَ المَاضِي؟

Who **borrowed** my car last weekend?

1466. محترف [adj] *professional*

إِنَّهُ مُحْتَرِفٌ جِداً.

He's so **professional**.

1467. سروري [n] *pleasure*

إِنَّهُ لَمِنْ دَوَاعِي سُرُورِي أَنْ أَكُونَ هُنَا.

It's my **pleasure** to be here.

1468. نحاول [v] *we are trying to*

نَحْنُ **نُحَاوِلُ** أَنْ نَكُونَ الأَفْضَلَ فِي مَجَالِنَا.

We are trying to be the best in our field.

1469. وسط [adj] *amid*

عَلَى الأَرْضِ، **وَسَطَ** أَكْوَامٍ مِنَ الكُتُب، كَانَ هُنَاكَ مِغْلَفَانِ صَغِيرَانِ.

On the floor, **amid** mounds of books, were two small envelopes.

1470. يملك [v] *has*

يَمْلِكُ بِيتَر كَلْبَيْنِ وَقِطَّةً وَاحِدَةً.

Peter **has** two dogs and one cat.

1471. أعترف [v] *admit*

أَنَا **أَعْتَرِفُ** أَنَّنِي مُعْجَبٌ بِمُثَابَرَتِكَ فِي هَذِه المَسْأَلَة.

I **admit** I admire your tenacity with this story.

1472. مجهول [adj] *anonymous*

لَقَدْ أَرْسَلَ لَنَا الفِيدْيُو مِنْ مَصْدَرٍ **مَجْهُولٍ**.

The video was sent to us by an **anonymous** source.

1473. أخمن [v] *I guess*

أُخَمِّنُ أَنَّهُ يَنْبَغِي عَلَيّ إِرْجَاعُ هَذَا لَك.

I **guess** I should give you this back.

1474. يصل [adv] *up*

لَمْ **يَصِلْ** فِي المَوْعِد.

He didn't show **up** on time.

1475. سأجد [v] *I'll find*

هذا مُؤَقَّتٌ. **سَأَجِدُ** لَنَا مَكَاناً آخَر.

It's just temporary, **I'll find** us a place.

1476. مكوك [n] *shuttle*

هَلْ سَبِقَ أَنْ كُنْتَ في **مَكُّوكٍ** فَضَائِيٍّ؟

Have you ever been in a space **shuttle**?

1477. أينما [adv] *whenever*

أَيْنَمَا تَذْهَبِينَ، سَأَجِدُك.

Whenever you go, I'll find you.

1478. الربيع [n] *spring*

هَلْ تُحِبُّ فَصْلَ **الرَّبِيع**؟

Do you like **spring**?

1479. بجانب [adv] *besides*

هَلْ تُمَارِسُ أَيَّ رِيَاضَة أُخْرَى **بِجَانِب** كُرَةِ القَدَم؟

Do you play any other sports **besides** football?

1480. أحد [n] *one*

يُمْكِنُكَ اسْتِعَارَة أَحَدَ الكُتُب.

I have a lot of books, you can borrow **one**.

1481. الجبن [n] *cheese*

هَلا أَعْدَدْتِ لِيّ **الجُبْنَ** المَشْوِيَّ، أَنَا جَائِع.

Will you make me a grilled **cheese**? I'm hungry.

1482. زجاج [n] *glass*

أَعْتَقِدُ أَنَّهُ لَدَيَّ مُنَظِّفُ زُجَاجٍ فِي مَكَانٍ مَا.

I think I have a clean **glass** around here somewhere.

1483. بقية [n] *the rest of*

سَأَقْرَأُ بَقِيَّةَ الكِتَاب.

I'll read **the rest of** the book.

1484. العالم [n] *world*

التكنُولوجيَا جَعَلَتْ العَالَمَ قَرْيَةً صَغِيرَةً.

Technology had made the **world** a small village.

1485. يدك [n] *your hand*

لا تَأْكُلْ بِيَدِكَ!

Don't eat with **your hand**!

1486. انتظار [n] *waiting for*

كُنْتُ بِانْتِظَارِكَ.

I was **waiting for** you.

1487. انقرضت [v] *extinct*

انقَرَضَتْ الدَّيْنَاصُورَات مُنْذُ مُدَّةٍ طَوِيلَةٍ.

Dinosaurs have been **extinct** since long ago.

1488. لرؤية [n] *to see*

سَأَبْقَى مُسْتَيْقِظاً اللَّيْلَةَ لِرُؤْيَةِ الشُّهُبِ.

I will stay up tonight **to see** the meteors.

1489. قميص [n] *shirt*

إنّهُ قَمِيصٌ جَمِيلٌ.

It's a nice **shirt**.

1490. أصعب [elat] *the most difficult*

سَأَقُومُ بِعَمَلِ أَصْعَبِ شَيْءٍ.

I will do **the most difficult** thing.

1491. روحي [adj] *spiritual*

جَمِيعُنَا لَدَيْنَا جَانِبٌ رُوحِيٌّ.

Everyone has a **spiritual** side.

1492. قررت [adj] *I decided*

قَرَّرْتُ الإقْلاعَ عَنْ التَّدْخِين.

I decided to quit smoking.

1493. يعرف [v] *knows*

إنّهُ يَعْرِفُ مَا يَفْعَلُهُ.

He **knows** what he's doing.

1494. اتصلت [v] *I called*

اتَّصَلْتُ بِكَ. لِمَاذَا لَمْ تَرُدَّ؟

I called you, why didn't you answer?

1495. انت [pro] *you*

أَنْتَ صَدِيقِي المُفَضَّل.

You are my best friend.

1496. ركوب الخيل [n] *riding*

هَلْ تُحِبُّ رُكُوبَ الْخَيْل؟

Do you like **riding**?

1497. حر [n] *free*

لَقَدْ قُلْتَ أَنَّني حُرٌّ بِالذَّهَابِ عِنْدَمَا أَسْمَعُ عَرْضَكَ.

You said I was **free** to go after I heard your offer.

1498. بطاقة [n] *card*

يُمْكِنُكَ اسْتِخْدَامُ بِطَاقَة فيزَا إِذَا كُنْتَ تَرْغَبُ في الشِّرَاء.

You can use a Visa **card** if you wish to purchase.

1499. خبير [adj] *expert*

يُمْكِنُكَ فِعْلُ ذَلِكَ. أَنْتَ خَبِيرٌ بِالاعْتِذَارَاتِ الْمُزَيَّفَة.

You can handle that. You're an **expert** at phony apologies.

1500. العبث [n] *tampering with*

لَمْ نَشُكَّ في احْتِمَالِ الْعَبَثِ بِالغِذَاء.

We did not suspect **tampering with** the food supply.

1501. السقف [n] *roof*

لَقَدْ تَسَرَّبَ الْمَاءُ، لِهَذَا، نَقُومُ بِتَرْمِيم السَّقْفِ.

It leaked earlier, so we're fixing the **roof**.

1502. ألعاب نارية [n] [adj] *fireworks*

لَدَيْنَا أَلْعَابٌ نارِيَّةٌ في السَّمَاء.

We got **fireworks** in the sky.

1503. اتفاق [n] *agreement*

سَأَكُونُ عَلَى اتِّفَاقٍ مَعَكُمْ.

I will be in **agreement** with you.

1504. ذاكرة [n] *memory*

إِنَّهُ يَمْلِكُ ذَاكِرَةً قَوِيَّةً.

He has a strong **memory.**

1505. قطة [n] *cat*

هَلْ لَدَيْكَ قِطَّةٌ؟

Do you have a **cat**?

1506. فرصة[n] *chance*

إِنَّهَا فُرْصَتُكَ الأَخِيرَةُ.

It's your last **chance.**

1507. المزيد [adv] *more*

هَلْ يُمْكِنُنِي الحُصُولُ علَى المَزِيد مِنْ فَضْلِكَ؟

Can I have **more**, please?

1508. جرعة [n] *dose*

أُرِيدُ جُرْعَةً أُخْرَى مِنَ الأَتْرُوفِين مِنْ فَضْلِكَ.

I need another **dose** of atropine, please.

1509. معرض [n] *exhibition*

هَلْ سَتَذْهَبِينَ إِلَى المَعْرِض؟

Are you going to the **exhibition**?

1510. كرة السلة [n] *basketball*

هَلْ تَلْعَبُ كُرَةَ السَّلَّة؟

Do you play **basketball**?

1511. حقوق [n] *rights*

هُنَالك حُقُوق ملكِيَّة فِكْرِيَّة تَعُودُ للرَّسَّام.

There are intellectual property **rights** that belong to the artist.

1512. وطني [adj] *national*

وُضِعَ بَرْنَامَجٌ وَطَنِيٌّ للنُّهُوضِ بِالسُّكَّانِ الأَصْلِيِّين.

The **National** Program for the Development of Indigenous Peoples had been designed.

1513. بساطة [adv] *simplicity*

مَا أَحْبَبْتُهُ حَقاً بِهَذَا المَشْرُوع كَانَتْ بَسَاطَةَ التَّعْبِير.

What I really loved about this project was its **simplicity** of statement.

1514. قمنا [adv] *we have*

لَقَدْ قُمْنَا بِتَطْوِيرِ المِلَفَّات للقَضَاءِ عَلَى الفَيْرُوسَاتِ.

We have developed files to eliminate viruses.

1515. اردت [v] *I wanted*

أَرَدْتُ أَنْ أُعْطِيَكَ هَذِه الوُرُودَ في عِيدِ الحُبِّ.

I wanted to give you these roses on Valentine's Day.

1516. من اجلي [prep] [n] for **me**

هَلْ يُمْكِنُكَ أَنْ تَفْعَلَ هَذَا مِنْ أَجْلِي؟

Can you do this **for me**?

1517. نوبة [n] **bout**

مَتَى كَانَتْ أَوَّلُ نَوْبَةٍ لَكَ بِالصَّرَع؟

When was your first **bout** with epilepsy?

1518. ساعدني [v] **help me**

سَاعِدْنِي لَوْ سَمَحْتَ.

Please, **help me**?

1520. الطلب [n] **demand**

الطلَبُ عَلَى الخَدَمَاتِ المَالِيَّةِ الخَارِجِيَّة كَبِيرٌ وَقَوِيٌّ وَمُتَنَوِّعٌ.

The **demand** for offshore financial services is extremely large, strong, and diverse.

1521. دراجة [n] **bike**

كَانَتْ دَرَّاجَة عَادِية وَلَكِنَّ القفْلَ كَانَ شَيْئاً مُمَيَّزاً.

It was an ordinary **bike**, but the lock was something special.

1522. اذهبي [v] **go**

اذْهَبِي، لا أُرِيدُ رُؤْيَتَكِ.

Just **go**, I don't want to see you.

1523. هاري [n] **Harry**

ابْنُ عَمِّي هَارِي قَادِمٌ.

My cousin **Harry** is coming.

1524. روبرت [n] *Robert*

رُوبِرتْ سَائِقُ سَيَّارَات مُحْتَرِف.

Robert is a professional car driver.

1525. رغم [v] *although*

قَرَّرَ الذَّهَابَ، رَغْمَ أَنَّنِي تَوَسَّلْتُ إِلَيْهِ أَلا يَفْعَلَ.

He decided to go, **although** I begged him not to.

1526. مزاج [n] *mood*

لِمَاذَا أَنْتَ فِي مِزَاجٍ سَيِّءٍ؟

Why are you in a bad **mood**?

1527. يضحك [v] *laugh*

كَيْفَ يُمكِنُنِي أَنْ أَكُونَ بِرِفْقَةِ أَحَدٍ لا يَضْحَكُ؟

How could I be with someone that doesn't **laugh**?

1528. كاملة [adj] *full*

لَقَدْ حَصَلْتُ عَلَى عَلامَاتٍ كَامِلَةٍ.

I got **full** marks.

1529. صفحة [n] *page*

هلْ قَرَأْتِ آخِرَ صَفْحَةٍ مِنَ الكِتَاب؟

Do you read the last **page** of the book?

1530. ساحر [adj] *charming*

أَنْتَ رَجُلٌ سَاحِرٌ وَمَوْهُوبٍ وَوسِيم وذَكِي.

You're this talented, **charming**, handsome, and smart man.

1531. سحر [n] *magic*

أنتِ تنشرين سحراً بِعُيُونِكِ.

You spread **magic** with your eyes.

1532. بصمة [n] *fingerprint*

كلُّ شَخْصٍ لَهُ بَصْمَةٌ خَاصَّةٌ بِه.

Everyone has their own **fingerprint**.

1533. تعبير [n] *expression*

كُلُّ تِلْكَ الأَسْئِلَةِ مُجَرَّدُ تَعْبِيرٍ عَلَى غَيْرَتِكِ.

All these carping questions are the **expression** of your jealousy.

1534. فهي [prep] [pron] *it is*

الشَّمْسُ هي إحْدَى مَصَادِرِ الطَّاقَة، فَهِيَ طَاقَةٌ مُتَجَدِّدَةٌ.

The sun is one of the energy resources; **it is** renewable energy.

1535. جمهور [n] *public*

بَدَأْتُ التَّدْرِيسَ وَكُنْتُ مَرْعُوباً مِنَ الحَدِيثِ أَمَام جُمْهُور.

I started teaching and was terrified of **public** speaking.

1536. مفيد [adj] *handy*

هَذَا تَذْكِيرٌ مُفِيدٌ.

That's a **handy** reminder.

1537. معدل [n] *rate*

حَالِياً، يَبْلُغُ مُعَدَّلُ تَوْظِيفِ الإِنَاثِ 32,6 فِي المَائة.

The female employment **rate** as it stands presently is 32.6 percent.

1538. الآنِسة [n] *miss*

فِلْمِي المُفَضَّلُ هُوَ الآنِسَةُ سُلْوان.

My favorite movie is **Miss** Sloane.

1539. فايروس [n] *virus*

إِنَّنَا نَتَعَامَلُ مَعَ فايْرُوسٍ عَصَبِيٍّ.

We're dealing with a neurotropic **virus**.

1540. الفائز [v] *winner*

مُبَارَك! أَنْتَ الفَائِز.

Congratulations! You're the **winner**.

1541. قطط [n] *cats*

هَلْ تُحِبُّ القِطَطَ؟

Do you love **cats**?

1542. مريحة [adj] *ergonomic*

هَذِهِ أُرْجُوحَةٌ مُرِيحَةٌ.

This is an **ergonomic** work hammock.

1543. مروحة [n] *fan*

عَبِير لَدَيْهَا مِرْوَحَةٌ مَصْنُوعَة مِنَ الأوْرَاق.

Abeer has a **fan** made of palm leaves.

1544. تقدم [v] *progress*

أَحْسَنْتَ، أَحْرَزْتَ تَقَدُّماً عَظِيماً!

Well done, you made significant **progress**!

1545. قرد [n] *monkey*

لَدَيَّ قِرْدٌ.

I have got a **monkey**.

1546. دب [n] *bear*

هَلْ أَعْطَانِي أَيَّاً مِنْكُمْ دُمْيَةَ دُبٍّ؟

Did anyone give me a toy **bear**?

1547. وسادة [n] *pillow*

أَيَّتُهَا المُمَرِّضَة، طَلَبْتُ وسَادَةً إِضَافِيَّةً مُنْذُ سَاعَة.

Nurse, I asked for an extra **pillow** an hour ago.

1548. محرج [adj] *embarrassed*

أَنَا مُحْرَجٌ جِداً.

I am so **embarrassed**.

1549. رسم [n] *drawing*

كَانَتْ مُتَّجِهَةً نَحْوَ الحَرَم الجَامِعِيِّ لتحضُرَ دُرُوسَ رَسْمٍ مُتَقَدِّمَة.

She was headed to campus for an advanced **drawing** class.

1550. حجر [n] *stone*

كَان هُنَاكَ حَجَرٌ فِي حِذَائِي.

I had a **stone** in my boot.

1551. مصنع [n] *factory*

هَيَّا، لِنَذْهَبْ إِلَى مَصْنَع المَعْكَرُونَة.

Come on, let's go to the spaghetti **factory**.

1552. الأصوات [n] *votes*

كَمْ عَدَدُ **الأَصْوَات** اللازِمَة لِرَفْضٍ مَطَالِبِ الفِرْقَة المُوسيقِيَّة؟

How many **votes** to reject the orchestra's demands?

1553. تتجاوز [v] *exceed*

لا **تَتَجَاوَزْ** حُدُودَك!

Don't **exceed** your limits!

1554. الحفرة [n] *hole*

نحْنَ عَلَى وَشكِ مَلء هَذِهِ **الحُفْرَة** الآن.

We are about to fill this **hole** now.

1555. بصدق [adv] *sincerely*

أَوَدُّ أَنْ أَشْكُرَكَ **بِصِدْقٍ** عَلَى هَذَا اليَوْم.

I wanted to thank you, **sincerely**, for today.

1556. تلمس [v] *touch*

لا **تَلْمَسْ** هَاتِفِي!

Don't **touch** my phone!

1557. خارجي [adj] *external*

تَحْتَاجُ إلَى مُحَفِّزٍ **خَارِجِيٍّ** لِتَبْقَى مُهْتَمَّاً.

You need some **external** stimulation to keep up your interest.

1558. دائم [adj] *durable*

سَيَسْعَى المَكْتَبُ إلَى إيجَاد حَلٍّ **دَائِم** لِمِحْنَتِهِم.

The Office will attempt to find a **durable** solution to their plight.

1559. خبرة [n] *experienced*

أَنْتَ الرَّجُل الأَكْثَرُ خِبْرَةً هُنَا.

You are the most **experienced** guy here.

1560. أداء [v] *performance*

كَانَ أَدَاؤُكَ رَائِعاً.

Your **performance** was great.

1561. موهوب [n] *talented*

أَنْتَ شَخْصٌ مَوْهُوبٌ.

You're a **talented** person.

1562. تحتفظ [n] *reserve*

بَعْدَ أَنْ تَحْظَى بِأطفَالٍ، تَحْتَفِظُ بِرَغَبَاتِكَ مِنْ أجْلِ أطْفَالِكَ.

After you have kids, you **reserve** your wishes for your kids.

1563. يدير [v] *run*

لا أَسْتَطِيعُ أَنْ أَسْمَحَ لِلخَوْفِ أَنْ يُدِيرَ حَيَاتِي.

I can't let fear **run** my life.

1564. علمي [adj] *scientific*

لَيْسَ هُنَالِكَ مُبَرِّرٌ عِلْمِيٌّ قَوِيٌّ لِهَذِه الدِّرَاسَة.

There is no strong **scientific** justification for this study.

1565. الحزن [v] *grief*

يَجِبَ عَلَيْكَ أَلَّا تُهْلِكَ نَفْسَكَ في الحُزْن.

You must not allow yourself to be consumed with **grief**.

1566. فاز [v] *won*

لا يَتَعَلَّقُ الأَمْرُ بِمَنْ فَازَ وَمَنْ خَسِرَ.
It's not about who **won** or who lost.

1567. مساحة [n] *space*

أَعْطِني مَسَاحَةً للتَّفْكِير.
Give me **space** to think.

1568. وسائل [n] *means*

عَلَيَّ اسْتِخْدَامُ وَسَائِلَ أُخْرَى لإيقَافِه.
I'll have to use other **means** to stop him.

1569. عالق [a.p.] *stuck*

إنَّهُ عَالِقٌ في مَاضِيه.
He's **stuck** in his past.

1570. استراحة [n] *break*

نَحْتَاجُ إلَى اسْتِرَاحَةٍ.
We need a **break**.

1571. إعلان [n] *announcement*

هَلْ قَرَأْتَ الإعْلان؟
Did you read the **announcement**?

1572. وكيل [n] *agent*

أَيْنَ هُوَ وَكِيلُكَ؟
Where's your **agent**?

1573. المدى [n] *range*

أَنْتَ تَعْرِفُ مَاذَا يَتَطَلَّبُ الْأَمْرُ لِإِصَابَةِ هَدَفٍ بِهَذَا الْمَدَى؟

Do you know what it takes to make a shot at that **range**?

1574. محكمة [n] *court*

لَمْ أَذْهَبْ إِلَى الْمَحْكَمَةِ مِنْ قَبْلُ.

I'd never even been to **court.**

1575. الأساس [adj] *the foundation*

نَوَايَاكَ مُخْلِصَة، لَكِنَّ أَسَاسَهَا هُوَ الْأَكَاذِيبُ.

Your intention is sincere but its **foundation** is lies.

1576. المخلوقات [n] *creatures*

أَنْتَ سَتُخْبِرُنِي بِكُلِّ شيء عَنْ هَذِهِ الْمَخْلُوقَاتِ.

You're going to tell me all about these **creatures.**

1577. داخلي [adj] *internal*

إِنَّ الشَّيء الْأَكْثَر تخْوِيفاً هُوَ تَنَافُسٌ دَاخِلِيٌّ.

The most dreaded thing is an **internal** rivalry.

1578. غنى [v] *needless to*

كَانَتْ هُنَالِكَ مَخَاطِرُ مُعَيَّنَةٌ، وَهَذَا غَنِيٌّ عَنِ الْقَوْل.

Needless to say, there were certain risks.

1579. فستان [n] *dress*

أَمِيرَتِي، مَا أَجْمَلَ فُسْتَانَ التَّتْوِيجِ الذِي تَرْتَدِينَهُ.

Princess, what a beautiful coronation **dress** you are wearing.

1580. التخرج [n] *graduation*

أَتَيْتُ لِإِعْطَائِكِ هَدِيَّةَ التَّخَرُّجِ.

I came by to give you a **graduation** gift.

1581. فظيعة [adj] *awful*

كَانَتْ الوَالِدَةُ **فَظِيعَةً**، وَلَكِنَّ الفَتَاةَ بَدَتْ بِخَيْرٍ.

The mom was **awful**, but the girl seemed fine.

1582. ملاك [n] *angel*

أَنتِ **مَلَاكٌ** جَمِيلٌ، أَتَعْلَمِينَ هَذَا!

Whoo! You are a beautiful **angel**!

1583. متعلق [a.p.] *related*

إِنَّهُ سُؤَالٌ مُخْتَلِفٌ قَلِيلاً، وَلَكِنَّهُ **مُتَعَلِّقٌ** بِنَفْسِ المَوْضُوع

It is a slightly different question but **related** to the same subject.

1584. ينبغي [v] *should*

يَنْبَغِي عَلَيْنَا تَحْدِيدُ يَوْمٍ لِنَقُومَ بِالتَّنْظِيف.

We **should** set a date and do a major cleaning.

1585. أصابع [n] *fingers*

لَدَيْنَا خَمْسَةُ أَصَابِعَ.

We have five **fingers**.

1586. الرهان [n] *betting*

لا مَزِيدَ مِنَ الرِّهَان.

No more **betting**.

1587. أفسدت [v] *corrupted*

أَنَا أُحَارِبُ مِنْ أَجْلِ مَا **أَفْسَدْتَ**.

I fight for what you've **corrupted**.

1588. وإلا [part] *otherwise*

أَحْسِنِي التَّصَرُّفَ، **وَإِلَّا** فَلَنْ يُمْكِنَكِ البَقَاءُ فِي الفِرْقَة.

Lighten up. **Otherwise**, you can't stay in the choir.

1589. مسار [n] *path*

حَدِّدِي **مَسَارَكِ** بِعِنَايَةٍ.

Set your **path** carefully.

1590. نشر [v] *published*

نُشِرَ الكِتَابُ عَامَ أَلفٍ وتِسْعُمائَة وخمسٍ وثَمَانِين.

The book was **published** in 1985.

1591. الخشب [n] *wood*

جَمِيعُ الأَشْكَالِ مَنْحُوتَةٌ مِنْ **الخَشَبِ** بِشِقِّ الأَنْفُسِ.

All the figures are just painstakingly carved out of **wood**.

1592. الزي [n] *uniform*

لا يَنْبَغِي أَنْ أَرْتَدِيَ هَذَا **الزِّيَّ** هُنَا.

I'm not supposed to wear this **uniform** here.

1593. الاحترام [n] *respect*

كُلَّ **الاحْتِرَام** وَالحُبِّ.

All **respect** and love.

1594. دمية [n] *doll*

أَبِي، هَلْ سَأَحْصُلُ عَلَى دُمْيَةٍ نَاطِقَةٍ؟

Dad, do I get a talking **doll**?

1595. الفخ [n] *trap*

بَدَأْتُ أَشْعُرُ بِشُعُورٍ غَرِيبٍ، وَكَأَنَّ مَا أَنَا فِيه فَخٌّ.

Starting to get a weird feeling like this whole thing's some kind of **trap**.

1596. شأني [n] *my business*

لَيْسَ مِنْ شَأْنِي!

It's not **my business**!

1597. أرسل [v] *send*

أَرْسِلْ أَحَداً لِيُنَظِّفَ هَذَا المَكانَ حَالاً.

Send someone up here to clean this place.

1598. حجز [v] *book*

هَلْ حَجَزْتَ غُرْفَة فِي الفُنْدُق؟

Did you **book** at the hotel?

1599. ضيوف [n] *guests*

يَجِبُ أَنْ تُغَادِرَ، فَلَدَيَّ ضُيُوفٌ عَلَى العَشَاءِ.

You have to leave. I've got **guests** for dinner.

1600. انتقلت [v] *I moved*

انْتَقَلْتُ الأُسْبُوعَ المَاضِي إلَى شُقَّةٍ جَدِيدَة.

Last week, **I moved** to a new apartment.

1601. الأكواخ [n] *huts*

انْتَهَى بِنَا الأَمْرُ إِلَى هَذِهِ الأَكْوَاخِ.

We ended up being taken aside into these **huts**.

1602. بقي [v] *left*

نَسْتَطِيعُ مُسَاعَدَتَكَ عَلَى الحِفَاظِ عَلَى مَا بَقِي.

We can help you keep what's **left** of it.

1603. صنعت [v] *manufactured*

هُنَاكَ شَرِكَةٌ صَنَعَتْ الأَحْذِيَةَ التي تَمْلِكُهَا.

There's a company that **manufactured** the shoes that you have.

1604. الوحدة [n] *unity*

إِنَّ تَعْزِيزَ الوِحْدَةِ الوَطَنِيَّةِ وَاجِبٌ.

Reinforcing national **unity** is a duty.

1605. التنفس [n] *breathing*

نَحْنُ لا نَفْعَلُ شَيئاً غَيْرَ التَّنَفُّسِ وَعَدَمِ التَّحَرُّكِ.

We're not doing anything other than **breathing** and not moving.

1606. اكتشفت [v] *I discovered*

كُنْتُ أَصْغَرَ مِنْكَ بِكَثِير عِنْدَمَا اكْتَشَفْتُ هِوَايَتِي.

I was a lot younger than you when **I discovered** my hobby.

1607. لوحدك [prep] [n] *on your own*

أَنْتَ لا تَستَطِيعُ مُوَاجَهَة العالِمِ لِوَحْدِكَ.

You can't take on the world **on your own**.

1608. حيوان [n] *animal*

أَخْطَرُ حَيَوانٍ هُوَ البَعُوضِ.

The most dangerous **animal** is the mosquito.

1609. أعترف [v] *admit*

مِنَ الصَّعْبِ عَلَيَّ أَنْ أَعْتَرِفَ عِنْدَمَا أَكُونُ مُخْطِئاً.

It's difficult for me to **admit** when I'm wrong.

1610. الجمال [n] *beauty*

لَقَدْ وَجَدْنَا الجَمَالَ مَعاً، وَلَنْ نَفْقِدَهُ أَبَداً.

We had found **beauty** together, and we could never lose it.

1611. أعني [v] *meant*

لَقَدْ أَخْبَرْتُكَ أَنّني أُحِبُّكَ، وَأَنَا أَعْني ذَلِكَ.

I told you I love you, and I **meant** it.

1612. طرق [n] *methods*

يمْكِنُنا اعتِمَادُ طُرُقٍ عديدَةٍ لإنْهاءِ هَذَا.

We can follow different **methods** to get this done.

1613. حدث [n] *occurrence of*

لِيَسَتْ المَجَاعَةُ حَدَثاً طَبِيعِيّاً لا مَفَرَّ مِنْهُ.

Famine is not a natural **occurrence** and is not inevitable.

1614. حقّ [adj] *right*

أنتَ عَلَى حَقٍّ.

You're **right**.

1615. تقع [v] *is located*

أيٌّ مِنَ البُحَيْرَاتِ العُظْمَى الخَمْسِ **تَقَعُ** فِي الوِلايَاتِ المُتَّحِدَة؟

Which of the five Great Lakes **is located** entirely in the United States?

1616. غرفتي [n] [pron] *my room*

اخْرُجْ مِنْ غُرْفَتِي حَالاً!

Leave **my room** at once!

1617. فراش [n] *bedding*

سَتَجِدُ فِرَاشاً فِي الدُّولاب.

You'll find **bedding** in the closet on the shelf.

1618. مناسبة [adj] *suitable*

هَذِهِ أَرِيكَةٌ مُحْتَرَمَةٌ ومُنَاسِبَةٌ لِجَمِيعِ أَفْرَادِ العَائِلَة.

This is a good, decent couch. **Suitable** for the whole family.

1619. ممتعة [adj] *enjoyable*

كَانَتْ رِحْلَةً مُمْتِعَةً لِلْغَايَة.

It was the most **enjoyable** trip.

1620. توقعت [v] *I expected*

أَبْلَيْتَ حَسَناً، أَكْثَرَ مِمَّا تَوَقَّعْتَ.

I did well, better than **I expected**.

1621. الرصاص [coll. n] *lead*

هَلْ يُمْكِنُكَ أَنْ تَصْنَعَ لِي قِلادةً بِهَا رَمْزُ رَصَاصٍ؟

Can you make me a pendant with a **lead** symbol?

1622. اليسار [adj] *left*

هَلْ تَسْتَخْدِمُ يَدَكَ اليَسَارَ في الكِتَابَة؟

Do you use your **left** hand to write?

1623. شبكة [n] *network*

هُنَاكَ شَيْء عَجِيبٌ يَحْدُثُ مَعَ شَبَكَةِ الكَمْبُيوتَر.

There's something weird going on with the computer **network**.

1624. دورك [n] [pron] *your turn*

الآنَ هُوَ دَوْرُكَ للإبتِسَامِ لآلَات التَّصْوِير.

Now it's **your turn** to smile for the cameras.

1625. الأوان [n] *late*

جَعَلْتَني أُدْرِكُ بأَنَّ الأوَانَ لَا يَفُوتُ أَبَداً.

You made me realize it's never too **late**.

1626. عصابة [n] *gang*

تَدَقَّقْتُ مِنْ صُوَرٍ لأعْضَاءِ عِصَابَةٍ مَعْرُوفِينَ.

I've checked security photos of known **gang** members.

1627. حدود [n] *border*

هَذِه الصُّورَةُ أُخِذت عَلَى حُدُود"هَنْغَارْيَا"

This picture was taken at the **border** of Hungary.

1628. أسواق [n] *markets*

أُغْلِقَتْ جَمِيعُ الأسْوَاق بِسَبَبِ الوَبَاء.

All **markets** were closed due to the epidemic.

1629. قواعد [n] *rules*

يَجِبُ عَلَيْنَا اتِّبَاعُ الْقَوَاعِدِ دَائِماً.

We must always follow the **rules**.

1630. مستشفى [n] *hospital*

هَلْ ذَهَبْتَ إِلَى الْمُسْتَشْفَى الْيَوْم؟

Did you go to the **hospital** today?

1631. انتبه [v] *be aware*

هَلْ هُنَاكَ أَمْرٌ عليَّ أَن أَنْتَبِهَ إِليه؟

Is there something I need to **be aware** of?

1632. غضب [adv] *anger*

عَلَيْكَ أَنْ تَتَحَكَّمَ بِغَضَبِكَ.

You have to control your **anger**.

1633. البشرية [n] *human*

دَاخِلَ هَذِهِ الأَدْمِغَةُ الجَمِيلَةُ، يَكْمُنُ السِّرُّ لِفَهْمِ ظَلام الرُّوح البَشَرِيَّةِ.

Inside those beautiful brains lies the secret to understanding the darkness of the **human** psyche.

1634. رائعة [adj] *brilliant*

إِنَّها فَتَاةٌ رَائِعَة.

She is a **brilliant** girl.

1635. مشتبه [a.p.] *suspected*

أصبح صَدِيقِي مُشْتَبهاً بِه. كَيْفَ أَنَامُ جَيِّداً؟

My friend is **suspected**, how can I sleep well?

243

1636. تمكنت [v] *managed*

تَمَكَّنَتْ الإمْبَرَاطُورِيَّةُ العُثْمَانِيَّةُ مِنْ السَّيْطَرَة على الحَرْب.

The Ottoman Empire **managed** to turn the war.

1637. فخور [adv] *proud*

أَنَا **فَخُورٌ** بِكَ.

I'm **proud** of you.

1638. مالك [a.p.] *owner*

أَنَا **مَالِكُ** الحَقِيبَة التي كُنْتُم تحْمِلُونَها!

I'm the rightful **owner** of that briefcase you've been carrying around!

1639. مسألة [n] *issue*

أُرِيدُ أَنْ آخُذَ دَقِيقَةً لِمُنَاقَشَةِ مَسْأَلَةٍ أَمْنِيَّةٍ.

I want to take a second to address an **issue** of security.

1640. طوارئ [n] *emergency*

هَلْ لَدَيْكَ رَقْمٌ لِخَدَمَات **طَوَارِئ** الطُرُق؟

Do you have the number for **emergency** road service?

1641. القرية [n] *village*

يَبْدُو أنَّهُمْ يَرْغَبُونَ في المَجِيء لِهَذِه **القَرْيَة**.

It appears they're willing to come to this **village**.

1642. متجر [n] *store*

سَتَجِدِينَ هَذَا التَّطْبِيقَ في **المَتْجَر**.

You'll find this app in the play **store**.

1643. يَسير [v] *walking*

رَأَيْتُ ابنَكِ يَسِيرُ في الحَدِيقَة.

I saw your son **walking** in the garden.

1644. مجتمع [n] *community*

نَحْنُ مُجْتَمَعٌ وَاحِدٌ رغْمَ مَشَاكِلِنَا.

Despite our troubles, we are one **community**.

1645. حائط [n] *wall*

أُحِبُّ الكِتَابَاتِ المَوجُودَةِ عَلَى الحَائِطِ.

I love the writing on the **wall**.

1646. سباحة [n] *swimming*

هَلْ تَوَدُّ الذَّهَابَ للسِّبَاحَةِ مَعِي؟

Do you want to go **swimming** with me?

1647. تبكي [v] *crying*

لِمَاذَا تَبْكِي؟

Why are you **crying**?

1648. حديقة [n] *garden*

عِنْدَمَا تَبْدَأ الأَعْشَابُ بِالنُّمُوِّ، تَبْدُو السَّاحَةُ مِثْلَ حَدِيقَةٍ مَلِيئَةٍ بِالثَّلْجِ.

When the weeds begin to grow, it's like a **garden** full of snow.

1649. سيعود [prep] [v] *will return*

سَيَعُودُ الأَمَانُ يَوْماً.

Security **will return** one day.

1650. القلق [n] *anxiety*

نَحْنُ بِحَاجَةٍ إِلَى مَعْرِفَةٍ مَا يُسَبِّبُ هذَا القَلَق.

We need to find out the cause of this **anxiety**.

1651. خمر [n] *wine*

لا تَشْرَب الخَمْرَ!

Don't drink **wine**!

1652. كتابة [n] *writing*

تَعِبْتُ مِنْ كِتَابَةِ الرَّسَائِل.

I'm tired of **writing** letters.

1653. يطلب [v] *ask*

لايَعْتَرِفُ الرَّجُلُ إلا إذَا كَانَ مُخْطِئاً، وَهَا هُوَ يَطْلُبُ الاعْتِذَار.

A man can only admit when he was wrong and **ask** forgiveness.

1654. مسكين [adj] *poor*

إنَّهُ رَجُلٌ أَعْمَى مِسْكِينٌ يُحِبُّ قِطَّهُ.

He's just a **poor** blind guy who loves his cat.

1655. تخيل [v] *imagine*

العَالَمُ الحَقِيقِيُّ هُوَ لِمَنْ لا يَسْتَطِيعُونَ تَخَيُّلَ أَفْضَلَ مِنْهُ.

The real world is for people who can't **imagine** anything better.

1656. أسوء [elat] *worst*

رَنِينُ الهَاتِفِ فِي سَاعَةٍ مُتَأَخِّرَةٍ مِنَ اللَّيْلِ هُوَ أَسْوَءُ كَوابِيسِ الآبَاء.

Late night phone call, every parent's **worst** nightmare.

1657. مخيف [adj] *scary*

أَنَا لَا أُحِبُّ المَكَانَ هُنَا. إِنَّهُ مُخِيفٌ.

I don't like this place; it's **scary**.

1658. مريض [n] *patient*

حَسَناً، إِذَا كَانَ أَحَدُكُمْ مُتَفَرِّغاً، فَلَدَيْنَا مَرِيضٌ قَادِمٌ.

Okay, if anyone's free, we have an incoming **patient**.

1659. كعك [n] *cake*

لَدَيْنَا كَعْكُ الشُّوكُولَاتَةِ لِلفُطُور.

We have chocolate **cake** for breakfast.

1660. حمام [n] *bath*

أَيُمْكِنُكَ أَنْ تَأْخُذَهَا بَيْنَمَا آخُذُ أَنَا حَمَّاماً؟

Can you take her while I take a **bath**?

1661. تقبل [v] *accept*

يَصْعُبُ عَلَيْنَا أَحْيَاناً تَقَبُّلُ المَدِيح، أَلَيْسَ كَذَلِكَ؟

Sometimes it's hard for us to **accept** a compliment, right?

1662. دفعت [v] *I paid*

دَفَعْتُ 500 دُولَارٍ فَقَط لِسَيَّارَتِي الأُولَى.

I paid 500 bucks for my first car.

1663. كوب [n] *cup*

أَيُمْكِنُنِي الحُصُولُ عَلَى كُوبِ قَهْوَة والاسْتِرْخَاءُ لِدَقِيقَةٍ؟

Can I have a **cup** of coffee and relax a minute?

1664. إيقاف [n] *stop*

نَحْنُ أَحِبَّةٌ، وَلا أَحَدَ يُمْكِنُهُ إِيقَافُ ذَلِكَ.

We're soul mates, and nothing can **stop** that.

1665. اختبار [n] *test*

هَلْ لَدَيْكَ اخْتِبَارٌ غَداً؟

Do you have a **test** tomorrow?

1666. نقاط [n] *points*

أَهُنَاكَ نِقَاطٌ تَوَدِّينَ مُنَاقَشَتَهَا قَبْلَ التَّوْقِيعِ؟

Are there any **points** you'd like to discuss before you sign?

1667. رسائل [n] *messages*

مَنْ أَرْسَلَ لَكَ هَذِهِ الرَّسَائِلِ؟

Who sent you these **messages**?

1668. طبيعية [adj] *natural*

جَمِيعِ العَنَاصِرِ وَالإِجْرَاءَاتِ تَحْكُمُهَا قَوَانِينٌ طَبِيعِيَّةٌ عَالَمِيَّةٌ.

All the constituents and actions are governed by universal **natural** laws.

1669. باسم [prep] [n] *on behalf of*

يُشَرِّفُنِي، باسْمِ مَجْمُوعَتِنَا، أَنْ أُؤَيِّدَ هَذِهِ الفِكْرَة.

It is an honor **on behalf of** our group to support this idea.

1670. شمال [adj] *north*

هُنَاكَ مَنْظَرٌ أَخَّاذٌ فِي شَمَالِ الغَابَة.

There is a breathtaking view in the **north** of the woods.

1671. خنزير [n] *pork*

لا يَأْكُلُ المُسْلِمُونَ لَحْمَ الخِنْزِيرِ.

Muslims do not eat **pork.**

1672. شرب [v] *drink*

هَلْ تَرْغَبُ في شُرْبِ بَعْضِ المَاءِ؟

Would you like to **drink** some water?

1673. دجاج [n] *chicken*

هَذِه أَفْضَلُ سَلَطَةِ دَجَاجٍ أَتَنَاوَلُهَا عَلَى الإِطْلاقِ.

This is the best **chicken** salad I've ever had.

1674. الموعد [n] *the deadline*

قُدِّمَتْ طَلَبَاتٌ أُخْرَى بَعْدَ المَوْعِدِ المُحَدَّدِ.

Other applications had been submitted after **the deadline.**

1675. الأطباء [n] *physicians*

لا يُمْكِنُ للأَطِبَّاءِ مِنْ دُونِ تَرْخِيصٍ مُمَارَسَةُ الطِّبِّ.

Physicians without a license cannot practice medicine.

1676. ليلتك [n] [pron] *your night*

كَيْفَ قَضَّيْتَ لَيْلَتَكَ؟

How was **your night**?

1677. الأمير [n] *prince*

أَفْعَلُ هَذَا لأَجْلِ الأَمِيرِ، وَلَيْسَ لأَجْلِكَ.

I do it for the **prince**, not for you.

1678. أخيراً [adv] *finally*

أَعْتَقِدُ أَنَّني فَهِمْتُ أَخِيراً عِبْءَ الْقِيَادَة الْكَامِلَة.

I think I **finally** understand the burden of full command.

1679. قابل للنقاش [a.p.] [n] *negotiable*

الْعَرْضُ غَيْرُ قَابِلٍ للنِّقَاشِ.

The offer is not **negotiable**.

1680. أصغر [elat] *smaller*

أَحْيَاناً أُفَكِّرُ في الإنْتِقَالِ إلَى مَنْزِلٍ أَصْغَرَ.

Sometimes I think about moving to a **smaller** house.

1681. البنك [n] *bank*

ذَهَبْتُ لأَخْذِ الأَمْوَالِ مِنَ الْبَنْكِ.

I went to take money out of the **bank**.

1682. خطأي [n] [pron] *my fault*

أَعْتَقِدُ أَنَّ مَا حَدَثَ اللَّيْلَة كَانَ خَطَئِي جُزْئِياً.

I guess what happened tonight is partly **my fault**.

1683. المطار [n] *airport*

سَأَذْهَبُ لأَجلُبَ وَالِدَتي مِنَ الْمَطَارِ عَلى السَّاعَة الثَّانِية.

I'm going to pick my mom up at the **airport** at 2:00.

1684. عقلي [adj] *mental*

إنَّ الْمَكَانَ جَمِيلٌ جِداً هُنَا وَمُنَاسِبٌ لِبِنَاء مصحَّةٍ عَقْلِيَّة.

It's really pretty here, for a **mental** institution.

1685. التنضيد [n] *typesetting*

كَانَتْ آلَةُ **تَنْضِيدِ** الحُرُوفِ الأكْثَرَ اسْتِعْمَالاً قَبْلَ اخْتِرَاعِ الحَاسُوب.

Manual **typesetting** was the only typing method before the invention of computers.

1686. ضحايا [n] *victims*

أَنْقِذْهَا. لا تُحَوِّلْهَا إِلَى ضَحِيَّةٍ من **ضَحَايَاك**.

Don't turn her into another one of your heartbroken **victims**.

1687. شريك [n] *partner*

أَنْتَ تَمْلِكُ أَفْضَلَ **شَرِيكٍ** فِي العَالَم.

You have the best **partner** in the world.

1688. سمين [adj] *fat*

أَنَا لَا أَحْتَاجُ للحِمْيَةِ لأَنَّني لَسْتُ **سَمِيناً**.

I don't need to go on a diet, because I am not **fat**.

1689. تستمر [v] *continue*

أُرِيدُك أَنْ **تَسْتَمِرَّ** فِي صَقْلِ هَذِه القُدُرَاتِ.

I want to see you all **continue** to polish those abilities.

1690. الأحد [n] *Sunday*

كُنْتُ أَتَسَاءَلَ إِنْ كُنْتَ سَتَأْتِي للْمُبَارَاةِ **الأَحَدَ** القَادِمَ.

I was wondering if you're planning on coming to the match next **Sunday**.

1691. اهدا [v] *calm down*

اهْدَأْ. أَنَا أُحَاوِلُ مُسَاعَدَتَكَ عَلَى أَدَاءِ عَمَلِكَ.

Just **calm down**, I'm trying to help you do your job.

1692. حذر [v] *aware of*

يَجِبُ أَنْ تَكُونَ **حَذِراً** مِنْ أَيِّ شَخْصٍ حَوْلَكَ.

You should be **aware of** anyone around you.

1693. جسم [n] *body*

جِسْمُ المَرْأَةِ مُهَيَّئٌ لِكَيْ يُنْتِجَ الأَطْفَال.

A woman's **body** is designed to have babies.

1694. اجتماع [n] *meeting*

لَدَيْنَا **اجْتِمَاعُ** عَمَلٍ.

We have a business **meeting**.

1695. تعاني [v] *suffer*

لا أُرِيدُهَا أَنْ **تُعَانِي**.

I don't want her to **suffer**.

1696. العلم [n] *science*

العِلْمُ هُوَ أَعْظَمُ رَغَبَاتِي فِي الحَيَاة.

Science is my great passion in life.

1697. مذهلة [adj] *amazing*

لَدَيْهِ بَصِيرَةٌ **مُذْهِلَةٌ** اكْتَسَبَهَا مِنْ حَيَاةٍ طَوِيلَةٍ فِي الغَابَة.

He had **amazing** insight acquired during his long life in the forest.

1698. سباق [n] *race*

أَنَا وَاقِفٌ بِجَانِبِ سَيَّارَةٍ سِبَاقٍ حَمْرَاءَ رَائِعَةٍ.

I'm standing right next to a bright red **race** car.

1699. صعوبة [v] *difficulty*

وَاجَهْتُ صُعُوبَةً عَظِيمَةً كَيْ أَجِدَكَ، لَكِنَّنِي سَعِيدٌ بِذَلِكَ.

I had great **difficulty** finding you, but I'm glad I did.

1700. إجابة [n] *answer*

أَنَا أَحْتَاجُ إِلَى إِجَابَةٍ عَنْ سُؤَالِي.

I need an **answer** to my question.

1701. الطبيعة [n] *nature*

هُنَاكَ إِحْسَاسٌ قَوِيٌّ بِأَنَّنَا نَسْمَعُ الطَّبِيعَةَ وهِيَ تُكَلِّمُنَا.

There is a strong sense that we are hearing **nature** talk to us.

1702. تقود [v] *leads*

المُثَابَرَةُ تَقُودُ إِلَى النَّجَاحِ.

Diligence **leads** to success.

1703. اللوحة [n] *painting*

عِنْدَمَا يَنْظُرُ النَّاسُ إِلَى هَذِهِ اللَّوْحَةِ، يَرَوْنَ مَلِكاً وَمَلِكَة.

When people look at this **painting**, they see a king and a queen.

1704. عشرون [n] *twenty*

أَتَحَدَّاكَ بِعِشْرِينَ دولاراً أَنَّهُمْ كَتَبُوا اسْمِي بِشَكْلٍ خَاطِئٍ.

I bet you **twenty** dollars they spell my name wrong.

1705. أكتب [v] *write*

لَمْ أَكْتُبْ رِسَالَةً لِأَخِي.

I didn't **write** a letter to my brother.

1706. الأوراق [coll. n] *leaves*

تَسَاقُطُ الأوراقِ هُوَ جُزْءٌ مِنَ الدَّوْرَةِ الطَّبِيعِيَّةِ.

Shedding **leaves** is a part of the natural cycle.

1707. جد [n] *grandfather*

هَلْ ذَهَبْتَ لِزِيَارَةِ جَدِّكَ؟

Have you gone to visit your **grandfather**?

1708. تحميل [v] *upload*

لا نَسْتَطِيعُ تَحْمِيلَ هذَا الفِيدِيُو عَلَى اليُوتْيُوبْ.

We can't **upload** that video to YouTube.

1709. سرعة [adj] *speed*

سُرْعَةُ الضَّوْءِ ثَابِتَةٌ وَتَتَبَايَنُ بِالنِّسْبَةِ لِكُلِّ شَيْءٍ آخَرَ.

Speed of light is constant, relative to everything else.

1710. الرئيسية [n] *home*

أُرِيدُ مِنْكَ إِعَادَةَ تَصْمِيمِ الصَّفْحَةِ الرَّئِيسِيَّةِ.

I want you to redesign the **home** page.

1711. ظهرت [v] *appeared*

لَقَدْ ظَهَرَتْ مُؤَخَّراً بَعْضُ بَوَادِرِ الأَمَلِ.

Some reasons for hope have recently **appeared**.

1712. القمامة [n] *garbage*

مازَال عَلَيْنَا أَنْ ننظّفَ المَكَانَ ونأْخُذَ القُمَامَةَ إِلَى الخَارِج.

We still have to clean up and take the **garbage** out.

1713. تشغيل [v] *run*

أُرِيدُكَ أَمِنْكَ تَشْغِيلَ هَذَا العَرْضِ اليَوْمَ.

I want you to **run** this presentation today.

1714. جعلتني [v] [pron] *made me*

لَمْ أُخْبِرْكِ بِهَذَا أَبَداً، وَلَكِنَّكَ جَعَلْتَنِي أَشْعُرُ بالأَمَانِ.

I never told you this, but you **made me** feel safe.

1715. منطقي [adj] *logical*

نُرِيدُ حَلاً مَنْطِقِياً.

We want a **logical** solution.

1716. الشرف [n] *honor*

هَذَا تَصَرُّفُ الفَارِسِ الحَقِيقِيّ بِالبُطُولَةِ وَالشَّرَف.

This is how a true knight behaves, with gallantry and **honor**.

1717. الذنب [n] *guilt*

أَشْعُرُ بِقَلِيلٍ مِنَ الذَنْبِ حَوْلَ كَيْفِيَّة انْتِهَاء مُحَادَثَتِنَا.

I feel a bit **guilty** about how our conversation ended.

1718. رائحة [n] *smelled*

كُنْتُ أُحِبُّ رَائِحَةَ شَجَرَةِ المِيلادِ في صِغَرِي.

I used to love the way our Christmas tree **smelled** when I was little.

1719. الصين [n] *China*

أَنْتَ بِالتَّأْكِيدِ تَعْرِفُ الصِّينَ أَكْثَرَ مِنِّي.

I'm sure you're more familiar with **China** than me.

1720. مرت [v] *passed*

أَنَا لَمْ أَعْرِفْ كَمْ عَدَدُ السَّاعَاتِ الِّتِي مَرَّتْ.

I don't know how many hours **passed**.

1721. أمامك [adv] *in front of you*

لَا يَجِبُ أَنْ نُنَاقِشَ الْأُمُورَ الْعَائِلِيَّةَ أَمَامَكَ.

We shouldn't discuss family business **in front of you**.

1722. تقييم [adj] *valuation*

حَظِيَ تَقْيِيمُ الْعُمْلَاتِ، وَلَا سِيَّمَا رنمينبي الصِّينِي، بِمَزِيدٍ مِنَ الِاهْتِمَام.

The **valuation** of currencies, especially the Chinese renminbi, has attracted increased attention.

1723. اسبوعين [n] *two weeks*

أُسْبُوعَانِ فِي طُوكْيُو، سَنَحْظَى بِوَقْتٍ رَائِعٍ.

Two weeks in Tokyo. We'd have a great time.

1724. مجموعة [n] *collection*

سِلْسِلَةُ أَفْلَامٍ هِيَ عِبَارَةٌ عَنْ مَجْمُوعَةٍ مِنَ الْأَفْلَامِ ذَاتِ الصِّلَةِ عَلَى التَّوَالِي.

A film series is a **collection** of related films in succession.

1725. المرء [n] *one*

لِلْبُؤْسِ وَسِيلَتُهُ لِتَوْضِيحِ قَنَاعَاتِ الْمَرْءِ.

Well, misery has a way of clarifying **one**'s convictions.

1726. الكلية [n] *college*

فِي أَيِّ **كُلِّيَّةٍ** تَدْرُسُ؟

Which **college** are you studying at?

1727. فكرة [n] *idea*

يَا لَهَا مِنْ **فِكْرَةٍ** عَظِيمَة!

What a great **idea**!

1728. لاعب [n] *player*

أَنْتَ أَكْثَرُ **لاعِبٍ** مُتَحَمِّسٍ شَاهَدْتُهُ فِي حَيَاتِي.

You are the most exciting **player** I have ever seen.

1729. الشر [adj] *evil*

عَلَيْنَا دَائِماً أَنْ نَتَّحِدَ ضِدَّ **الشَّرِ**.

We must always unite against **evil**.

1730. مجلس [n] *council*

أُرِيدُ أَنْ أُرْسِلَ رِسَالَةً إِلَى أَصْدِقَائِي فِي **مَجْلِسِ** المَدِينَة.

I want to send a message to my friends on the city **council**.

1731. النفس [n] *self*

الكَمَالِيَّةُ تَتَعَلَّقُ بِاسْتِكْمَالِ **النَّفْسِ**.

Perfectionism is about perfecting the **self**.

1732. إجراء [n] *action*

لا أَحَدَ مِنْكُمْ يَأْخُذُ أَيَّ **إِجْرَاءٍ** نِيَابَةً عَنِّي.

None of you should take any **action** on my behalf.

1733. فرق [n] *teams*

سَأَحْشُدُ فِرَقَ البَحْثِ وَأَنْضَم إلَيْكَ قَرِيباً.

I'll get the search **teams** mobilized and join you shortly.

1734. مفقود [p.p.] *missing*

بَرْنَامَجُ دَعْمِ وِيِنْدُوزْ تَالِفٌ أَوْ مَفْقُودٌ.

The Windows support software is corrupted or **missing**.

1735. العقيد [n] *colonel*

أَعْرِفُ أَنَّ هَذَا صَعْبٌ عَلَيْكِ أَيَّتُهَا العَقِيدُ.

I know this must be difficult for you, **colonel**.

1736. الطيور [coll. n] *bird*

حُلْمُ البَشَرِيَّةِ هُوَ أَنْ تَطِيرَ مِثْلَ الطُّيُورِ.

It is a dream of humankind to fly like a **bird**.

1737. قبلة [n] *kiss*

كَيْفَ تَقُولُ "قِبْلَةٌ" بِلُغَةِ الإِشَارَة.

How do you say "**kiss**" in sign language?

1738. شريط [n] *bar*

لَدَيْنَا شَرِيطٌ خَاصٌّ مَفْتُوحٌ عَلَى مَدَارِ السَّاعَة.

Our private **bar** is open round the clock.

1739. آمنة [adj] *safe*

هَذِهِ المِنْطَقَةُ آمِنَةٌ، لا تَقْلَقْ.

Don't worry, this place is **safe**.

258

1740. نتائج [n] *results*

هَلْ خَرَجَتْ **نَتائِجُ** الاخْتِبَارِ؟

Did the test **results** come out?

1741. مبلغ [n] *amount*

لا يُوجَدُ **مَبْلَغٌ** مِنَ المَالِ يُمْكِنُهُ إصْلاحُ هَذَا.

No **amount** of money is going to fix this.

1742. حصان [n] *horse*

هَلْ سَبَقَ لَكَ أَنْ رَكِبْتَ **حِصَاناً**؟

Have you ever ridden a **horse**?

1743. صف [n] *row*

كُنْتُ أَزْرَعُ **صَفّاً** جَدِيداً مِنَ الشُّجَيْرَاتِ بِالحَدِيقَةِ الخَلْفِيَّةِ.

I was planting a new **row** of squash in the back garden.

1744. وقود [n] *fuel*

رُبَّمَا يَكُونُ الغَضَبُ **وَقُوداً** شَافِياً، لَكِنَّهُ سَيُغَيِّبُ العَقْلَ.

Anger can be a potent **fuel**, but it does cloud the mind.

1745. تصرف [v] *behaved*

يَسُرُّنِي أَنَّك تَتَمَتَّعُ بِالعَمَلِ الدَّؤُوبِ وَحُسْنِ **التَّصَرُّفِ**.

I am so pleased that you're hardworking and well-**behaved**.

1746. شعب [n] *people*

إنَّهُمْ **شَعْبٌ** قَرَوِيٌّ يَشْعُرُ بِأَثَرِ العَوْلَمَةِ.

They are village **people** feeling the impact of globalization.

1747. للغاية [adv] *extremely*

أَنَا مُتْعَبٌ لِلْغَايَة.

I am **extremely** tired.

1748. أذن [v] *authorization*

لا أَحَدَ يَدْخُلُ أَوْ يَخْرُجُ دُونَ إِذْنِي.

No one comes or goes without my **authorization**.

1749. تهانينا [n] *congratulations*

تَهَانِينَا! لَقَدْ اجْتَزْتَ الاخْتِبَار.

Congratulations! You passed the exam.

1750. مائة [n] *one hundred*

طَلَبَتْ مِنِّي أُمُّكَ إِخْبَارَكَ بِأَنَّها تَدْعَمُكَ **مَائَةً** بالمَائَةِ.

Your mother told me to tell you that she's behind you one **hundred** percent.

1751. كلمة السر [n] [adj] *password*

هَلْ يُمْكِنُكَ إِعْطَائِي **كَلِمَةَ السِرِ**؟

Can you give me a **password**?

1752. رصاصة [n] *bullet*

يَبْدُو أَنَّنا تَفَادَيْنَا **رَصَاصَةً** يَا سَيِّدِي الرَّئِيس.

It looks like we dodged a **bullet**, Mr. President.

1753. احداث [n] *events*

يَتَعَيّنُ عَلَيْنَا أَنْ نُحَوِّلَ مُصِيبَاتِنَا إِلَى **أَحْدَاثٍ** تُعَزِّزُ الحَيَاة.

We both have to transform our misfortunes into life-enhancing **events**.

1754. علامات [n] *marks*

كَيْفَ كَانَتْ **عَلامَاتُ** اخْتِبَارَاتِكَ؟

How are your test **marks**?

1755. مسموح [p.p.] *allowed*

لَيْسَ **مَسْمُوحاً** لِي بِالسَّفَرِ خَارِجَ البِلادِ.

I'm not **allowed** to travel abroad.

1756. عقل [n] *mind*

لَدَيْهِ قَلْبٌ جَبَانٌ، وَلَكِنَّ **عَقْلَهُ** مَاكِرٌ.

He has a coward's heart but a cunning **mind**.

1757. تستطع [v] *could*

بَعْضُ أَصْدِقَائِكَ قَالُوا لِي أَنَّكَ **تَسْتَطِيعُ** مُسَاعَدَتِي.

Some of your friends told me that you **could** help me.

1758. سحب [v] *pull*

أَيُمْكِنُكَ **سَحْبُ** الإِسْطِوَانَة؟

Can you **pull** the cylinder?

1759. وسيم [adj] *handsome*

إِنَّهُ شَابٌ **وَسِيمٌ**.

He's a **handsome** man.

1760. طفلي [n] *my baby*

عِنْدَمَا أَرْقُصُ عَلَى هَذِهِ المُوسِيقَى، يَسْتَمْتِعُ **طِفْلِي** أَيْضاً.

When I dance to this music, **my baby** likes it, too.

1761. تشبه [v] *similar to*

وَسَائِلُ النَّقْلِ المَحَلِّيَّة المَائِيَّة **تُشْبِهُ** المَرَاكِب.

Local waterborne public transport is **similar to** the ferry.

1762. تصوير [n] *filming*

كنتُ أتمنّى التحدّث مَعَك بِخُصُوصِ **تَصْوِيرِ** فلمٍ وثائقيّ هنا.

I was hoping to talk to you about **filming** a documentary here.

1763. أشك [v] *I doubt*

أنْتَ غَيَّرْتَ عَادَاتِك. **أَشُكُّ** في أنَّها سَتُغَيِّرُ عَادَاتَها.

You change your habits, but **I doubt** she'll change hers.

1764. المطر [n] *rain*

تتَدَفَّقُ الكَلِمَاتُ مِثْلَ **المَطَرِ** الدَّائِمِ في كَأْسٍ وَرَقِيٍّ.

Words are flowing out like endless **rain** into a paper cup.

1765. القومي [adj] *national*

لا تخْبِرْني بِذَلِك إذَا كَان الأمْرُ يُعَرِّضُ الأمْنَ **القَوْمِيَّ** للخَطَر.

Don't tell me if it compromises **national** security.

1766. أقترح [v] *I suggest*

لَنْ **أَقْتَرِحَ** شَيْئاً في غَيْرِ مَصْلَحَتِك أَبَداً.

I would never **suggest** anything that is not in your best interest.

1767. هوية [n] *identity*

سَتَحْتَاجُ إلَى **هُوِيَّةٍ** جَدِيدَة لِكَيْ تَعْمَلَ مَعَنَا.

You'll need a new **identity** to work with us.

1768. آثار [n] *effects*

تَخْتَلِفُ آثَارُ الفَسَادِ، كَمَا تَتَنَوَّعُ مَظَاهِرُه.

The **effects** of corruption vary, as do its manifestations.

1769. الطقس [n] *weather*

لَقَدْ كَانَ الطَّقْسُ سَيِّئاً لِلْغَايَة، فَطَلَبْتُ مِنْهُ المَبِيتَ.

The **weather** was so bad I asked him to stay overnight.

1770. عبقري [n] *intelligent*

أنْتَ رجُلٌ عبقَرِيٌّ وَشَخْصٌ لَطِيفٌ جِدّاً.

For an **intelligent** man, you are very nice.

1771. نضع [v] *keep*

لَنْ نَضَعَ الكَثِيرَ مِنَ الأشْيَاء فِي الصَّالَة.

We won't **keep** too many things in the hall.

1772. يتطلب [v] *require*

لَدَيَّ مَشْرُوعٌ صَغِيرٌ قَدْ يَتَطَلَّبُ مَوَاهِبَكَ الخَاصَّةَ.

I have a little project that might **require** your special talents.

1773. ضعيف [adj] *weak*

أنْتَ قَوِيٌّ، وَلَكِنَّهُمْ يَجْعَلُونَكَ ضَعِيفاً.

You are strong, but they make you **weak**.

1774. تحقق [v] *check*

تَحَقَّقْ مِنْ فِقْدَانِ الاتِّصَال.

Check if there's a loose connection.

1775. يشير [v] *refer*

إِلَامَ يُشِيرُ هَذَا النَّصُّ؟

What does that text **refer** to?

1776. ورقة [n] *paper*

لَا يُمْكِنُكَ اسْتِخْدَامُ حِبْرٍ وَرْدِيٍّ عَلَى وَرَقَةٍ حَمْرَاءَ.

You can't use pink ink on red **paper**.

1777. بالجوار [adv] *close by*

هَلْ تَبْحَثِينَ عَنْ شَخْصٍ مَا أَمْ تَسْكُنِينَ بِالجِوَارِ هُنَا؟

Are you looking for someone, or you live **close by**?

1778. طويل [adj] *long*

أَنَا لَا أَنْفِي أَنَّ الطَّرِيقَ كَانَ طَوِيلاً وَصَعْباً.

I am not denying that the road has been **long** and rocky.

1779. حبي [n] *my love*

إِنَّهَا حُبِّي.

She is **my love**.

1780. مناسبة [adj] *appropriate*

هَلْ هَذِهِ الهَدِيَّةُ مُنَاسِبَةٌ لَهُ؟

Is this an **appropriate** gift for him?

1781. لنبدأ [prep] [v] *let's start*

لِنَبْدَأْ بِالإِسْتِرْخَاء مَعَ القِيَامِ بِبِضْعَةِ تَمَارِينِ تَنَفُّسٍ بَسِيطَةٍ.

Let's start by relaxing with a few simple breathing exercises.

1782. بِلِقائِك [prep] [n] [pron] *to meet you*

أَنَا سَعِيدَةٌ بِلِقائِكَ.

I'm so happy **to meet you.**

1783. عامل [a.p.] *factor*

لَدَيَّ مَا يُسَمَّى "عَامِلُ المُفَاجَأة".

I have what is called "the surprise **factor**".

1784. لصالح [prep] [n] *in favor of*

نَادِراً مَا تَنْتَهِي قَضَايَا الوِصَايَة لِصَالِحِ الأَبِ.

Custody cases rarely turn out **in favor of** the father.

1785. العليا [adj] *high*

أَنَا مُتَأَكِّدٌ أَنَّنَا سَنَشْعُرُ بِالعَظَمَةِ حَوْلَ مَعَايِيرِنَا الأَخْلاقِيَّة العُلْيَا.

I'm sure we'll all feel great about our **high** moral standards.

1786. أستمع [v] *listen*

اسْتَمِعْ، أُرِيدُ إِخْبَارَكَ عَنْ شَيْء سَيَحْدُثُ اليَوْمَ.

Listen, I need to tell you something that happened today.

1787. يستغرق [v] *it takes*

يَسْتَغْرِقُ العَمَلُ المُوجَزُ وَالمُفَصَّلُ بَعْضَ الوَقْتِ.

It takes time to do detailed and precise work.

1788. قاعة [n] *hall*

يَبْدُو أَنَّهُمَا هُنَا لِيَحْجِزَا قَاعَةَ زَفَافِ ابْنَتِهِمَا.

It seems they're here to check out their daughter's wedding **hall**.

1789. رئيسي [adj] *major*

أُرَجِّحُ أَنَّنا عَلَى وَشْكِ أَنْ نَشْهَدَ تَغَيُّراً رَئِيسِيّاً فِي المُنَاخ.

I think we're on the verge of a **major** climate shift.

1790. زهور [n] *flowers*

هُنَاكَ زُهُورٌ وَشَمْسٌ مُشْرِقَةٌ حَتَّى فِي الشِّتَاء.

The sun shines and there are **flowers** even in winter.

1791. استيقظ [v] *wake up*

أَسْتَيْقِظُ مُبَكِّراً لأُمَارِسَ بَعْضَ الرِّيَاضَة.

I usually **wake up** early to practice sport.

1792. اختفى [v] *disappeared*

كَمْ كَانَ عُمُرُ ابنِكَ عِنْدَمَا اخْتَفَى؟

How old was your son when he **disappeared**?

1793. سلسلة [n] *series*

إِنَّها سِلْسِلَةٌ مُمْتِعَةٌ حَوْلَ مُغَامَرَاتِ البَائْدَا الصَّغِير.

It's a delightful **series** about an adventurous little panda.

1794. أغلب [adv] *most of*

أَذْهَبُ هُنَا وَهُنَاكَ، حَائِراً أَغْلَبَ الوَقْتِ.

I here and there and wander **most of** the time.

1795. علبة [n] *tray*

يَجِبُ تَعْبِئَةَ عُلْبَةِ الوَسَائِطِ.

Media **tray** needs to be filled.

266

1796. قصص [n] *stories*

أُرِيدُكَ أَنْ تُخْبِرَنِي **قِصَصاً** حَوْلَ مَاضِيكَ.

I want you to tell me **stories** about your past.

1797. خاتم [n] *ring*

إِذَا تَقَدَّمْتَ لِلزَّوَاجِ مِنِ امْرَأَةٍ، فَيَجِبُ أَنْ تُقَدِّمَ لَهَا **خَاتَماً** لِلخُطُوبَةِ.

You propose marriage to a woman, you should offer her an engagement **ring**.

1798. جسر [n] *bridge*

هَيَّا، عَلَيْنَا أَنْ نَعْبُرَ **الجِسْرَ**.

Let's cross the **bridge**.

1799. متزوج [a.p.] *married*

إِنَّهُ رَجُلٌ **مُتَزَوِّجٌ**.

He's a **married** man.

1800. يدل [v] *indicate*

النَّصُّ الَّذِي يَسْبِقُهُ سَهْمٌ **يَدُلُّ** عَلَى مُتَابَعَةٍ مُمْكِنَةٍ.

Text preceded by arrows will **indicate** possible follow-up.

1801. قارب [n] *boat*

أَقَمْتُ حَفْلَةً عَلَى **القَارِبِ** فِي عُطْلَةِ الأُسْبُوعِ المَاضِي.

Well, last weekend, I had a party on a **boat**.

1802. سنتان [n] *two years*

مَا كَانَ يَسْتَغْرِقُ **سَنَتَيْن** لا يَسْتَغْرِقُ سِوَى أُسْبُوعٍ الآن.

What used to take about **two years** for discovery takes them about a week now.

1803. مهتم [n] *interest*

لِمَ أَنْتَ مُهْتَمٌّ؟

Why does it **interest** you?

1804. زعيم [n] *leader*

مَنْ هُوَ زَعِيمُكُم؟

Who is your **leader**?

1805. مجلة [n] *magazine*

قِرَاءَةُ مَجَلَّةِ رَقْصٍ لا يَجْعَلُ مِنْكَ رَاقِصاً.

Reading a dance **magazine** doesn't make you a dancer.

1806. ملفات [n] *files*

أَحْضِرِي تِلْكَ المَلَفَّاتِ وَاتبَعِيني إلَى مَكْتَبِي.

Grab these **files** and follow me back to my office.

1807. نَمَت [v] *grown*

لَقَدْ نَمَت الأَزْهَارُ بِسُرْعَةٍ كَبِيرَة.

Flowers have **grown** rapidly.

1808. أوامر [n] *orders*

هَلا تَوَقَّفْتَ عَنْ إلقَاءِ الأَوَامِرِ لِلَحْظَةٍ؟

Would you stop giving **orders** for a moment?

1809. جنوب [n] *south*

أَنَا ذَاهِبٌ إلَى الأَنْدَلُس، جَنُوبَ إسْبَانِيا.

I'm going to Andalusia, **south** of Spain.

1810. شرف [n] *Sharaf*

شَرَف شَابٌّ مُؤَدَّبٌ.

Sharaf is a gracious man.

1811. متكبّر [prep] [n] *entitled*

لا تُكَلِّمْه مُجَدَّداً. إنَّهُ مُتَكَبِّرٌ جِدّاً.

Don't talk to him anymore. He's so **entitled**!

1812. شجاعة [adj] *courage*

أَحْيَاناً، يَتَطَلَّبُ الأَمْرُ شَجَاعَةً لِمَعْرِفَةِ الأُمُورِ غَيْرِ السَّارَّةِ.

Sometimes, it takes **courage** to assume unpleasant attitudes.

1813. رفع [v] *lifting*

لَمْ أَفْقِدْ مَوْهِبَتِي فِي رَفْعِ المَعْنَوِيَّات.

I haven't lost my gift for **lifting** spirits.

1814. حجم [n] *size*

أُرِيدُ أَنْ أَعْلَمَ بالضَّبْطِ حَجْمَ وَشَكْلَ تِلْكَ الحَقِيبَة.

I need to know the exact **size** and shape of that case.

1815. لاحقاً [adv] *later*

أَرَاكَ لاحِقًا!

See you **later**!

1816. غريب الأطوار [n] *eccentric*

إنَّهُ غَرِيبُ الأَطْوَار!

He's a little **eccentric**!

1817. مسلسل [n] *series*

هَلْ سَبَقَ وَشَاهَدْتَ مُسَلْسَلاً كَرْتُونِياً؟

Have you ever seen a cartoon **series**?

1818. الكبرى [adj] *grand*

حَسَناً، حَانَ الوَقْتُ لِلتَّصْوِيتِ لِلجَائِزَةِ الكُبْرَى.

All right, it's time to vote for the **grand** prize.

1819. بطل [adj] *hero*

أَنْتَ بَطَلٌ رَائِعٌ!

You're an amazing **hero**!

1820. فشلت [v] *failed*

لَقَدْ فَشِلْتَ، وَلَكِنَّ هَذَا لا يَعْنِي الاسْتِسْلام.

You **failed**, but that doesn't mean surrender.

1821. صالح [n] *Saleh*

سَأَذْهَبُ لِزِيَارَة صَالِح غَداً.

I'm going to visit **Saleh** tomorrow.

1822. خيار [n] *option*

لا نَمْلِكُ أَيَّ خِيَارٍ آخَر.

We have no other **option**.

1823. مثير الشفقة [adj] *pathetic*

لا تَكُنْ شَخْصاً مُثِيراً لِلشَّفَقَة.

Don't be a **pathetic** person.

1824. للحد [n] *reduction*

سَوْفَ يُعَدُّ بَرْنَامَجٌ وَطَنِيٌّ شَامِلٌ **للحَدِّ** مِنَ العُنْفِ.

A comprehensive national program for the **reduction** of violence will be prepared.

1825. الكهرباء [n] *electricity*

لا يُمْكِنُنَا العَيْشُ دُونَ **كَهْرَبَاء**.

We can't live without **electricity**.

1826. مالم [part] *unless*

المُشْكِلَةُ لَيْسَتْ حَقِيقِيَّة **مَا لَمْ** تُؤَثِّر عَلَيْنَا مُبَاشَرَةً.

The problem isn't real **unless** it affects us directly.

1827. نموذج [n] *sample*

أَحْتَاجُ إِلَى **نَمُوذَج** جَدِيدٍ مِنْ هَذَا الاخْتِبَار.

I need a new **sample** of this exam.

1828. رفض [v] *refused*

كَانَ رَسَّاماً، لَكِنَّهُ **رَفَضَ** أَنْ يَبِيعَ عَمَلَهُ.

He was a painter but he **refused** to sell his work.

1829. فصل [n] *separate*

حَاوِلِي **الفَصْلَ** بَيْنَ حَيَاتِكِ الشَّخْصِيَّةِ وَالمِهَنِيَّةِ.

Try keeping your private life and work life **separate** for a change.

1830. إقامة [n] *accommodation*

أَعْتَقِدُ أَنَّنِي سَأَتَمَكَّنُ من الحُصُولِ عَلَى **إقامة**.

I think I can get **accommodation**.

1831. ببطء [adv] *slowly*

تَكَلَّمْ **بِبُطْءٍ** وَوُضُوحٍ، وَسَأَتَمَكَّنُ مِنْ أَنْ أَقْرَأَ شِفَاهَكَ.

You can just speak **slowly** and articulate and I can read your lips.

1832. طب [n] *medicine*

هَلْ سَتَدْرُسُ **الطِّبَّ**؟

Are you going to study **medicine**?

1833. وعدت [v] *promised*

وَعَدْتُ بِأَنْ أَجْعَلَ العَالَمَ مَكَاناً أَفْضَلَ.

I **promised** to make the world a better place.

1834. حارس [n] *guard*

لَقَدْ عَيَّن الامبَرَاطُورُ **حَارِساً** لِيُرَافِقَكَ.

The emperor assigned a **guard** to accompany you.

1835. تعديل [v] *amendment*

أَطْلُبُ **تَعْدِيلاً** عَلَى المَادَّةِ.

I'm asking for an **amendment** to the article.

1836. رياح [n] *wind*

لا تُوجَدُ **رِيَاحٌ** حَتَّى الآن، الوَقْتُ مُبَكِّرٌ.

There is no **wind** yet. It's early.

1837. كلية [n] *faculty of*

تَخَرَّجْتُ من **كُلِّيَّةِ** الآدَاب.

I graduated from the **Faculty of** Arts.

1838. عمدة [n] *Mayor*

كَيْفَ يُمكِنُني المُسَاعدة يَا سَيّدَتِي **العُمْدَة**؟

So, what can I do to help, Madam **Mayor**?

1839. الطلاق [n] *divorced*

أَعْتَقِدُ أَنَّنَا نَسْتَطِيعُ حَلَّ المُشْكِلَةِ دُونَ **الطَّلاق**.

I think we can solve the problem without getting **divorced**.

1840. قدرة [n] *capacity*

لَدَيَّ سُؤَالٌ حَوْلَ **قُدْرَتِكُمْ**.

I have a question about your **capacity**.

1841. الدين [n] *religion*

الدِّينُ عُنْصُرٌ مُكَمِّلٌ لِلْحَيَاة.

Religion is an integral part of life.

1842. طاقة [n] *energy*

لا تُهْدِرْ **طَاقَتَكَ** يَا أَخِي.

Brother, don't waste your **energy**.

1843. بدونك [n] *without you*

لا أَسْتَطِيعُ العَيْشَ مِنْ **دُونِكَ**!

I can't live **without you**!

1844. قانوني [adj] *legal*

لَدَيْهِمْ نِظَامٌ **قَانُونِيٌّ** مُخْتَلِفٌ هُنَا.

They have a totally different **legal** system here.

1845. مؤلم [adj] *painful*

هَلْ الحَدِيثُ عَنْ هَذا الأَمْرِ مُؤْلِمٌ؟

Has this been so **painful** to talk about?

1846. الفارغ [adj] *empty*

لَدَيْنَا الكَثِيرُ مِنَ الفَضَاء **الفَارِغ** هُنَاكَ.

We've got a lot of **empty** space up there.

1847. تحسن [v] *improvement*

إِنَّ وَضْعَهُم الحَالِي لَمْ يَكَدْ يَطْرَأُ عَلَيْهِ أَيُّ تَحَسُّنٍ.

Their present situation shows little **improvement.**

1848. فيديو [n] *video*

لَقَدْ قُمْتُ بِتَصْوِيرِ **فِيدْيُو** عَنْ عِيدِ الكِرِيسْمَاسْ.

I made a **video** about Christmas day.

1849. شهادة [n] *certificate*

هَلْ يُمْكِنُكَ أَنْ تُعْطِيَنِي شَهَادَةَ مِيلادِي؟

Could you give me my birth **certificate**?

1850. علاقات [n] *relations*

لا تُوجَدُ لَدَيَّ **عَلاقَاتٌ** كَثِيرَةٌ مَعَ الأَشْخَاصِ في الخَارِج.

I don't have many **relations** with people abroad.

1851. انسان [n] *human*

لَنْ تَكُونَ إِنْسَاناً إِنْ لَمْ تَشْعُرْ بالخَوْف.

You wouldn't be **human** if you didn't feel scared.

1852. لسنوات [prep] [n] *for years*

لَقَدْ كُنْتُ أُشَاهِدُ عَمَلَكَ لِسَنَوَاتٍ.

I have been watching and admiring your work **for years.**

1853. بأسرع [adv] *as soon as*

سَأُحْضِرُ لَكَ بَعْضَ المُسَاعَدَة فِي أَسْرَع وَقْتٍ مُمْكِنٍ.

I'll get you some help **as soon as** possible.

1854. لذيذ [adj] *delicious*

سَوْفَ أَشْتَرِي شَيْئاً لَذِيذاً.

I'll buy something **delicious** to eat.

1855. جلسة [n] *sessions*

إِنَّها تُرِيدُ أَنْ تَعْرِفَ كَيْفَ تَسِيرُ جَلْسَةُ التَّصْوِير.

She wants to know how the photo **sessions** are going.

1856. اجازة [n] *vacation*

قَضَّيْتُ أَفْضَلَ إِجَازَةٍ مَعَكُمْ جَمِيعاً!

I've had the greatest **vacation** with you all!

1857. انسى [v] *forget*

وَقَفْتُمْ إِلَى جَانِبِي، وَلَنْ أَنْسَى ذَلِكَ أَبَداً.

You guys were there for me, and I will never **forget** that.

1858. تأكد [v] *ensure*

تَأَكَّدْ مِن ارْتِدَاء جَمِيعِ الرُّكَّاب لِحِزَام الأَمَان.

Ensure all passengers wear a seat belt.

1859. التهرّب [n] *evasion*

الآنَ، لِنَحْسِمِ الأَمْر، لا مَزيدَ مِن **التَّهَرّب**.

Now, let's get down to it. No more **evasion**.

1860. طبية [adj] *medical*

هَلْ أَحْضَرْتَ مُعِدّاتٍ **طِبّيّة**؟

Did you bring **medical** equipment?

1861. خبز [n] *bread*

أُريدُ أَنْ آكُلَ أَيَّ **خُبْزٍ** حَتَّى تَنْفَجِرَ مَعِدَتي.

I would like to eat **bread** until my stomach explodes.

1862. مساحة [n] *square*

كَمْ قَدَماً مُرَبّعاً **مَسَاحَةُ** هَذَا المَكَان؟

How many **square** feet is this place?

1863. تدمير [n] *destruction*

عَلَيْنَا أَنْ نُوقِفَ **تَدْميرَ** الجَدَاوِلِ وَالزُّهُور وَالأَشْجَار.

We must stop the **destruction** of the streams, the flowers and the trees.

1864. مرور [n] *passage*

شُكْراً عَلَى تَوْفيرِ **مُرورٍ** آمن لي يَا أَخِي.

Thank you for providing safe **passage**, brother.

1865. شأن [n] *issue*

سَنَتَوَاصَلُ المُشَاوَرَاتُ بِ**شَأن** هَذِهِ المَسْأَلة.

Consultations on this **issue** will continue.

1866. تركيز [v] *concentration*

هَذَا العَمَلُ يَتَطَلَّبُ تَرْكِيزاً عَالياً.

This work requires a high degree of **concentration**.

1867. الجنسية [n] *nationality*

مَا هي جِنْسِيَّتُكَ؟

What is your **nationality**?

1868. حبوب [n] *grain*

لَدَيْنَا شُحْنَةٌ من الحُبُوب قَادِمَة مِن الجَنُوب.

We've got a shipment of **grain** coming in from the south.

1869. معجبة [adj] *impressed*

والدي معجبٌ دائما بالرِّجَالِ الأَتْقِيَاء.

My father has always been **impressed** with biased men.

1870. أموال [n] *funds*

أَعْطِني الرَّقْم وَمِنْ ثَمَّ سَنَبْدَأُ بِإيدَاعِ أَمْوال إلَى حسَابَاتِكُم.

Get me the number, and then we'll start depositing **funds** into your accounts.

1871. دوري [adj] *league*

لَقَدْ فَوَّتت الدَوْرِي لِمُدَّة ثَلاثَة أَسَابِيع عَلَى التَّوَآلي.

She's missed **league** night three weeks running.

1872. الأوغاد [adj] *rascals*

مَاذَا فَعَلَ هَؤُلاء الأَوْغَاد مُجَدَّداً؟

What did those **rascals** do now?

1873. النظرية [n] *theory*

إِثْبَاتُ **النَّظَرِيَّةِ** لَمْ يَعُدْ ضَرُورِيّاً.

Once the **theory** was proved, it was no longer needed.

1874. زيادة [n] *increase*

تَمَكَّنْتُ مِنْ **زِيَادَةِ** المِيزَانِيَّةِ لِتَعْيِين عَمِيلٍ جَدِيدٍ.

I was able to **increase** the budget to hire a new agent.

1875. الدعم [n] *support*

سَوْفَ أُوَفِّرُ لَكِ أَيَّ **دَعْمٍ** تَحْتَاجِينَهُ.

Whatever **support** you need, I will get for you.

1876. لحظات [n] *moments*

لَقَدْ قَضَّيْنَا **لَحَظَاتٍ** مُمْتِعَةً لِلْغَايَةِ.

We spent very enjoyable **moments**.

1877. زهري [adj] *pink*

اللَّوْنُ **الزَّهْرِيُّ** هُوَ لَوْنِي المُفَضَّلُ.

Pink is my favorite color.

1878. تحول [v] *turning*

الجَمِيعُ لَدَيْهِ نُقْطَةُ **تَحَوُّلٍ** فِي حَيَاتِه.

Everybody has a **turning** point in his life.

1879. مكالمة [n] *call*

تَلَقَّيْتُ **مُكَالَمَةً** مِن أُخْتِي.

I got a **call** from my sister.

1880. حارس [n] *sentinel*

أَنَا هُنَا في انْتِظَار **الْحَارِسِ** الجَدِيد.

I am awaiting the new **sentinel**.

1881. الجنة [n] *paradise*

يُمْكِنُكِ فِعْلُ مَا تُحِبِّينَ فِعْلَهُ في **الجَنَّة**.

You can do what you like in **paradise**.

1882. تحميل [v] *download*

إِنَّ **تَحْمِيلَ** هَذَا البَرْنَامَج مَجَّانيٌّ تَمَاماً.

It's completely free to **download** this application.

1883. دقيقة [n] *minute*

أَمْهِلِيني **دَقِيقَةً** مِنْ فَضْلِكِ.

Just give me a **minute**, please.

1884. التسجيل [n] *registration*

هل من المَمْكِن أَنْ تُخبِرَني أَيْنَ أَجِدُ مَبْنَى إدَارَة **التَّسْجِيلِ**؟

Can you tell me where the **registration** building is?

1885. الصيد [n] *fishing*

نَحْنُ ذَاهِبُونَ **للصَّيْدِ**.

We are going **fishing**.

1886. تفسير [n] *interpretation*

أُرِيدُ **تَفْسِيراً** لِمَا يَحْدُثُ هُنَا!

I need an **interpretation** of what's happening here!

1887. الدرج [n] *stairs*

رَأَيْتُكَ اللَّيْلَة المَاضِيَة عَلَى الدَّرج.

I saw you the other night, on the **stairs**.

1888. دواء [n] *drug*

لا يُوجَدُ دَوَاءٌ لِعلاج فِقْدَان الذَّاكِرَة.

There's no **drug** therapy for amnesia.

1889. قذر [adj] *dirty*

لا أَسْتَطِيعُ البَقَاءَ بِمَنْزِلك لأَنَّهُ قَذِرٌ جِدّاً.

I can't stay at your house because it's so **dirty**.

1890. مثالية [adj] *ideal*

هَلْ تَعْتَقِدُ أَنَّ هُنَاكَ حَيَاةً مِثَالِيَّة؟

Do you think there is an **ideal** life?

1891. عسل [n] *honey*

أَعْطِني بَعْضَ العَسَلِ من فضلِك.

Give me some **honey**, please.

1892. مساعد [a.p.] *assistant*

أَيْنَ هُوَ مُسَاعِدُك؟

Where is your **assistant**?

1893. سبعة [n] *seven*

هَلْ قَرَأْتَ قِصَّة "فلة والأقزام السبْعَة"؟

Did you read the "Snow White and the **Seven** Dwarves" story?

1894. الوزارة [n] *Ministry*

تُقَدِّمُ **الوَزَارَةُ** كَافَّةَ الخَدَمَاتِ للأَطْفَال المعاقينَ مَجَّاناً.

All these services that the **Ministry** provides for disabled children are free of charge.

1895. التعرف [n] *recognize*

أَنْتِ تَبْدِينَ رَائِعَةً، لَمْ أَسْتَطِعْ **التَّعَرُّفَ** عَلَيْكِ.

You're looking beautiful, I couldn't **recognize** you.

1896. مجال [n] *domain*

المُعْجَمُ هُوَ مَجْمُوعَةٌ مِنَ الكَلِمَاتِ تَصِفُ **مَجَالاً** مُعَيَّناً.

A lexicon is a body of words that describes a **domain**.

1897. لازم [adj] *necessary*

يَجِبُ أَنْ تَفْعَلُوا كُلَّ شَيْء **لازِمٍ** لِتَحْمُوا أَنْفُسَكُم.

You must do everything **necessary** to protect one another.

1898. الرفاق [n] *comrades*

من الرّائِع قَضَاءُ بَعْضِ الوَقْتِ مَعَ **الرِّفَاق**.

It's always nice to spend time with **comrades**.

1899. زجاجة [n] *bottle*

هَلْ أَسْتَطِيعُ الحُصُولَ عَلَى **زُجَاجَةٍ** مِنَ المَاء؟

Can I have a **bottle** of water?

1900. تتبع [v] *track*

لِنَرَى إن كَان بِإِمْكَانِكَ أَنْ **تَتْبَعَ** تِلْكَ السَّيَّارَة.

Let's see if you can **track** that vehicle.

1901. يشتري [v] *buy*

ذَهَبَ أَحْمَدُ لِيَشْتَرِيَ الحَلَوِيَّاتِ.

Ahmed went to **buy** sweets.

1902. سائق [n] *driver*

أَنَا مُجَرَّدُ سَائِقٍ.

I'm just a **driver**.

1903. الظروف [n] *conditions*

أَنْتَ مُدْهِشٌ لِأَنَّك تَعْمَلُ تَحْتَ هذهِ الظُّرُوفِ الصَّعْبَةِ.

You have been doing such an incredible job under such difficult **conditions**.

1904. أزرق [n] *blue*

لَوْنُ السَّمَاءِ أَزْرَقُ.

The sky is **blue**.

1905. أنقذت [v] *saved*

أَنْقَذْت حَيَاتِي، شُكْراً لَك.

You **saved** my life, thank you.

1906. مصعد [n] *elevator*

هُنَاكَ مِصْعَدٌ آخَرُ يُمْكِنُنَا أَنْ نَسْتَخْدِمَهُ.

There's another **elevator** we can use.

1907. كاميرا [n] *camera*

كَانَ يَوْماً مَجِيداً عِنْدَمَا اشْتَرَتْ كَامِيرا مِن أجلِ عَمَلِهَا.

A memorable day, when she bought a **camera** for their work.

282

1908. المزرعة [n] *farm*

لَقَدْ ذَهَبْتُ مَعَ وَالِدِي إِلَى المَزْرَعَة.

I went with my father to the **farm**.

1909. محتمل [p.p.] *potential*

كَانَ لَدَيَّ زَوَاجٌ مُزَيَّفٌ مُحْتَمَلٌ وَقَدْ فَشِلَ.

I had a **potential** fake marriage that fell apart.

1910. مثال [n] *example*

أَعْطِنِي مِثَالاً.

Give me an **example**.

1911. يفكر [v] *think*

عليكِ مَعْرِفَة كَيْفِيَّةُ تَيْسِيرِ الأُمُورِ وَكَيْفَ يُفَكِّرُ النَّاسُ.

You have to know how the world works, how people **think**.

1912. غاز [n] *gas*

لَقَدْ اشْتَرَيْتُ الأُسْبُوعَ المَاضِي عُلْبَةَ غَازٍ جَدِيدَةٍ.

Just last week I had to buy a new **gas** tank.

1913. ملاحظة [n] *note*

لَقَدْ أَرْسَلْتَ لِي مُلاحَظَةً رَائِعَةً.

You sent me a lovely **note**.

1914. نجم [n] *star*

أَنْتَ نَجْمٌ مَشْهُورًا!

You are a rock **star**!

1915. كرسي [n] *chair*

كَانَتْ مَلَابِسُهَا عَلَى كُرْسِي حَيْثُ أَلْقَتْ بِهِمْ.

Her clothes were on a **chair** where she'd dumped them.

1916. خصام [n] *fight*

أَنَا لَا أُرِيدُ أَنْ أُجَادِلَ. دَعْنَا نَتَجَنَّب الخِصَام.

I don't want to argue. Let's not **fight**.

1917. صلة [n] *link*

ثَمَّةَ صِلَةٌ وَاضِحَةٌ بَيْنَ انتهاكَاتِ حُقُوق الإنسَانِ وَالفَسَاد.

There is a clear **link** between human rights abuses and corruption.

1918. ذاته [n] *the same*

نَشَأْنَا في المَنْزِلِ ذَاتِهِ لِثَمَانِية عَشَرَ عَامَاً.

We grew up in **the same** house for 18 years.

1919. حوض [n] *basin*

هَلْ سَمِعْتَ يَوْماً عَنْ حَوْضٍ شَافْلْيَاسْ؟

Have you ever heard of Atchafalaya **Basin**?

1920. جائزة [n] *award*

سمِعْتُ أَنَّكَ سَتَسْتَلِمُ جَائِزَةً مِنْ وَزِير التَّعْلِيم.

I've heard you will receive an **award** from the Education Minister.

1921. الأحياء [n] *neighborhoods*

بَعْضُ الأَحْيَاءِ تَشِيخُ بِسُرْعَة.

Some **neighborhoods** are aging rapidly.

1922. شبح [n] *ghost*

كانَ يَبْكِي مُصِرّاً عَلَى أَنَّهُ رَأَى شَبَحاً.

He was crying, insisting he'd seen a **ghost**.

1923. مدرب [n] *coach*

مَنْ هُوَ مُدَرِّبُكَ؟

Who's your **coach**?

1924. الحمل [n] *pregnancy*

أَثْنَاءَ الحَمْلِ، يَتَشَارَكُ الأُمُّ وَالطِّفْلُ الخَلَايَا وَالحِمْضِ النَّوَوِيِّ.

During **pregnancy**, a mother and child share cells and DNA.

1925. أشاهد [v] *watch*

لَيْسَ مِن المَسْمُوحِ لِي أَنْ أُشَاهِدَ التِّلْفَازَ لِأُسْبُوعٍ.

I'm not allowed to **watch** TV for a week.

1926. أصيب [v] *injured*

يَبْدُو أَنَّ سَائِقَ شَاحِنَتِنَا أُصِيبَ فِي الحَادِثِ.

Looks like our trucker was **injured** in the accident.

1927. تنظيف [v] *clean*

عَلَيْنَا تَنْظِيفُ البَيْتِ!

We have to **clean** the house!

1928. سئمت [v] *fed up*

أَنَا سَئِمْتُ مِنْ تَنَاوُلِ نَفْسُ الطَّعَامِ كُلَّ يَوْمٍ.

I'm **fed up** of eating the same food every day.

1929. مقعد [n] *seat*

اجلِسْ في مَقْعَدِكَ.

Take a **seat**.

1930. سابقًا [adv] *previously*

هَذَا التَّصَرُّفُ يَخْتَلِفُ عَمَّا فَعَلْتَهُ سَابِقاً.

This behavior isn't the same as the troubles you created **previously**.

1931. حلقة [adj] *episode*

كُلُّ حَلْقَةٍ أَفْضَلُ مِنَ التي تَسْبِقُهَا.

Every **episode** is better than the one before.

1932. يهرب [v] *flee*

رَأَيْتُهُ وَهوَ يَهْرُبُ.

I saw him **flee**.

1933. مؤخراً [adv] *recently*

مَاذَا فَعَلْتَ مُؤَخَّراً؟

What have you done **recently**?

1934. عديم اللون [adj] *colorless*

المَاءُ عَدِيمُ اللَّوْنِ وَالرَّائِحَة.

Water is **colorless** and odorless.

1935. منظمة [n] *organization*

سَتَتَحَمَّلُ كُلُّ مُنَظَّمَةٍ تَكَالِيفَ سَفَرِ مُمَثِّلِيهَا.

Each **organization** will cover the travel expenses of its representatives.

بالتأكيد [adv] *certainly* 1936

تَحسَّنَتْ في الماكيَاج بالتَّأْكِيد.

Well, she **certainly** became better at doing her makeup.

1937. إشارة [n] *signal*

لَدَيْنَا إشَارَةٌ قَويَّةٌ، لَكِنْ لا أَحَدَ يُجِيبُ.

We have a strong **signal**, but no one's answering.

1938. ساحرة [n] *witch*

سَأَكُونُ سَاحِرَةً طَيِّبَةً للغَايَة.

I am going to be a very good **witch**.

1939. عادي [adj] *normal*

أَوَدُّ أَنْ يَكُونَ هَذَا اليَوْمُ الدِّرَاسِيُّ عَادِياً.

I'd like this to be a **normal** school day.

1940. إضافية [adj] *additional*

لَقَدْ طَلَبُوا مَوَادّاً إضَافِيَّةً، وَنَحْنُ نُحَاولُ تَوْفِيرَهَا.

They asked for **additional** material and we're trying to supply it.

1941. الغناء [n] *singing*

عَلَيْكَ بِمُوَاصَلَةِ الغِنَاءِ فَقَط حَتَّى نَعْلَمَ مَكَانَكَ.

Just keep on **singing** so we know where you are.

1942. قوانين [n] *laws*

هُنَاكَ قَوَانِينَ تَسْتَعْبِدُ البَشَرَ وَقَوَانِينَ تُحَرِّرُهُمْ.

There are **laws** that enslave people, and **laws** that set them free.

1943. عربة [n] *wagon*

إِنَّهُ ثَقِيلٌ حَقّاً، لِذَا، وَضَعْتُهُ في عَرَبَةٍ.

It's really heavy so I put it in a **wagon**.

1944. سيد [n] *mister*

أَنْتَ تَجْعَلُني مُتَوَتِّراً، يَا سَيِّد.

You're making me nervous, **mister**.

1945. مركزية [adj] *central*

حُقُوقُ الإِنْسَانِ مَسْأَلَةٌ مَرْكَزِيَّةٌ في عَمَلِيَّةِ الإِصْلاح.

Human rights are a **central** matter in the process of reform.

1946. النجاح [n] *success*

إِذَا كُنْتِ تُرِيدِينَ النَّجَاحَ بِشِدَّةٍ، فَسَوْفَ تَحْصُلِينَ عَلَيْهِ.

If you want **success** so badly, then you will get it.

1947. الشمال [n] *north*

هَلْ تَعِيشُ في الشَّمَالِ أو الجَنُوب؟

Do you live in the **north** or the south?

1948. للأمام [adv] *forward*

تَطَلَّعْ للأَمَامِ دَوْماً!

Look **forward** always!

1949. بحثت [v] *examined*

بَحَثْتُ في الصَّالَة بالأَمْسِ. لَمْ يَكُنْ هُنَاكَ شَئٌ.

I **examined** the hall yesterday, it was clear.

1950. عالمية [adj] *global*

الفَقْرُ مُشْكِلَةٌ عَالَمِيَّةٌ.

Poverty is a **global** problem.

1951. يقصد [v] *intend*

والدِي بالتَّبَنِّي لَمْ يَقْصُدْ تَغْيِيرَ حَيَاتِي.

My foster father didn't **intend** to change my life.

1952. كدت [imp. v] *I almost*

كِدْتُ أَنْسَى يَا أُمِّي. أَحْضَرْتُ بَعْضَ الهَدَايَا الصَّغِيرَة لَكِ.

I almost forgot. Mother, I've got some little presents for you.

1953. حليب [n] *milk*

أُحِبُّ حَلِيبَ الشُّوكُولاتَة.

I love chocolate **milk**.

1954. قاسية [adj] *harsh*

لِمَاذَا أنتِ قَاسِيَةٌ جِدّاً مَعِى؟

Why do you have to be so **harsh** to me?

1955. الجبل [n] *mountain*

اعْتَدْتُ عَلَى صُعُودِ الجَبَلِ مَعَ أبي وَأخِي.

I used to go up to the **mountain** with my father and brother.

1956. بارع [adj] *witty*

أَنْتَ بَارِعٌ جِدّاً وَلَطِيفٌ.

You are so **witty** and charming.

1957. عبقري [adj] *genius*

أَعْلَمُ أَنَّهُ يُمْكِنُكَ فعْلُ هَذَا لِأَنَّكَ عَبْقَرِيٌّ.

I knew you could do it, because you're a **genius**.

1958. تهديد [v] *threatened*

هَلْ تَعَرَّضْتَ لْلتَّهْدِيد؟

Have you been **threatened**?

1959. آلي [adj] *automatic*

تَمَّتْ إِعَادَةُ تَوْجِيهِ مُكَالَمَتِكَ إِلَى نِظَام الرَّسَائِل الآلي.

Your call has been forwarded to an **automatic** message system.

1960. الوعي [n] *awareness*

عَلَيْنَا زِيَادَةُ الوَعْي بَيْنَ النَّاس.

We need to raise **awareness** among people.

1961. أقدام [n] *feet*

كُنْتُ عَلَى بُعدِ ثَلاثَة أَقْدَام.

I was about 3 **feet** away.

1962. المختبر [n] *laboratory*

أَعْتَقِدُ أَنَّا مَحْظُوظُونَ بِكَوْنِنَا جُزْءاً مِنْ ذَلِكَ المُخْتَبَر.

I believe we are all privileged to be part of that **laboratory**.

1963. نفسي [adj] *psychological*

كُنْتُ أَتَطَلَّعُ إِلَى القِيَام بِنِقَاشٍ نَفْسِيٍّ يَخُصُ شَخْصِيَّتِي.

I've been looking forward to having that **psychological** discussion about my personality.

1964. DNA [adj] [n] الحمض النووي

هَلْ فَحَصْتَ الحِمْضَ النَّوَوِيَّ؟

Have you examined the **DNA**?

1965. read [v] تقرأ

كَانَتْ **تَقْرَأُ** رَسَائِلَكَ القَدِيمَة كَمَا لَوْ أَنَّهَا وَصَلَتْ للتَّوِّ.

She would **read** your old letters as if they'd just come.

1966. violence [n] العنف

لَقَدْ حَارَبْتُ **العُنْفَ** في هَذِهِ المَدْرَسَة لِوَقْتٍ طَوِيل.

I've fought against **violence** at this school for too long.

1967. insurance [n] التأمين

هَلْ سَيُلْغِي عِقْدُ **التَّأْمِينِ** العِقْدَ القَدِيمَ؟

Will the new **insurance** contract cancel out the old one?

1968. cancer [n] السرطان

الخَبَرُ الجَيِّدُ هُوَ أَنَّنا تخلَّصْنا مِنَ **السَّرَطَان**.

Well, the good news is that we got all the **cancer** out.

1969. imposed [p.p.] المفروض

السَّلامُ **المَفْرُوضُ** بِقُوَّةِ السِّلاحِ مَآلُهُ الفَشَلُ.

Peace **imposed** by force of arms is always doomed to failure.

1970. radio [n] الراديو

لَقَدْ وَجَدْنَا هَذَا **الرَّادْيُو** وَلَكِنَّهُ لا يَعْمَلُ.

We found this **radio**, but I don't think it works.

1971. سيارة أجرة [n] *taxi*

أَنَا تَعِبْتُ من انْتِظَارِ سَيَّارَةِ أُجْرَةٍ.

I am tired of waiting for a **taxi**.

1972. أوروبا [n] *Europe*

قَدِمْتُ من أُورُوبَا لِزِيَارَةِ أُخْتِي.

I'm here from **Europe** visiting my sister.

1973. قطعت [v] *cut off*

يبدو الأمْرُ كَمَا لَوْ أَنَّهَا قَطَعَتْ عَلاقَتَهَا مَعَ الحَيَاة.

It's as if she has **cut** herself **off** from life.

1974. عصير [n] *juice*

مَا عَصِيرُكَ المُفَضَّلُ؟

What is your favorite **juice**?

1975. عظام [n] *bones*

مُرُونَتُكَ تَجْعَلُكَ تَبْدُو وَكَأَنَّكَ بِلَا عِظَامٍ.

Your fluidity makes it appear that you have no **bones**.

1976. أفلام [n] *films*

لَقَدْ عَمِلَ عَلَى أَفْلامٍ أَكْثَرَ وَأَصْبَحَ نَجْماً كَبِيراً.

He made a dozen more **films** and became a big star.

1977. تراجعوا [v] *step back*

تَرَاجَعُوا. فَلْنَفْسَحْ لَهُ المَجَالُ.

Step back. Let's give him room.

1978. يواجه [v] *face*

يَجِبُ عَلَيْهِ أَنْ يُوَاجِهَ عَاقِبَةَ أَفْعَالِهِ.

He'll have to **face** the consequences.

1979. إثبات [n] *proof*

أَبْقِي الْأَمْرَ لِنَفْسِكَ حَتَّى تَحْصُلَ عَلَى إِثْبَاتٍ.

I would keep it to yourself until you have **proof**.

1980. رمز [n] *code*

أَعْطِنِي الرَّمْزَ.

Give me the **code**.

1981. يصلح [v] *repair*

لَقَدْ حَصَلا عَلَى مَوْلُودٍ وَيَتَمَنَّيانِ أَنْ يُصْلِحَ ذَلِكَ زَوَاجَهُمَا.

They just had a baby, hoping it would **repair** their marriage.

1982. مشهد [n] *scene*

أَنَا نَجْمَةٌ فِي كُلِّ مَشْهَدٍ مِنْ حَيَاتِي.

I am a star in every **scene** of my life.

1983. المفتش [n] *inspector*

أَخْبَرْتَ الْمُفَتِّشَ أَنَّنَا ذَهَبْنَا إِلَى الْمَلْهَى، صَحِيحٌ؟

You told the **Inspector** that we went to the club, right?

1984. قارعة [n] *corner*

لِمَ يَعْزِفُ شَخْصٌ مِثْلُكَ عَلَى قَارِعَةِ الطَّرِيقِ؟

Why would a guy like you play on a street **corner**?

1985. حار [adj] hot

ذَلِكَ الكُوبُ حَارٌّ جِداً، وَقَدْ يَحْرِقُكَ!

That cup is very **hot** and might burn you!

1986. عجلة [n] wheel

اضْطَرُّوا إِلَى التَّوَقُّفِ لِتَغْيِيرِ عَجَلَةِ السَّيَّارَةِ.

They were compelled to stop to change the **wheel** of the car.

1987. عكس [n] *unlike*

عَلَى عَكْسِ شَرِيكَتِكَ، لَدَيْكَ سِجِلٌّ نَظِيفٌ.

Unlike your partner, you've got an immaculate record.

1988. الشرق [n] *East*

أَكْمَلَ سَنَتَيْنِ خِدْمَةً فِي الشَّرْقِ الأَوْسَطِ.

He completed two years of service in the Middle **East**.

1989. أؤكد [v] *I assure*

أُؤَكِّدُ لَكَ، صَدِيقِي مَوْثُوقٌ بِهِ.

I **assure** you, my friend is reliable.

1990. صبي [v] *boy*

كُلُّنَا نَعْرِفُ بِأَنَّهُ أَجْمَلُ صَبِيٍّ فِي القَرْيَةِ.

We all know he is the sweetest **boy** in the village.

1991. بقرة [n] *cow*

مِنَ أَيْنَ أَشْتَرِي بَقَرَةً؟

Where do I buy a **cow**?

1992. عاصفة [n] *storm*

يَقُولُونَ أَنَّهَا أَسْوَءُ **عَاصِفَةٍ** صَيْفِيَّةٍ مُنْذُ سَنَوَات.

They say it's the worst summer **storm** we've had in years.

1993. السلطة [n] *authority*

أَعْتَقِدُ أَنَّ الشَّرِكَةَ مَنَحَتْكَ **السُّلْطَةَ** الكَامِلَةَ هُنَا.

I imagine that corporate has granted you unreserved **authority** here.

1994. بلطف [adv] *gently*

أَنَا أُحَاوِلُ أَنْ أُخْبِرَكَ **بِلُطْفٍ** قَدْرَ الإِمْكَانِ.

I'm trying to tell you as **gently** as possible.

1995. اللغة [n] *language*

بَعْدَ قِرَاءَة هَذَا الكِتَاب، سَتَسْتَطِيعُونَ التَّحَدُّث **بِاللُّغَةِ** العَرَبِيَّةِ.

After reading this book, you will be able to speak the Arabic **language**.

1996. حذاء [n] *shoes*

سَأَشْتَرِي **حِذَاءً** جَدِيداً.

I'll buy new **shoes**.

1997. نوبة قلبية [n] *heart attack*

لِلأَسَفِ، أُصِيبَ **بِنَوْبَة قَلْبِيَّةٍ**.

Unfortunately, he had a **heart attack**.

1998. مزعج [adj] *annoying*

هَذَا مُزْعِجٌ، لَكِن هَذا لَيْسَ ذَنْبَكَ.

It's **annoying**, but that's not your fault.

1999. مقابلة [n] *interview*

سَأَقُومُ بِإِجْرَاء أَوَّلِ مُقَابَلَةٍ صُحُفِيَّةٍ لِي كَمُرَاسِلَة.

I'm conducting my first **interview** as a reporter.

2000. بالتوفيق [prep] [v] *good luck*

بِالتَّوْفِيق، أَتَمَنَّى لَكُمْ النَّجَاحَ!

Good luck, I wish you all success! ☺

CONCLUSION

And thus, we've finally reached the very end of this wonderful list of the *2000 Most Common Arabic Words in Context*!

If you feel you've made progress in Arabic, we're happy to have helped you and hope to see you again soon; we'll surely meet again in future books and learning material.

So, take care and study hard, and don't forget the four tips we gave you at the beginning if you want to become a pro in Arabic!

Practice hard!

Don't limit yourself to these 2000 words!

Grab a study partner!

Write a story!

Keep an eye out for more books like this one; we're not done teaching you Arabic! Head over to www.LingoMastery.com and read our free articles, sign up for our newsletter and check out our YouTube channel. We give away so much free stuff that will accelerate your Arabic learning and you don't want to miss that!

If you liked the book, we would really appreciate a little review wherever you bought it.

MORE BOOKS BY LİNGO MASTERY

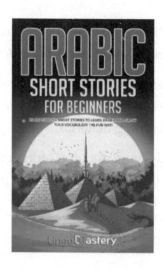

Are you looking for a fun and effective way to grow your Arabic language skills?

Some languages can be a real challenge to learn, and Arabic is definitely no exception. After all, it's not easy to find easy, fun and accessible reading material in Modern Standard Arabic that caters to ALL audiences. However, this book has been created to change that.

A beautiful, enchanting and ancient language spoken by over 420 million people worldwide, Arabic is a language that will allow you to build your professional career and open up the world for you. Modern Standard Arabic, which we will deal with in this book, is the standardized, literary Arabic that is used in print and mass media.

The Arabic world is known for its excellent storytelling. Because of this, in this book we have compiled 20 easy-to-read, compelling and fun stories that will allow you to expand your vocabulary and give you the tools to improve your grasp of the wonderful Arabic tongue.

How Arabic Short Stories for Beginners works:

- Each chapter possesses a funny, interesting and thought-provoking story based on real-life situations, allowing you to learn a bit more about the Arabic culture.
- The summaries follow a synopsis in Arabic and in English of what you just read, both to review the lesson and for you to see if you understood what the tale was about. Use them if you're having trouble.
- At the end of those summaries, you'll be provided with a list of the most relevant vocabulary involved in the lesson, as well as slang and sayings that you may not have understood at first glance! Don't get lost trying to understand or pronounce it all, either, as all of the vocabulary words are translated for your ease of use!
- Finally, you'll be provided with a set of tricky questions in Arabic, allowing you the chance to prove that you learned something in the story. Whether it's true or false, or if you're doing the single-answer questions, don't worry if you don't know the answer to any — we will provide them immediately afterwards, but no cheating!

We want you to feel comfortable while learning the tongue; after all, no language should be a barrier for you to travel around the world and expand your social circles!

So look no further! Pick up your copy of **Arabic Short Stories for Beginners** and level up your Arabic language learning right now!

Want more Arabic books? Head over to LingoMastery.com/Arabic

Made in United States
Troutdale, OR
03/19/2024

18587526R00169